New Mexico's Buffalo Soldiers

Monroe Lee Billington

New Mexico's
Buffalo Soldiers, 1866–1900

University Press of Colorado

Copyright © 1991 by the University Press of Colorado
P.O. Box 849
Niwot, Colorado 80544

The University Press of Colorado is a cooperative publishing enterprise supported, in part, by
Adams State College, Colorado State University, Fort Lewis College, Mesa State College,
Metropolitan State College of Denver, University of Colorado, University of Northern Colorado,
University of Southern Colorado, and Western State College.

Library of Congress Cataloging-in-Publication Data

Billington, Monroe Lee.
    New Mexico's buffalo soldiers, 1866–1900 / Monroe Lee Billington.
        p.   cm.
    Includes bibliographical references and index.
    ISBN 0-87081-233-5
    1. Afro-American soldiers —New Mexico — History — 19th century. 2. New Mexico
— History — 1848– 3. United States. Army — Afro-American troops — History — 19th
century. 4. United States. Army. Cavalry — History — 19th century. 5. Frontier and
pioneer life— New Mexico. 6. Indians of North America — New Mexico — Wars. 7. Indians
of North America — Wars — 1866–1895. I. Title.
E185.93.N55B55 1991
978.9'04—dc20   91-12001
                                                                              CIP

The paper used in this publication meets the minimum requirements of the American National
Standard for Information Sciences—Permanence of Paper for Printed Library Materials. ANSI
Z39.48–1984

∞

10 9 8 7 6 5 4 3 2 1

7696627

Dedicated to Wilma

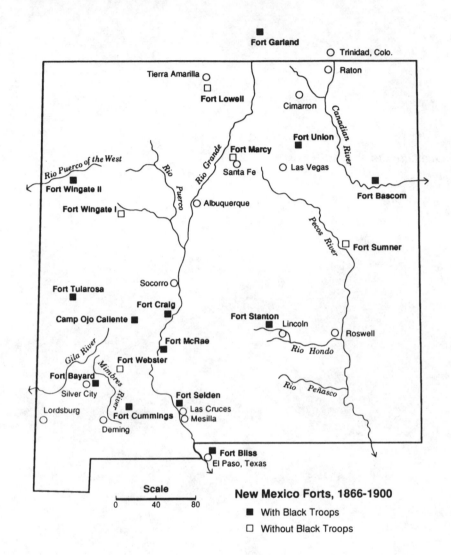

Fort Garland

○ Trinidad, Colo.

Tierra Amarilla ○
□ **Fort Lowell**

○ Raton

Cimarron ○

Fort Union ■

Canadian River

Rio Grande

Fort Marcy □
Santa Fe ○

○ Las Vegas

Rio Puerco of the West

Fort Wingate II ■

Fort Bascom ■

Rio Puerco

Fort Wingate I □

○ Albuquerque

Pecos River

□ **Fort Sumner**

Socorro ○

Fort Tularosa ■

Fort Craig ■

Fort Stanton ■ Lincoln ○
○ Roswell

Camp Ojo Caliente ■

Rio Hondo

Gila River

Fort McRae ■

Fort Webster □

Rio Peñasco

Fort Bayard ■
Silver City ○

Mimbres River

Fort Selden ■
Las Cruces ○

Lordsburg ○

Fort Cummings ■
Deming ○

Mesilla ○

Fort Bliss ■
El Paso, Texas ○

Scale

0   40   80

New Mexico Forts, 1866-1900

■ With Black Troops
□ Without Black Troops

Contents

Illustrations

Maps

Preface

The term "buffalo soldier" originated with the Indians, who saw that the hair of the black soldiers resembled the fur of the buffalo and that the soldiers' fighting spirit made them a worthy opponent. The soldiers accepted the name as complimentary, and the Tenth Cavalry incorporated a likeness of a buffalo on its regimental crest. Although the Indians first applied the name to members of the cavalry, it became a term that referred not only to cavalrymen but also to infantrymen.

In recent years many books have been written on the roles of blacks in the American West, including W. Sherman Savage, *Blacks in the West* (Westport, Conn.: 1976), William Loren Katz, *The Black West* (Garden City, N.Y.: 1973), and Kenneth Wiggins Porter, *The Negro on the American Frontier* (New York: 1971). These volumes, however, essentially ignore blacks in the military. Though historians and popular writers have produced countless volumes on the post–Civil War conflict between U.S. military forces and the Indians, the great majority of them either totally ignore or make only passing references to black soldiers. Otherwise excellent volumes that include hardly more than occasional references to black soldiers are Robert M. Utley, *Frontier Regulars: The United States Army and the Indians, 1866–1891* (New York: 1973), Donald E. Worcester, *The Apaches: Eagles of the Southwest* (Norman, Okla.: 1979), Dan L. Thrapp, *The Conquest of Apacheria* (Norman, Okla.: 1967) and *Victorio and the Mimbres Apaches* (Norman, Okla.: 1974). Edward M. Coffman, *The Old Army: A Portrait of the American Army in Peacetime, 1784–1898* (New York: 1986) has a long and detailed chapter on the army's enlisted men who served between the end of the Civil War and the beginning of the Spanish-American War. But because that chapter deals with a great variety of subjects in both time and space, it is able to give only minimal attention to the life of the black soldier in New Mexico.

Of the few volumes that have appeared that focus on black soldiers in the West, the most important are John M. Carroll, ed., *The Black Military Experience in the American West* (New York: 1971), Arlen L. Fowler, *The Black Infantry in the West, 1869–1891* (Westport, Conn.:

1971), and William H. Leckie, *The Buffalo Soldiers: A Narrative of the Negro Cavalry in the West* (Norman, Okla.: 1967). Yet neither Carroll nor Fowler devotes attention to blacks in the military in New Mexico Territory after the American Civil War. Although Leckie concentrates on Texas and Arizona, he does devote some attention to New Mexico. He limits his subject matter to the cavalry and the Indian Wars, and his work is more a military organizational history than a focus on the common troops. In addition, he chooses not to include the non-Indian–related activities of the black cavalrymen. Though Lenwood G. Davis and George Hill, comps., *Blacks in the American Armed Forces, 1776–1983: A Bibliography* (Westport, Conn.: 1985) has a chapter listing references to black soldiers in the West, its usefulness lies in its affirmation of how limited are the serious works on the subject: it has few entries referring to New Mexico.

In short, black soldiers in the West have received some attention, but their activities in New Mexico Territory have been neglected. Though Leckie has chronicled the black cavalrymen's pursuit of the Indians, no volume has detailed the similar experiences of black infantrymen who also chased Indians in New Mexico. Furthermore, works dealing with army life in the post–Civil War Southwest are in short supply, and they are essentially nonexistent in regard to black soldiers in New Mexico. In view of this neglect and in view of the significant contributions black soldiers made in post–Civil War New Mexico Territory, the time has come for that story to be told.

Though historians' neglect of the story of black soldiers in New Mexico justifies my writing this book, I have not written it to argue that their chronicle is unique. In fact, the lives of the black soldiers were not far different than those of their white counterparts. I have been struck by how similar were all soldiers' experiences in almost every realm — from chasing Indians to performing garrison duty to engaging in leisure activities. But white and black soldiers did have some different experiences, experiences primarily stemming from color. While whites felt the civilian population's prejudice because they were in the military, blacks received a double dose, both because they were soldiers and because of their skin color. Hence, the prejudice and discrimination visited upon the "buffalo soldiers" further justify their story being told.

A number of people have contributed to this work. The most

important is my wife, Wilma, to whom I give special thanks for her support. I also appreciate Ira Clark, Edward Coffman, Myra Ellen Jenkins, Simon Kropp, William Leckie, Darlis Miller, and Eugene Todd, each of whom gave me helpful reactions either to the work as a whole or to one or more chapters of the evolving manuscript. I am happy to express my gratitude for the contributions of staff members of the University Press of Colorado, especially Jody Berman for her general editorial supervision and Debbie Weed for her careful copyediting. I must thank my colleagues and graduate students in the Department of History at New Mexico State University, my family members, and my friends, not only for their assistance but also for their mostly silent suffering through several years of my introducing the subject of black soldiers into almost every conversation.

Introduction

During the American Civil War, the northern states and the U.S. government enlisted the help of blacks — both free northern blacks and former southern slaves — in the Union cause. One of the ways in which blacks conspicuously assisted the nation's victory was through their military service: by 1863 and 1864 various northern states fielded black regiments. In early May 1863 the U.S. Army had established the Corps d'Afrique (U.S. Colored Volunteers), composed of one cavalry regiment, one heavy artillery regiment, five regiments of engineers, and twenty-two infantry regiments. Despite considerable and powerful opposition, stemming primarily from racial prejudice, in late June 1863 the Lincoln administration approved the establishment of the Bureau of Colored Troops, which had the responsibility of organizing and filling regiments consisting of federal black troopers led by white commissioned officers. By the spring of 1864 these units came to be called U.S. Colored Troops.

Before the war was over, in addition to the twenty-nine volunteer black regiments, the army had over 130 conscripted black infantry regiments, thirteen regiments of heavy artillery, ten batteries of light artillery, and six cavalry regiments. The number of black men that the Union recruited and organized during the Civil War totaled at least 178,895 and may have approached two hundred thousand, numbers which excluded white officers. Thus, black men constituted approximately 10 percent of the total number of Union soldiers.[1]

From Virginia to the western frontier, black soldiers fought in 449 Civil War engagements, thirty-nine of which were major battles. They won enviable reputations for their ability, courage, and devotion, proving themselves worthy of the confidence their advocates had expressed when they first argued for black men in the military. The black soldiers' actions and contributions during the war proved that the prejudiced reservations some people had concerning their presence in the armed forces were totally unjustified.[2]

Despite the fact that black men had made significant contributions to the Union military effort during the Civil War, when that conflict came to an end many military and political leaders of the nation did not relish the prospect of blacks in the peacetime army. Members of Congress and others argued long hours over whether black soldiers should be included in the postwar regular army; because of racial prejudice many people believed that the army should be all white.

The most historically significant development in the composition of the regular army in the post–Civil War era was the inclusion of black enlisted personnel. When the Congress passed a bill in 1866 to reorganize the U.S. Army, it provided for an army of 54,300 in ten regiments of cavalry, five regiments of artillery, and forty-five regiments of infantry. The cavalry and artillery regiments were to be composed of twelve companies each, while infantry regiments were to have ten companies. The legislation designated two of the cavalry regiments (the Ninth and Tenth) and four of the infantry regiments (the Thirty-eighth through the Forty-first) for blacks. In 1869 the Congress reduced the army's enlisted personnel to not more than 37,300 and its total number of infantry regiments from forty-five to twenty-five, the new Twenty-fourth being composed of the former Thirty-eighth and Forty-first, and the new Twenty-fifth being made up of the former Thirty-ninth and Fortieth.[3] Although these various black regiments had assignments in a number of locations, many companies of both cavalry and infantry served in the postwar American West. As had been true during the Civil War, white commissioned officers led these black units, while noncommissioned officers were of the same race as the other enlisted men.

Between 1866 and 1900 from 3,300 to 3,800 black infantrymen and cavalrymen in the U.S. Army served at one time or another at eleven of the sixteen military installations in New Mexico Territory.[4] From 1866 to 1869 parts of the old Fifty-seventh and One Hundred Twenty-fifth Infantry Regiments and the then-new Thirty-eighth Infantry were stationed at eight forts: Bascom, Bayard, Craig, Cummings, McRae, Selden, Stanton, and Union. From 1875 to 1881 companies of the Ninth Cavalry were stationed at all of the above forts except Bascom, as well as at Wingate and Tularosa and Camp Ojo Caliente. Between 1887 and 1892 units of the Tenth Cavalry were located at Bayard, and from 1888 to 1896 a large part of the Twenty-fourth Infantry was there as well. Also, small detachments of the Twenty-fourth were at Selden from 1888 to 1891 and at Stanton for three months in 1896. Two companies of the Twenty-fifth Infantry were stationed at Bayard and Wingate in 1898 and 1899. Finally, men of the Ninth Cavalry were at Bayard in 1899 and at Wingate in 1899 and 1900.[5]

Despite many obstacles, including an unfamiliar environment, inclement weather, backbreaking work, Indian dangers, poor housing, inferior animals, worn-out equipment, bad food, loneliness, boredom, and racial prejudice, black soldiers made significant contributions in New Mexico Territory. Primarily they helped subdue and control the hostile Indians. In the process, they escorted trains and stages, built military roads and telegraph lines, guarded water holes and railroad construction workers, and watched over animals and supply lines. They protected immigrants and other travelers and workers not only from Indians but also from other dangers, including robbers, horse thieves, and cattle rustlers. They escorted farmers, miners, and cattlemen who migrated from the East, and they watched over these groups while they were in the West. The black soldiers' presence discouraged lawlessness among both Indians and unruly whites.

Wherever the army went, important developments followed: military spending stimulated the civilian economy; military roads became civilian roads; geographic and boundary surveys assisted land development and settlement. Black soldiers contributed to these advances, participating in a military society and culture that influenced the New Mexico territorial scene. One authority has argued that the western military establishments were stepping stones to permanent civilian settlements.[6] To the extent that black soldiers were at these posts, they aided in this evolutionary process. While at the various posts, they had more than occasional contact with the civilian population and thus had impact upon the developing social and economic environment of New Mexico. In short, they aided in bringing a new civilization to New Mexico.[7]

New Mexico's Buffalo Soldiers

I. Infantrymen and Indians, 1866–1869

Before the outbreak of the American Civil War, many of the eighteen thousand enlisted men of the U.S. Army were scattered throughout the trans–Mississippi West, protecting travelers and settlers from hostile Indians who resented and resisted white intrusion into their homelands and hunting grounds. Upon the beginning of the war in 1861, army officials recalled the vast majority of these soldiers to the East. In view of the lower military profile, Indians in the West stepped up their attacks upon white settlements and settlers. The Sioux outbreak in Dakota Territory in 1862 was the most famous of these, but other Indians, including the Apaches and the Comanches in the Southwest, also went on the warpath. Such action on the part of the Indians convinced the nation's political and military leaders that if that vast area was to be made safe, a great segment of the army must be relocated in the West upon the conclusion of the war.

In July 1865 — three months after the end of the Civil War — the Union army had 123,156 black soldiers in 130 infantry regiments, thirteen regiments of heavy artillery, ten batteries of light artillery, and six regiments of cavalry.[1] During the next few months as men were mustered out of military service, the total numbers of both white and black soldiers in the army declined rapidly, creating a dangerously small military organization. The need for a military force on the western frontier, however, demanded a great portion of this peacetime strength. In response, the army began to require conscripted Civil War personnel to complete their obligations, and in 1866 it initiated diligent recruitment practices. The novel result was a peacetime increase in the army's total manpower. A number of the Civil War veterans who remained in the army for several months following the end of the war or who reenlisted were stationed in the western regions of the country.

In the immediate postwar years, black troopers who served in New Mexico Territory were members of one of twenty companies of the Fifty-seventh, One Hundred Twenty-fifth, or Thirty-eighth Infantry Regiments. Organized in March 1864, the Fifty-seventh Infantry grew out of the Fourth Arkansas Infantry (African Descent). Until August 1864 the regiment's members did garrison duty at Little Rock and Helena, during which time some of them served as a train guard and most of them were involved in three separate Civil War skirmishes near Little Rock. From August 1864 until June 1865 its members did duty at Brownsville, Duvall's Bluff, and Little Rock, and for another year the entire regiment spent time guarding property in Arkansas. While part of the regiment continued this duty for the remainder of 1866, in August six companies traveled to new stations in New Mexico, Companies A, B, and D going to Fort Union and Companies C, E, and G going to Fort Bascom. The companies at Bascom joined those at Union in early October, and in the following month they were all transferred out of New Mexico. On December 31, 1866, the Fifty-seventh Infantry was disbanded and its members mustered out of the army.[2]

The One Hundred Twenty-fifth Infantry was organized in the spring of 1865 in Louisville, Kentucky. Obligated to three years of military service, all its members had garrison and guard duty at Louisville and other places in Kentucky and nearby Ohio and Illinois.[3] In August 1866 eight companies of the One Hundred Twenty-fifth were transferred to New Mexico, and by the end of the year they were serving at seven of the territory's forts.[4] In October 1867 these companies gathered at Fort Union. Then they moved on, most of them going to Fort Riley, Kansas, for discharge from military service.[5] On December 20, 1867, the One Hundred Twenty-fifth was disbanded and its members mustered out of the army.

As a part of the postwar regular army, the Thirty-eighth Infantry was formed in 1866. Some of the men in this new regiment were veterans of the Civil War, reenlisting in the army immediately upon being mustered out of their Civil War units. Others were untrained recruits who found adjustment to military life difficult. Though some of these enlisted men were recruited from northern states where they had lived free before the war, others were southern blacks who had been enslaved until only recently. Apparently many young black men willingly enlisted because the army provided them with economic security in a society where they were not accepted equally. Thirteen dollars a month was not much money, but blacks could expect to earn less as civilians. In addition, army life included free food, clothing, and shelter.

Almost as soon as the Thirty-eighth Infantry was formed, army authorities sent it to the western frontier to repulse Indian attacks. Under the direction of Gen. Winfield S. Hancock, men of the Thirty-eighth joined with elements of the Third, Sixth, and Thirty-seventh Infantry Regiments and the Seventh and Tenth Cavalry Regiments to defend Kansas, Colorado, and Indian Territory. Approximately four thousand officers and enlisted men of these regiments held down eighteen forts and camps and guarded more than 1,500 miles of major roads.

In 1867 black infantrymen were involved in a series of skirmishes and engagements collectively called Hancock's War.[6] During this conflict, a detachment of the Thirty-eighth assisted in the defense of Fort Wallace, Kansas, against an attack led by Cheyenne Chief Roman Nose. The black troopers were assigned to picket duty when this battle began, but when they realized they were needed on the skirmish line, without authority they jumped into a wagon pulled by four mules, all of the men standing up and firing in the direction of the Indians as their wagon rushed to the scene. Once there, they leaped out of the wagon and began firing again.[7]

As the One Hundred Twenty-fifth Infantry moved out of New Mexico, six companies of the Thirty-eighth Infantry arrived to replace it between September and December 1867.[8] To reach New Mexico these men of the Thirty-eighth had marched from Fort Leavenworth, Kansas, at that time the terminus of the nearest railroad. Asiatic cholera struck the men as they marched across the plains of Kansas, and those fit for duty reportedly had to bury the victims each morning before the day's march.[9] After serving in New Mexico until September and October 1869, these soldiers transferred to Fort McKavitt, Texas, where their regiment combined with the Forty-first to form the new Twenty-fourth Infantry.[10]

Serving concurrently in New Mexico with the Thirty-eighth Infantry was the white Thirty-seventh. From the middle of 1867 until late 1869 nine companies of the Thirty-seventh were at three forts

(Sumner, Marcy, and Lowell) at which blacks were not located. They were also stationed at Forts Bascom, Wingate, Union, and Stanton during this two-and-a-half-year period, but not when black troopers were present.[11]

Between August 1866 and October 1869 the number of black soldiers in New Mexico averaged about 522 per month. About 290 enlisted men of the Fifty-seventh Infantry, 440 men of the One Hundred Twenty-fifth Infantry, and 640 men of the Thirty-eighth Infantry served in the territory during that time.[12] New recruits may have raised the number of black soldiers to nearly 1,500. White officers led these black troopers, and they were often designated as commanders at their various posts.

Most of New Mexico's forts, even the smaller ones, usually contained at least two companies of soldiers, white and black enlisted men often serving simultaneously. At various times and stations (Fort McRae excepted) between 1866 and 1869, one or more companies of white Third cavalrymen served along with the black infantrymen. In the middle of 1860 the white Fifth Infantry had moved into New Mexico, where it was destined to remain not only throughout the Civil War but also for more than two years after its end. For short periods of time in 1866 and 1867 some of its men served with black infantrymen at Forts Bayard and Union. When taking up new assignments, these black infantrymen sometimes replaced white volunteer groups such as the First Infantry, New Mexico Volunteers; First Cavalry, New Mexico Volunteers; or First Cavalry, California Volunteers. Not uncommonly these white groups remained at a post for a few days or weeks after the black men had arrived before moving out.[13]

In 1866 black troopers had hardly arrived at the eight New Mexico forts to which they were assigned when Indians made them conscious of the hazards of their new duty. In late August forty Indians attacked two privates of the First Cavalry, California Volunteers, as they were carrying mail to Camp Mimbres, eight miles west of Fort Cummings. The Indians killed one man and badly wounded the other, capturing the dead man's horse, saddle, and equipment. The commander and fifteen men at Mimbres retrieved the stripped and mutilated body, the torn mailbag, and some of the scattered mail. They pursued the Indian band into the nearby mountains but failed to overtake it.[14]

Two months later Cummings's commander reported that on October 20 Pvt. Samuel Taylor of Company D, One Hundred Twenty-fifth Infantry, had been killed.[15] The cause of death was not listed, but Indians may have been responsible. Taylor may have the dubious distinction of being the first black soldier killed in New Mexico Territory in the post–Civil War era.

The U.S. government placed soldiers on the American frontier in order to subdue the Indians, and one might assume that the Indians would thus avoid the areas where soldiers were concentrated. The opposite was often true. The Indians coveted the soldiers' horses and other animals, and various groups in New Mexico made a number of attempts to capture such stock. A few days after Company D of the One Hundred Twenty-fifth Infantry arrived at Fort Cummings, about thirty Apache Indians, advancing in small parties and from different directions, approached the post, evidently to stampede the post's cattle. Twenty-five mounted black infantrymen drove the Indians away and pursued them, skirmishing through the canyons and over the mountains around Cooke's Peak. Cummings's post commander wrote: "They could run faster and hide quicker than we could and it being impossible to get them to fight, we failed to kill any, or if we did they carried their dead along with them."[16]

Two weeks later near Mimbres fifteen Indians made an attack on four herders and the government animals under their care, killing one herder and successfully running off with eleven horses and eight mules. Fort McRae's commander immediately tried to recapture the herd but failed. This incident prompted him to plan an attack on nearby Indian camps (called *rancherias*) with fifty infantrymen carrying twenty days' rations. He was interested both in retrieving the stolen stock and in breaking up the rancherias.[17]

Similar Indian raids continued for the duration of the black infantrymen's stay in New Mexico. In May 1867 while a white sergeant of the Third Cavalry and one corporal, six unmounted herd guards, and four mounted herders, all of the One Hundred Twenty-fifth Infantry, were watching government-owned animals near Fort Bayard, about twenty Indians attacked, driving off forty-four mules, one horse, and five beef cattle. The guards chased the Indians for a mile, shooting at them until they exhausted their ammunition. Upon their return, the guards took the remainder of the herd (ten mules and 139 beef cattle) to Fort Bayard for protection. A contingent of Third cavalrymen spent forty-eight hours attempting to find the Indians and the stolen animals, but they were not successful.[18]

In a similar incident, in November 1867 from twenty-five to seventy-five Apache Indians seized Fort Selden's quartermaster herd of thirteen horses and thirty mules. White cavalrymen and a few black infantrymen quickly mounted, chasing the Indians into the Doña Ana Mountains east of the fort. They killed three Indians and captured eight or ten Indian ponies and all the stolen stock, except for three horses and three mules that had been killed during the fight. The Indians, by contrast, killed a cavalryman's horse. During this episode, the soldiers shot and killed a Hispanic hay cutter whom they mistook for an Indian.[19]

Indian violence did not abate. In February 1869 Indians seized a herd of cattle two miles south of Selden, and in March they cut the ferry cable across the Rio Grande near the site of the fort, shot an officer's cow, killed a steer, and unsuccessfully attacked the fort's wood train within the military reservation.[20]

Military men were not the only ones to suffer, for the Indians took animals from private citizens as well. In November 1866 the commander at Fort Bascom wrote that "there has been for several weeks straggling bands of Indians . . . who are roaming over the country, killing and stealing citizen's stock, in the vicinity of this post." He sent out soldiers, who at times got close enough to the Indians to exchange shots with them, but the soldiers were unable to kill or capture any of the enemy, "owing to the impassable character of Mesa Rica, which seems to be the general rendezvous [for the Indians]."[21]

Soldiers at other forts protected citizens' stock, too. At sunset on January 17, 1868, about thirty Indians "mounted on American horses" dashed into Central City and drove away seven oxen, seven mules, and three horses. The commander of Fort Bayard, two miles away, heard of the raid an hour after it occurred and directed Thirty-eighth Infantry Lt. Bethel M. Custer immediately to pursue the raiders with "all the troops able to mount mules," each with three days' rations and forty rounds of ammunition.[22] Infantrymen mounted on mules had little chance to catch horse-mounted Indians. Five months later a party of Indians drove off a number of cattle and horses belonging to the citizens

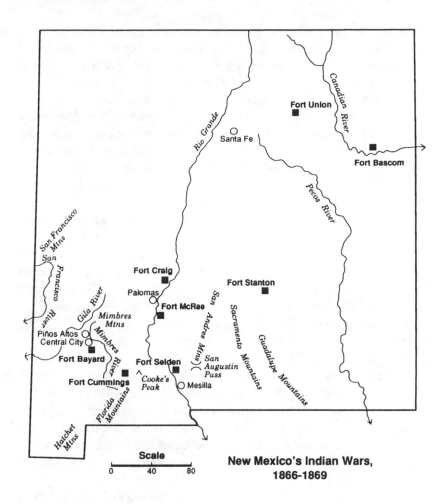

New Mexico's Indian Wars,
1866-1869

of Central City. A detachment of Third cavalrymen pursued the Indians to the nearby mountains, but they were no more successful than the infantrymen had been earlier.[23]

Resentful of white settlers' encroachment upon their lands, Indians did not hesitate to kill the intruders. In March 1867 about thirty members of the Rio Mimbres Apache tribe attacked the white settlements on the Mimbres River about forty miles from Fort Cummings, killing one citizen and wounding another.[24] The commander at Cummings reported that in August near Pinos Altos, Indians shot and killed

one citizen and wounded another. However, he reported that he knew
of no persons who, between April and September 1867, had been killed
or wounded within forty miles of Fort Cummings.[25] Such a statement
may appear self-serving, but providing protection for citizens in the
area of his post was a major task for a post commander.

In September 1869 Cummings's new commander, Capt. Alexander
Moore of the Thirty-eighth Infantry, found the task no easier, reporting
that Indians had recently shot and seriously wounded a Hispano, who
at that time lay in the post hospital with little chance to survive. When
a band of Indians murdered a white woman and her child near Hot
Springs, after which they stole thirty cattle and fifteen mules and
horses, the commander wrote: "I have men to scout for these Indians
but I must have a guide. I don't want to chase Indians with a detachment of men and a number of animals through an unknown country
totally without water. I just want superiors to know it is perfectly useless
for the soldiers at Cummings to try to protect the settlers here without
a guide. I can be in no way held responsible for Indian outrages." To
support his argument further, Moore reported that "last night the
Indians tried to take alive our sentinel at post no. 4 at this fort, and he
only escaped through his own watchfulness and the prompt actions of
the guard."[26] These were not the words of a coward or a whimperer. A
tough native of Ireland, Moore had been cited for gallantry and highly
meritorious conduct in the Civil War Battle of Gettysburg.[27] He was a
seasoned veteran who led his infantrymen on a number of scouts
against the Indians and who never flinched in the face of hardship or
danger. Indeed, a spirit of "go get 'em" pervaded his actions and his
reports. No doubt his black troopers reflected that spirit.

In efforts to protect New Mexico's law-abiding citizens and their
property, black soldiers attended not only to Indians but also to white
cattle thieves. In April 1867 when soldiers discovered a fresh cattle
trail leading away from the Fort Bascom military reservation, an investigation revealed that government-owned cattle were missing. Lt. John
D. Lee, serving as temporary commander of Bascom for Capt. George
W. Letterman, immediately sent a sergeant and five enlisted men to
follow the trail. After a forty-mile ride, the detachment caught sight of
two white men and the missing cattle. When the men saw the approaching soldiers, they fled.

The soldiers recovered the cattle a few miles from a ranch owned by Charles M. Hubbell, who served as agent for a contractor who supplied beef to Fort Bascom. They continued to chase the two thieves, the trail leading them to Hubbell's Ranch. At the ranch they learned that Hubbell and his partner Sam Smith had arrived a short time previously, but they were not there when the detachment arrived, so the sergeant and his men followed Hubbell and Smith's trail, which led from the ranch to Fort Bascom. Hubbell and Smith arrived at Bascom on April 20, the day before they were to make a beef delivery. Letterman concluded that the circumstantial evidence indicated that Hubbell and Smith were guilty of theft and that apparently Hubbell had hoped to fill his beef contract with cattle he had stolen from the post.[28]

In addition to thwarting Indian raids and cattle thieves, black soldiers were used to clamp down on illegal commerce. In August 1867 a detachment of seventeen men was sent from Fort Bascom to investigate reports of the presence of a large body of Comanche Indians. Approximately sixty miles east of the fort, the troopers overtook six Mexicans and eleven donkeys loaded with five hundred pounds of beans, forty butcher knives, and many pounds of lead and powder. The Mexicans did not have papers authorizing them to trade with the Indians, but they claimed that other members of their party — who had preceded them into the Indian lands — had the proper permits. Doubting the story, the soldiers' leader compelled the Mexicans to accompany the detachment to Bascom. There the traders were released, but their goods were confiscated. Although some such traders had legal permits, others did not. Captain Letterman had little regard for any of them, believing they were all scoundrels who smuggled contraband goods to the Indians and received stolen cattle in return, notwithstanding the military's deterrent efforts.[29] Such policing actions added to the workload of the black soldiers.

In general the presence of soldiers on the frontier was a protection to white settlers and travelers. For instance, when a civilian desired to sink a water well at the halfway point on the fifty-five-mile-long road between Forts Cummings and Selden "for the use and convenience of all persons traveling that road," he applied to Cummings's commander, Capt. R. B. Foutts, for military protection while workers dug the well. Foutts knew that no water was available on that well-traveled road, except during the rainy season in July and August, and he was aware that if a well was dug, water from it would be of great benefit to the public. He therefore willingly supplied protection for the diggers.[30]

In addition, Foutts helped a citizen in an emergency. When Navarro Chavez accidentally seriously wounded himself, and the surgeon at Fort Cummings did not have the necessary instruments to operate, the commanding officer ordered the Hispanic man to be taken to Fort Bayard, accompanied by a detail composed of a corporal and three privates from Company F of the Thirty-eighth.[31]

Not everyone, however, was satisfied with the performance of the soldiers — or that of their commanding officer. When Indians killed Charles Young, a mail courier, a few miles from Fort Cummings in November 1867, black soldiers retrieved the body and buried it in the post cemetery. Because this death was so close to a military post, citizens of Pinos Altos called upon Cummings's newly appointed commander, Lt. James N. Morgan, to express their concern about inadequate protection, relating their irritations at what they considered less than satisfactory relationships between themselves and the black soldiers and their officers. When these citizens did not receive reasonable reassurances from Morgan, they held a public meeting at which they expressed their doubt about Morgan's competence, proclaiming that "the officer commanding colored troops now stationed in the vicinity is utterly destitute of truth." They claimed that Morgan had told them that the black troopers stationed at Cummings were not there to protect citizens.

Morgan disclaimed having made such a statement. He was quoted as claiming that "no insult offered by the troops under my command to citizens of this County has ever been reported to me, nor did I know of any officer using the language imputed to officers of Colored troops."[32] Despite Morgan's protests, the army replaced him with Capt. Charles E. Clarke as commander of Cummings. Young's death had triggered citizens' criticisms not only of Morgan but also of the black soldiers under his command, awakening the latent racism that lay just beneath the surface of the society of New Mexico.

As control of the Indian population was the major reason for the presence of soldiers in post–Civil War New Mexico Territory, both white cavalrymen and black infantrymen went on numerous scouts to seek out and subdue Indians by capturing or killing them. One officer indicated that his instructions were to scout thoroughly for Indians and to kill every Indian capable of bearing arms.[33] Many of these scouts were of short duration, lasting only a few hours, as, for example, when troopers chased away Indians from a post or a settlement. Other scouts were planned in advance and lasted from a few days to several weeks. Black participation in these excursions was substantial: official military records reveal that when black infantrymen were in New Mexico between August 1866 and October 1869, many of them went on numerous small-scale scouts, several major scouts, and the following grand expedition.

On March 6, 1867, Lt. Col. Alexander Duncan, commander of Fort Bayard, two other commissioned officers, and fifty-eight men of the One Hundred Twenty-fifth left their post with twenty-five days' rations on a scout of the Gila River and the country northwest of that stream. The column confronted disagreeable snow and rain, as well as treacherous high waters in the rivers. At one point they had to build a raft to transport rations and men across the San Francisco River. Duncan wrote: "The inclemency of the weather and high waters made the trip a rough one." Horses and pack mules died from exhaustion, and guide Juan Arroyos confessed it was the roughest scout he had ever made. Miners accompanying the soldiers found some gold in Chase's Gulch, but not in sufficient quantities to justify expending large amounts of labor or capital. The soldiers saw no Indians, although they observed smoke signals in the San Francisco Mountains. After traveling three hundred miles, on March 28 Duncan and his men returned to Bayard.[34]

The Gila River scout, however, was not the most physically taxing expedition for black infantrymen in New Mexico. The superiors of Lt. Henry F. Leggett ordered him to leave Fort Cummings on January 1, 1868, in command of the Thirty-eighth Infantry Company A (twenty-five men) to join and cooperate with a detachment leaving Fort Bayard on the same day. The united detachment was to break up a rancheria of Indians supposed to be about forty miles southwest of Fort McRae.[35] Leggett, however, never made contact with the Bayard contingent, and the latter carried through on its orders without him. Led by Captain Moore, the Bayard detachment was composed of seventy-two enlisted men of Companies D and F of the Thirty-eighth. Moore and his men traveled northwest of Bayard to the Mimbres River country, where their "axes were in constant use cleaving timber and small brush which obstructed the march." The Mimbres Mountains environment proved to be even more of an obstacle. A severe snowstorm revealed that the black soldiers were "exceedingly sensitive to low degrees of temperatures," and "the necessary absences of fire in the exposed positions . . . aggravated the discomfort." At times they marched through snow two feet deep. As snow continued to fall, on a very steep decline both "men and animals rolled and slid with frightful velocity," causing much damage to the mules' packs. Moore reported that the terrain over which his infantrymen traveled would make it difficult for a cavalry unit to scout the country.

At the close of this seventeen-day march a considerable number of troops were without shoes or had only remnants thereof. These barefooted infantrymen led into Bayard unshod mules that were becoming lame. In his final report on this scout, Moore recommended that in the future, extra shoes be taken for both men and mules and that a blacksmith join such scouts. Incidentally, the detachment had found some stolen cattle, but it had seen no Indians. Despite its hardships, the scout was not without positive results. In his nine-page report, Moore included a map of the terrain covered. His superiors recognized that information about the terrain, Indians, and Indian trails was valuable for the future, and they praised Moore for the information he had gathered and reported.[36]

Apparently the army was unconcerned about the severity of the weather and the hardships of scouting. The day after Moore and his half-frozen and nearly shoeless men stumbled into Bayard while snow was still falling upon them, superiors ordered Lt. Bethel Custer and ten enlisted men of Company D of the Thirty-eighth to pursue a band of Indians who had stolen some cattle. Joining them were the guide Juan Arroyos and three citizens from whom the cattle had been taken. They were able to follow the Indians in a southwesterly direction because the latter left a clearly marked trail in the snow, despite attempts to hide it by moving over steep and rough rocky ridges.

The Indians were well mounted and drove the stolen herd along at a rapid gait. Mounted on mules, Moore's men kept their animals at a slow trot for a day and a half. When they heard a noise similar to a coyote's bark (a noise they recognized as an Indian signal), the black troopers moved forward preparing for an attack. At that point they discovered that the Indians had scattered the stolen animals in all

"A Camp Fire Sketch." (Courtesy Frederic Remington Art Museum, Ogdensburg, New York.)

directions in an attempt to throw the soldiers off their trail. When the military detachment accidentally came upon a mounted Indian, the guide fired a rifle at him, "which did not appear to have any effect, other than to accelerate his speed."

Early the next morning, the detachment came upon the Indians driving the stolen cattle. But the Indians were in such a position that the detachment could not attack without moving into a canyon, where it would be at a considerable disadvantage "because the Indians could roll down boulders upon us." With such a small force, the lieutenant and his men returned to Bayard, having ridden about 128 miles and having been in the saddle twenty-eight hours. In his report Custer suggested that pocket compasses be provided for scouting parties, as their cost was little and their advantages were great. He could have saved twenty miles on his return trip if he had carried a compass.[37]

In August 1868 Capt. Edward Bloodgood and a party of forty men from Company K, Thirty-eighth Infantry, and Company K, Third Cavalry, including a Hispanic guide and an interpreter (all mounted and with fifteen days' rations), rode out of Fort Selden in search of

Indian raiders. Marching about sixty miles in four days, they crossed the Rio Grande two miles north of the fort and traveled on northward to Palomas, a Hispanic settlement at the mouth of the Palomas River. At Palomas they found a scouting detachment of twenty enlisted men of Company C of the Thirty-eighth from Fort McRae under the unlikely command of a quartermaster's clerk named William Ellis. Ellis reported that he and his men had accidentally encountered a party of one hundred or more Apache Indians in a dry canyon twenty-five miles west of Palomas. When an army surgeon from McRae arrived at Palomas to care for Ellis, who was badly wounded in the Apache encounter, Captain Bloodgood assumed temporary command of Ellis's men and led the unified column on a night march after their Apache prey. However, they lost the Indians' trail in a thunderstorm.[38]

From August through November 1868 the army made extra efforts to subdue the Indians in southwestern New Mexico, mounting several sizable scouts from Forts Bayard and Cummings. Some of the scouts out of Bayard were composed of men from both the Third Cavalry and the Thirty-eighth Infantry who, on one occasion battled some Indians, killing and wounding a few of them and destroying some of their property. James Francis, a black private, was wounded in this engagement.[39]

Capt. Alexander Moore and his infantrymen continued to chase Indians to the south and southwest of Fort Cummings. Convinced that Mexicans from south of the border encouraged Indians in New Mexico to steal cattle and to drive them across the international border, Moore and eighty-five enlisted men of the Thirty-eighth scouted the Hatchet and Florida mountains, attempting to stop this practice. On a scout that lasted from August 23 to September 14, this group traveled four hundred miles, during which time it surprised an Indian rancheria near Ojo Alamo and then attacked another band of Indians a few days later in the same vicinity. As a result of these encounters, the detachment killed three Indians and several animals and destroyed many pounds of powder, about one ton of preserved mescal, and some cooking utensils and water jars. They captured three Indian children, four rifles, and seventeen horses, mules, and burros and took for their own use wheat, peas, corn, and dried venison, as well as some blankets and skins. The soldiers must have wounded several Indians for the trails and rocks were sprinkled with blood.

Returning to Cummings, Moore had with him eleven Indian animals (the other six were wounded and had to be killed), three Indian children, and a large supply of Indian stores. He admitted he had problems with lack of water on this scout, but the detachment survived that inconvenience. Indeed, Moore reported that his men were in excellent health and spirits after this long and tough but successful march.[40]

The commander of Fort Selden had problems of his own. Indians sometimes interfered with immigrants moving through San Augustin Pass, a major route through the San Andres Mountains about twenty miles southeast of Fort Selden. Furthermore, they often attempted to steal the animals of the ranches near San Augustin Springs. Between September and December 1868 Selden's commander sent several scouting parties into that area, but despite these forays, Indians drove away at least one herd of horses and mules from a ranch near the pass.[41]

The troubles continued. In January 1869 Indians killed two civilians as they made their way through San Augustin Pass. Selden's commander responded by establishing at Shedd's Ranch near the eastern entrance to the pass a temporary picket guard and escort composed of Lt. Edwin A. Rigg and eleven men of Company K of the Thirty-eighth.[42] Shortly after this force was relieved, the Indians killed an Anglo named Thomas who was traveling alone on a mule over "what is considered the worst Indian country in this vicinity."[43]

In May 1869 thirty to fifty Indians attacked three cavalrymen as they escorted a citizen through the pass. The corporal was killed instantly, and one private, the citizen, and two horses were wounded. When word of this incident reached Fort Selden, all available cavalrymen and infantrymen rode to retrieve the dead soldier's body and to drive the Indians from the area of the pass.[44]

A larger picket of both white and black soldiers was stationed at the pass for a time following these events, causing the Indians to avoid the area.[45] In August 1869 Selden's commanding officer reported: "Nothing noteworthy has transpired in the vicinity of the picket."[46] But the peace was short-lived. In October Selden's commander reported that the pass "is regarded by all as the most dangerous place in this section of New Mexico."[47] He was surely correct. In a period of fifteen months Indians had killed twelve people near it.[48]

"The Sign Language." (Courtesy Frederic Remington Art Museum, Ogdensburg, New York.)

Although the officers and men of the army's black infantry companies and white cavalry companies had spent much time pursuing Indians during their first years in New Mexico, their efforts had been relatively uncoordinated. But in the late months of 1868 and the early months of 1869 the army attempted to implement a more coordinated and stepped-up effort to rout the Indians. The army's Division of the Missouri headquarters sent a large command into New Mexico to advance down the Canadian River to drive hostile Indians toward Fort Cobb in Indian Territory. Another command, operating out of Colorado, attacked hostile Indians wherever they were found.[49] During this main offensive, a formidable military force dealt a severe blow "to a notoriously bad and desperate band of Indians"[50] that went a long way toward ending Comanche and Kiowa difficulties in northeastern New Mexico. For a time thereafter, most of the Plains Indians remained on their reservations.[51] More importantly, even though the soldiers suffered winter hardships, the success of this operation convinced military leaders that winter was a practical season for punishing the Indians.[52] After this time, military forces made more winter attacks upon the Indians, thus placing yearlong pressure upon them.

In the spring of 1869 Captain Moore asked for and received permission to launch a massive expedition against the depredatory Mescalero Apaches in southeastern New Mexico and western Texas. Leaving Fort Cummings on April 4 with a detachment of Thirty-eighth infantrymen, Moore marched to Fort Selden, where he organized his expedition. He had to borrow or exchange mules and horses with other forts because so many of his animals were not able to make a long trip. Joining him were six companies of black enlisted men of the Thirty-eighth Infantry and their white leaders, Lts. Edwin A. Rigg of Fort Selden, Henry F. Leggett of Fort McRae, William E. Sweet of Fort Craig, and James N. Morgan of Bayard. The command contained Lt. Joseph C. McBride, one noncommissioned officer, and five privates, all of Company E, Third Cavalry, out of Fort Cummings. Moore took along Asst. Surgeon Charles Styer and a hospital steward, making a total of seven commissioned officers and 196 enlisted men.

This large command left Selden on April 11, marching through San Augustin Pass in the San Andres Mountains, across the Sacramento Mountains, and into the Guadalupe Mountains, where Moore established a supply camp at Pine Spring. On April 21 Moore met with

Gen. John R. Brooke out of Fort Stanton, who informed him that he
had recently burned an Indian rancheria. Because Brooke intended to
scout the northern range of the mountains, Moore decided to explore
to the south. He immediately ran into a band of Indians, which he
chased, pursuing it so closely that the Indians abandoned much of their
property, including sixteen horses, two mules, three oxen, twenty-
seven buffalo robes, a large quantity of dried meat, and all of their
cooking utensils and water vessels. From his supply camp Moore
scouted Delaware Creek, marching 209 miles. He found numerous
abandoned rancherias and evidence of large herds of cattle, but he
found no Indians.

Abandoning his supply camp in May and traveling farther south,
Moore viewed many large Indian trails. He found a good supply of water
in ponds but no running water. As he continued south he concluded
that few white men had been in this expansive and desolate land before,
and the Indians apparently felt quite safe. At one point Moore sent a
pack train into Fort Quitman, Texas, to obtain twenty days' rations.
While waiting for the rations, he made a thorough scout of the mesa
beside the Diablo Mountains, which convinced him that no Indians
were — or ever had been — permanently located in those mountains.
He found no large trails running through the region: the country was
barren and waterless except for one small spring.

Continuing to move, Moore and his men arrived at Barrel Springs,
Texas, from which he sent to Fort Davis, Texas, for ten days' rations
and a guide who was familiar with the mesas on the east side of the
Guadalupes. Lt. Col. Wesley Merritt, commanding Davis, obliged his
requests. After this, in extremely hot weather, Moore and his men
marched north along the eastern side of the Guadalupes, a sandy,
waterless route, barren of vegetation. They traveled westward across
the southern end of the Sacramento Mountains into the San Andres
Mountains, where at the San Augustin Springs they found water.
Climbing over the nearby pass, they then went directly to Fort Selden,
where their massive and exhaustive efforts ended, the officers and their
various companies returning to their home posts. In an expedition that
had lasted from April 11 to June 12, the main body of this command
had traveled 1,241 miles, an average of more than nineteen miles a day.

As a result of this expedition, Moore concluded that not more than
fifty Indian warriors were in the ranges he had scouted and that this

small band committed all the depredations recently reported. He recommended the establishment of a post in the area, which with regular scouting would compel the Indians to abandon that country and move south of the Pecos River and perhaps into Mexico. He praised both officers and enlisted men who made this march but stated: "All my experience in scouting with black troops goes to prove that the ordinary government ration is *not sufficient* for them when campaigning." He reported that the expedition resulted in no casualties and no desertions.[53]

A few months later Fort Bayard's commander, Maj. Henry C. Merriam, sent Capt. C.N.W. Cunningham and twenty-five men into the Mimbres Mountains, where the Indians often hid, to map the area for future scouts. Even though Merriam anticipated that this two-week scout would have no contact with Indians, he was aware of the hazards of such duty. "Owing to the inability of the Quartermaster Dept. to furnish extra shoes for troops," he wrote to Cunningham, "the greatest care must be taken to preserve by timely repairs with such material as may be at hand those now issued." He ordered a blacksmith to accompany this command, supplied with a shoeing hammer and extra mule shoes and nails.[54]

Cunningham and his men left Fort Bayard a day later than originally planned because first they had to kill and pack a beef. Once underway, this command marched through heavy rain that made even more difficult the tough ascents and descents in the mountains. Some of the men complained of cramps in their feet because of these marching conditions. At one time mosquitoes became so troublesome — especially to the command's animals — that the enlisted men kept a smoky fire going all night to keep their mounts from becoming unmanageable. In addition to rain and mosquitoes, this command also had to contend with extreme heat, which on one occasion delayed the troopers' daily march until 7 P.M. This night march ended at 4 A.M. after an eighteen-mile trek.[55] Yet these tribulations proved worthwhile, for Cunningham's map of the area helped others who later scouted for Indians.

Indians considered travelers of all kinds as fair game, especially those who had desirable animals. Because of this, mounted black infantrymen spent countless hours performing escort duty to protect citizens, military personnel, U.S. mail carriers, and supply trains.

Escorting citizens traveling from the East to California was a big job for the men at Fort Cummings, located on the Butterfield Overland Trail (a major trans-territorial route) and in an area occupied by particularly hostile Apache Indians. Cummings's position made it an appropriate place to station soldiers whose job was to protect travelers on their way to the mines at Santa Rita and Pinos Altos.[56] Military personnel needed protection, too. In April 1867, for example, enlisted men escorted officers from Fort McRae to Forts Craig and Selden.[57] The safekeeping of the U.S. mail necessitated soldierly escorts in many areas of New Mexico, especially in the vicinity of Fort Cummings.[58]

The number of entries referring to escorts in the military records indicates that soldiers most often provided escort services to protect quartermaster supplies; references to government trains filled with general supplies are numerous. In September 1866 a lieutenant, one sergeant, and seven privates of Company D, One Hundred Twenty-fifth Infantry, escorted six-mule-team wagons loaded with charcoal from the Santa Rita copper mines to Fort Cummings. The men carried twenty rounds of ammunition each, indicating their concern over Indian dangers.[59]

Other references to supply escorts abound. For example, in June 1867 a noncommissioned officer and eight privates of the One Hundred Twenty-fifth traveled round-trip with Lt. Joseph A. Corbett from Fort Cummings to Mesilla to pick up fifty bushels of lime for repairing the buildings on the post.[60] In August 1868 a noncommissioned officer and eight privates escorted a post train originating at Cummings to and from Pinos Altos, where it acquired lumber.[61]

"Escorting service" was sometimes a euphemism for "herding service." In August 1867 Cpl. Howard Lockett and three privates of Company D of the One Hundred Twenty-fifth at Cummings were ordered to Fort Bayard to escort beef cattle. A few months later a noncommissioned officer and nine privates of Company A of the Thirty-eighth at Cummings were detailed to travel to Fort Bowie with Hugh L. Hinds and his party in charge of a herd of cattle being delivered to troopers in Arizona.[62] No doubt such service was hot, dirty, and dangerous.

The black troopers at Fort Selden were regularly employed as escorts to Forts Craig and Bayard for civilians on their way to the mines at Pinos Altos.[63] In December 1866 they provided escort service for a district surveyor for the Territory of Arizona, and a month later they escorted a new custom-house officer on his way to Tucson.[64] In October 1868 they provided protection for Judge J. Houghton and his party between Selden and Forts Cummings and Craig when the group moved to and from Mesilla to attend the U.S. District Court session there.[65]

These men provided yet another type of escort service in 1867, when members of the One Hundred Twenty-fifth rode from Selden to another post with five horse thieves and robbers.[66] In 1869 a corporal of the Thirty-eighth was placed in charge of an escort for government teams of horses sent to Nesmith's Mills for lumber, the expedition requiring twelve days.[67] Finally, the post commander at Selden expressed his tacit confidence in a black soldier when he arranged for a private of the One Hundred Twenty-fifth to drive an ambulance carrying the commander's wife and her sister to Santa Fe.[68]

While white cavalrymen often scouted for hostile Indians and provided escort services specifically designed to thwart Indian attacks in the late 1860s in New Mexico Territory, mounted black infantrymen also devoted a considerable amount of time to these arduous and dangerous tasks. Through their early efforts partial control of the hostile Indians was possible, and they set the stage for the ultimate and total subjugation of the Indians during the era of the Indian Wars.

II. Infantry Camp Life, 1866–1869

The army's efforts to subjugate the Indians of New Mexico after the Civil War occupied a great deal of the average enlisted man's time. Even so, the men in the ranks spent countless hours performing duties in and around the posts. The hard and demanding garrison life of the black infantrymen who were in New Mexico from 1866 to 1869 was a significant part of their frontier experience in the post–Civil War era.

Conditions at small and isolated western posts may have justified the loosening of military regimen, but post commanders usually demanded that the soldiers perform the activities the army recommended or required. Insofar as conditions permitted, the men at these posts worked within a rigidly organized routine, beginning with early morning reveille and lasting until early evening taps. Almost every hour had one or more calls. Drills, parade assemblies, and fatigue details were everyday occurrences.

Some commanders gave attention to military formalities. For instance, within a few days after black troopers arrived at Fort Selden in August 1866, the commander requisitioned 150 pounds of powder for firing salutes at the post.[1] Occasionally, however, the men got a break from the work routine, as on July 4, 1868, when all drills and fatigue, with the exception of those necessary to police the post, were suspended at Fort Cummings and at noon the soldiers paraded and fired a national salute.[2] After learning of the death of former President James Buchanan, Cummings's troopers paraded at 11 A.M., after which all labor ceased for the day. On the next day, with the American flag at half-staff, thirteen guns were fired at dawn, one gun was fired at intervals of thirty minutes between the rising and setting sun, and at the close of the day thirty-seven guns were used in a national salute. Because of Buchanan's death, the troopers were ordered to wear crepe on their left arms and on their swords for a period of six months.[3]

Soldiers on the western frontier were often called upon to perform a considerable amount of both manual and skilled labor. Black infantrymen erected new buildings and repaired old ones at the New Mexico forts at which they served between 1866 and 1869. Military records indicate that these troopers served extra duty as carpenters, plasterers, painters, and bricklayers.[4] Simply because they performed skilled jobs did not always mean the men themselves had mastered the requisite skills. When Maj. Andrew J. Alexander became Fort Bascom's commander in January 1867, he reported that the newly constructed quarters were "not fit for dogs to live in." He wrote: "Every building in the place leaks badly, and the [quartermaster's] storehouse is in such a condition that I consider it in great danger of falling down [in] the first heavy rain." He implied that using enlisted men to build the post was a mistake.[5]

Because most of the New Mexico forts were great distances from railway facilities, the soldiers had to construct buildings from whatever materials were available locally. At Fort McRae, Company C of the One Hundred Twenty-fifth Infantry put a new roof on the post hospital and built a reading room, a corral, and a large warehouse for corn and other quartermaster stores. They also made twenty-five thousand adobe bricks, after which they built a large, four-room adobe house for officers' quarters.[6] Some of the soldiers who were employed as adobemakers in the immediate post–Civil War years were of Hispanic descent, and the use of black soldiers for the task at McRae was decidedly unusual. In any case, a few months later the army began contracting civilian laborers to furnish its adobe bricks.[7] Plenty of other construction tasks awaited the black troopers. For example, at Fort Bascom the fifty-five men of Company K of the One Hundred Twenty-fifth spent weeks in late 1866 building a corral for the horses of Company G, Third Cavalry.[8]

Black infantrymen made major contributions to the construction of the first buildings at the newly established Forts Selden and Bayard, men of the One Hundred Twenty-fifth joining white soldiers, civilian employees, and military prisoners in Selden's building program, which

Enlisted Men's Barracks, Fort Selden, built in part with black infantrymen's labor, 1867. (Photo #14929, Courtesy Arizona Historical Society, Tucson.)

Administration Building, Fort Selden, built in part with black infantrymen's labor, 1867. (Photo #14935, Courtesy Arizona Historical Society, Tucson.)

was essentially completed by January 1867.[9] Except for the administration building, Selden's original structures were one-story adobe buildings with dirt floors and roofs of rough cottonwood vigas covered with peeled willows and bulrushes, which in turn were covered with dirt and lime.[10] Such construction methods and materials must have seemed strange to men who had lived in the East or the South.

In January 1867 the commander at Fort Cummings indicated that post's buildings were "comfortable and sufficient for all officers and men likely to be stationed here."[11] But the deterioration of wood and adobe due to age, wind, and water soon caused him to purchase one thousand feet of lumber and fifty bushels of lime for building repair from the local economy. The next commander began to erect some new buildings, and in October 1867 he requested five thousand feet of lumber and two hundred bushels of lime to complete his building program. At that time, yet to be built were two sets of officers' quarters, earlier commenced and abandoned when the walls were approximately three feet high.[12]

When Cummings's building program faltered, a third commander indicated that no lumber was available at the post and requested more immediately to make the men's quarters comfortable during the next winter. He wrote: "At present the men's quarters are wholly destitute of suitable bunks."[13] By May 1869 Cummings's building program was finished except for the southern officers' quarters, which had only unfinished walls and a roof. The completed buildings were in fairly good shape at that time, although the commander acknowledged the necessity of almost constant repair of adobe construction.[14] The fact that men were used to construct and repair buildings led one western military officer later to write: "This 'labor of the troops' was a great thing. It made the poor wretch who enlisted under the vague notion that his admiring country needed his services to quell hostile Indians, suddenly find himself a brevet architect, carrying a hod and doing odd jobs."[15]

Even though soldiers supplied much of the labor for the building programs at the forts in New Mexico, the army was required to purchase some of the necessary building materials on the open market. The owners and operators of general mercantile companies and sawmills or lumber companies profited directly. By acquiring materials from civilian suppliers, the army became a major contributor to the economy of a region.[16]

Building problems often confronted the untrained construction crews. When black soldiers digging a well at Fort Bascom found a bed of sand five feet thick beginning about ten feet below the surface, they had to discontinue digging until they could acquire lumber to hold the sides of the deepening hole.[17] The men at Fort Cummings had the opposite problem. When their commander ordered them to dig a cellar to be used for storing pickled meats, molasses, pickles, and vegetables, they found that the fort had been built over almost solid rock just two feet below the surface; consequently, their assigned task took a great amount of hard labor.[18]

At Cummings, Cpl. Fredrick Wormley, a black noncommissioned officer of Company A, Thirty-eighth Infantry, was put in charge of a work party of eight or ten privates engaged in quarrying and hauling stone for the post garden and cemetery wall.[19] Since the earliest days of the army, standard procedure had allowed commissioned officers to give considerable responsibility to noncommissioned officers. In selecting Wormley for such responsibility, his superior officer afforded him the same treatment as the army gave whites.

The need for wood for fuel was a matter demanding attention at frontier forts in the Southwest. In an effort to economize, in November 1867 the War Department issued an order stipulating that "at every post where it is possible, fuel and hay shall be procured by the labor of the troops."[20] Enlisted men in New Mexico rarely cut their own hay, but many of them chopped and gathered their posts' wood supplies. At Selden the troopers spent hours digging mesquite roots to be used for fuel.[21] Because of the vast amount of labor required to furnish fuel for Cummings, the commander tried not to send men more than fifteen miles from the post in search of wood. He ordered that each day good axes be provided to the men cutting the wood and that wood racks rather than wagon beds be used for hauling wood or timber. So great were the fuel demands at Fort Cummings in January 1867 that the post commander used almost every available man for woodcutting and hauling duty.[22]

In the following fall, Cummings's commander used all available men to procure wood for the post. At that time he requested additional transportation to enable the soldiers to supply the post with fuel from timber taken from the banks of the Mimbres River, a distance of twenty-five miles. He wrote: "But if the troops are used to get this fuel

[wood] the strength of the garrison must be increased to furnish escorts, perform the labor, and leave at the post a sufficient number of troops for garrison duty."[23] Before the end of the winter of 1867–1868 the commander detailed Corporal Wormley for extra duty in the quartermaster department in charge of a wood train and the guard and working party accompanying it. Wormley was responsible for the axes furnished to the party and ensured that they were returned when the job was finished, but he was not held responsible for any damage to the tools incurred as the result of ordinary use. Finally, Wormley was in charge of the mules used by the woodcutting party.[24]

Post commanders other than the one at Fort Cummings complained to superiors that the use of troopers as woodcutters was inefficient and that contracting for fuel would cost less, as well as save wear and tear on army wagons, mules, and cutting tools. These arguments eventually won out; in 1873 the army decided that thereafter fuel was to be supplied by contract to all posts in the Southwest.[25]

Raw timber was sometimes used for repairs at isolated frontier posts. In January 1867 Lt. Joseph A. Corbett, one noncommissioned officer, and ten privates of Company D of the One Hundred Twenty-fifth took four of Fort Cummings's six-mule teams to the Mimbres River to gather and load timber to be used for repairing the public wagons at the post. The men took rations for themselves and forage for their mules for five days. Mindful of Indian dangers, each enlisted man carried thirty rounds of ammunition.[26]

Finished lumber was sometimes used for construction projects other than buildings. During the last year of the infantry's stay at Fort Bayard, the post commander ordered from a nearby sawmill five thousand feet of lumber, two thousand feet of which was extra good pine for making coffins. The records do not indicate whether black troopers were used for this project or whether other laborers were hired to do it. Nor do the records indicate why the commander ordered so many coffins to be built or how they were ultimately disposed of.[27]

Military authorities may not have raised questions about coffin building, but they did take notice of a report that the men of Company I of the One Hundred Twenty-fifth were being used as laborers in copper mines near Pinos Altos. An investigation revealed that the troopers — who were supposedly there to guard the mines and miners — were generally occupied in working in the mines for $3 to $5 a day with the knowledge and consent of both their company commander and Lt. Col. Alexander Duncan, commander of Fort Bayard. Military leaders immediately ordered Duncan to recall the company or any of its detachments and to keep the men at their military duties. When the investigators also learned that a number of the enlisted men of Company I had private horses that they hired out to citizens at the mines, they reminded the men that the army prohibited enlisted men from owning animals and ordered them to dispose of all such privately owned animals.[28]

An investigation revealed that Lieutenant Colonel Duncan had gone on a personal prospecting tour beyond the Gila River, taking with him fifty-eight enlisted men. On this trip Duncan was responsible for the deaths of seven army horses and mules and for "render[ing] permanently useless thirteen mules and about twenty horses." This command found a large quantity of cinnabar (red mercuric sulphide, the most important ore of mercury), after which Duncan staked out a large claim for himself, organized a mining company, built a monument to establish his claim, and enacted mining laws. The investigator concluded this report: "I think this use of soldiers and public property for private purposes injurious to discipline, beside the unwarrantable waste of the public means."[29]

On numerous occasions infantrymen served extra duty in quartermaster departments. This occurred not only with men who searched for, cut, and hauled wood but also with men who served as teamsters, blacksmiths' helpers, and corral builders.[30] Furthermore, from time to time some men served as bakers, as clerks or cooks in post hospitals, as acting hospital stewards, and as clerks in subsistence departments.[31] When these soldiers were detailed for more than ten consecutive days in these and similar departments, they were entitled to additional pay according to the work performed. By military order these men received from twenty cents to thirty-five cents a day, depending upon whether they were being used as common or skilled laborers.[32]

The food available to the army's enlisted men affected their efficiency, health, and psychological well-being. To those ends, the army arranged for subsistence stores for the garrisons. The commissary general of subsistence in Washington would advertise for bids in the newspapers and would give notice of the time and place at which commodities were to be delivered.

Fresh meat was an important staple. Assistant commissaries at the individual posts would make contracts for fresh beef after sealed bids had been received.[33] On one occasion, Fort Cummings acquired a large amount of fresh beef, which began to spoil because of the hot weather or the length of time between its acquisition and its use.[34] Other types of meat found their way to the soldiers' table, too. Because sheep were available and because mutton resisted heat spoilage better than beef, mutton was sometimes issued. In 1867 Cummings's commander purchased 850 pounds of mutton at twelve cents a pound and specifically ordered that this meat be issued to the men during warm weather.[35] Wild game was another source of meat. In the fall of 1867 the post commander at Cummings issued special permits for hunting game, fulfilling at least three objectives by this action: troopers were able to practice their shooting skills, troopers had pleasant diversion from work duties, and the men at the post had their army rations supplemented with fresh meat.[36]

Beans were the mainstay in the soldiers' daily diet; on one occasion a post commander in New Mexico ordered 3,333 pounds of beans.[37] Merchants in the vicinity of the posts usually won the contracts to supply the common but nutritious beans, and local farmers shared in the profits from the military market.[38] In efforts to provide a balanced and healthful diet to the men, post commanders often took measures to provide a generous supply of vegetables and other antiscorbutics for their enlisted personnel. Commissary departments made available pickles, kraut, dried fruits, and molasses, along with assorted seasonable vegetables.[39]

The considerable expense of obtaining fresh vegetables from distant sources led the Military Division of the Missouri to authorize New Mexican posts to purchase seed potatoes, garden seeds, and agricultural implements so that troopers could plant and cultivate their own vegetables.[40] Not only in New Mexico but also throughout the West, post and company gardens supplied most of the fresh produce eaten by both black and white soldiers. These gardens provided a valuable component of the officers' and enlisted men's diets.[41]

At Fort Cummings for a period of time the enlisted men were required to bake their own bread. As this was not in accord with War Department policy, the company bakery was ordered discontinued, to be replaced by a post bakery. Either the post bakery was never set up or it was established later, because six weeks after the order, no post bakery existed and the troopers were still baking their own bread.[42] At least one black enlisted man was recognized as a good cook. When Pvt. Henry Porter of Company D of the One Hundred Twenty-fifth went on escort duty from Fort Cummings to Fort Bayard, Lt. A. K. Kaiser illegally detained him at Bayard as his own private servant and cook. Special orders were issued to retrieve Porter from Kaiser and return him to Cummings for regular duty.[43]

Both men and animals at army garrisons in the West needed salt in their diets, and army cooks used large quantities of it to preserve meats and vegetables such as cabbage. Furnished under contract, most of the salt supplied to posts in New Mexico was obtained from local salt lakes. Some of this unrefined salt was of dark color, and neither officers nor men were particularly fond of it. But most of the con-tracted salt was white and of good quality, receiving praise from those who used it.[44]

Sometimes the posts did not rely upon contracted salt but obtained it themselves. A few weeks after the Fifty-seventh Infantry arrived at Fort Bascom, post commander Lt. Col. Silas Hunter took thirty of his 140 enlisted men and a train of wagons on a sixty-six-mile ride north-east of Bascom to a salt lake one hundred yards wide and two hundred yards long. In order to test the mineral qualities of the water contained in the pool, Hunter removed one gallon and boiled it down. The result was one quart of "beautiful white salt, equal in appearance and grain to the finest quality of lake salt." The men shoveled up the abundant caked salt from the bottom, washed it, and loaded it. While the September weather was pleasant, the men working in the water, which was three feet deep, had to be relieved every hour, for if they remained longer, they became chilled. After seven days had elapsed, Hunter and his men returned to Bascom, all wagons fully loaded with a total of eleven thousand pounds of the precious product.[45] No doubt other forts in the territory drew upon this supply of a necessary nutritional and preservative item.

Sickness, disease, death, and accidents were a part of frontier life for all U.S. soldiers, black men not excepted. When the army failed to regularly include fresh vegetables in the soldiers' diets, outbreaks of scurvy often occurred. In August 1866, when over 140 men of the Fifty-seventh Infantry arrived at Fort Union, some twenty men with scurvy were in the post hospital and a large number of less serious cases existed. Some of the affected men were black troopers. To remedy this situation the post commander requested permission to purchase six cows so that the men could have fresh milk. The sick men quickly responded to liberal allowances of milk and fresh vegetables.[46] Although scurvy was deadly when left untreated, it was easily cured and did not pose a serious problem at posts where vegetables were grown. Scurvy was not the most common illness among New Mexico's soldiers. Other potentially deadly diseases such as pneumonia, diarrhea, dysentery, and venereal diseases were more widespread. In 1867 at Fort Cummings, infantrymen James Bell and John Smith died of pneumonia and chronic diarrhea, respectively.[47]

Sickness sometimes incapacitated entire posts. In the early months of 1869 Fort Cummings experienced a smallpox epidemic resulting in the death of a captive Indian boy named Charley.[48] During this outbreak, the post surgeon was directed to disinfect the floors and bunks of the enlisted men's quarters once each day and to use other measures he believed would help prevent the spread of contagious diseases. He was told to move infected men to the post hospital upon the first appearance of symptoms, and only those "beyond the reach of the disease" were allowed in the ward. Men who had not been vaccinated were required to be.[49]

Post leaders took preventive actions to reduce the possibilities of sickness. In 1867 the surgeon at Fort Cummings recommended the removal and destruction of the vegetables in the company storehouse because they had spoiled and were dangerous to the health of the men.[50] Two years later Cummings's commander ordered kegs of spoiled whitefish and mackerel removed from the commissary storeroom and buried at a safe distance.[51]

Large numbers of men doing heavy manual labor together over a period of time invariably experienced various kinds of accidents. In July 1869 at Fort Selden Pvt. J. W. Williams of Company K, Thirty-eighth Infantry, received a serious cut in the foot with an axe. Because an artery was severed, the post commander, upon the recommendation of a hospital steward, urgently summoned an army assistant surgeon who was then in Las Cruces to tend to the wounded man.[52]

Most of the military personnel, however, were reasonably healthy. While in good health, these infantrymen in New Mexico in the 1860s spent time scouting for Indians, mapping the land, and escorting both military personnel and civilians, but these Indian-related activities were not all-consuming. Although they spent time with new building programs, repair and maintenance work, their regular work routine, and extra duty, periods occurred in the soldiers' schedules when they had time on their hands. Indeed, two of the greatest burdens borne by all men stationed throughout the West after the Civil War were the loneliness and almost unbearable tedium of garrison life. How did these men handle such heavy burdens? Occasionally their leaders ordered packages of newspapers for the men, and when such a package arrived it was considered a great boon to the garrison.[53] Some of the soldiers read these newspapers to help pass the time, but in view of the relatively high illiteracy rate among the black enlisted men, officers were more likely to read them.

The government did little to encourage formal entertainment or organized recreation for the enlisted men in the military. Soldiers not engaged in the performance of duties had few wholesome activities — mental or physical — to absorb them. Under the circumstances, sometimes even the best men sank into a dull apathy and became weary, discontented, and demoralized. Many men who probably would have become good soldiers became disgusted with military service and sought avenues of escape from the discomforts and monotony of their lives. In the absence of planned entertainment or recreation facilities, the means the enlisted men sought for occupying their leisure time were not always desirable; the New Mexico military records include numerous references to gambling, fighting, drinking, and stealing, as well as some to murder.[54] For example, members of the garrison at Fort Selden visited the nearby settlement of Leasburg and the town of Doña Ana, about twelve miles to the south, where diversions of various kinds, including women, dancing, gambling, and alcohol, were available.[55] Sometimes the soldiers fought with the settlers or with each other, after which they often spent time in the guardhouse.[56] As a result of such adventures, civilians killed at least seven Selden soldiers (some of whom were black) within the first year and a half of the fort's existence. In October 1869 Pvts. George Hammond and James Gibson of Company A of the Thirty-eighth were arrested for murdering Leandro Benardo (a Hispanic teamster) and dumping his body into the Rio Grande.[57]

Although army officials waged almost constant war against petty thievery, stealing was prominent among enlisted men. Infantrymen in New Mexico stole from each other, as at Fort Cummings when Pvt. Allen Townsend stole some trousers from Pvt. William Herron and a flannel sack coat from Pvt. Robert Berry, and at Fort Bayard when Pvt. William H. Russell stole trousers worth $3 from Sgt. Charles Southerner. All of the men involved in these thefts were members of Company F of the Thirty-eighth.[58]

Some men stole government property, as it was virtually impossible for the army to stop underpaid soldiers from such actions. Thirty-eighth infantrymen Pvts. Henry Perkins and William H. Russell stole three plugs of government tobacco and a government stable frock, respectively.[59] More serious were the actions of Pvt. Isam Logan of the Thirty-eighth's Company K, who, when on escort duty between Forts Selden and Cummings, traded his army-issued trousers to a Hispano for a dozen eggs.[60] Even more unacceptable were the actions of several enlisted men of the One Hundred Twenty-fifth at Bayard, who, along with a civilian, stole ordnance and public horses.[61]

Frequently soldiers sold or exchanged items of clothing, arms, and other supplies for money, whiskey, or sexual favors at off-reservation gambling houses or "hog ranches," the latter being places of prostitution on the frontier. An officer at Fort Selden described Leasburg as "entirely supported by selling mean whiskey to soldiers[,] by lewd women and . . . by purchasing government arms and clothing." He estimated that the army lost as much as $60 a day through these illegal exchanges.[62] Conditions grew so bad in Leasburg that Selden's commander placed it off-limits to the enlisted men.

If soldiers were discovered disposing of relatively small amounts of army goods, usually they were sentenced to forfeit some pay and were confined to the guardhouse or required to do hard labor. When Fort Selden's Private Logan was found guilty of a relatively minor charge of illegally disposing of his trousers, he was sentenced to forfeit his next month's paycheck.[63]

Enlisted men charged with more serious crimes, such as stealing large amounts of supplies or government animals, were locked in the guardhouse to await court-martial trials, which were often less than speedy. The men might spend several months waiting, during which time they — and sometimes their superiors — would become impatient with the delays. In March 1869 Cummings's commander, Capt.

Alexander Moore, pointed out that at his post several enlisted men of the Thirty-eighth's Company F were in confinement awaiting trial. As two of these men had been in the guardhouse for more than eight months, Moore requested that officers be sent to Cummings to hold a court-martial trial or, if that was not possible, that he be allowed to release the prisoners.[64]

When Thirty-eighth infantryman Pvt. Robert Booker and a private named Williams languished in the Cummings guardhouse for more than six months, Captain Moore wrote: "If there is no prospect of a trial of these men at an early date, I would respectfully request that I may be permitted to release them from confinement and return them to duty."[65] Booker wrote to higher military authorities in his own behalf, pointing out that court-martials had been in session at Forts Selden and Bayard and that men who had entered confinement after him had been tried. He wrote: "May I either be tried or released from confinement, having in vain complained about this so far."[66] Men who had been incarcerated and then tried while Booker languished included Thirty-eighth infantrymen Pvts. Henry White, William Lucas, and John Jones.[67]

For various minor offenses, enlisted men often were required to do onerous work or spend short periods in guardhouses. As punishment for neglect of duty, George McDonald of Company D of the One Hundred Twenty-fifth was relieved as a musician and ordered to carry a musket for a brief time.[68] Under the surveillance of a noncommissioned officer, six prisoners at Fort Cummings spent ten of their days in confinement sorting the post's supply of bacon and destroying what was unfit to eat.[69]

At least one black sergeant at Fort Bascom escaped his worldly environment by committing suicide,[70] but most men were more likely to desert than to take their own lives. Indeed, desertion was no small problem among the infantrymen in New Mexico, and some of the court-martials were held to try accused deserters. The records indicate that some of these men were caught as far away as St. Louis, Nashville, and Philadelphia, although some were captured in the region of the post where they served.[71] To be sure, men deserted for a variety of reasons, but for many men desertion was a way of protesting the conditions under which they lived and the officers under whom they worked.

Another form of protest was mutiny. In late 1867 at Fort Cummings, men of Company A of the Thirty-eighth did just that. Relieving a company of the One Hundred Twenty-fifth, which had been reassigned to Fort Union, Company A took station at Fort Cummings on October 1, 1867. Arriving with the company were its commander, Capt. Charles E. Clarke, and regimental adjutant Lt. William E. Sweet.[72] Also joining the company was Lt. Henry F. Leggett.

Most of the 101 enlisted men of the company were former slaves who had been recruited for the postwar army, and these freed blacks were not happy when they were transferred to the desert of New Mexico. They disliked the heat, the dry climate, the desert terrain, and the lack of plentiful green grass and trees; in short, physical conditions in New Mexico were far different from their native South, and the men were uneasy. Furthermore, the men were not always amenable to army discipline. Insubordination and incarceration were common.[73] The men often had little respect for their superiors, and they especially disliked Sweet and Leggett. Of Leggett, who was something of a martinet, one enlisted man said: "Before that damned son of a bitch [arrived], we were getting on like soldiers ought to."[74]

In view of this environment, tension prevailed. Company A became a powder keg waiting to explode. The fuse was lit on Sunday, December 1, when Lieutenant Leggett accused Mattie Merritt, a black camp follower of Company A in Leggett's employ as a domestic servant, of stealing a sum of money from his quarters. Lieutenant Sweet, apparently serving as officer of the day, ordered the maid searched, but the searchers found no money. Despite this lack of evidence, Sweet ordered her to leave the post. Because of the Indian menace and the lack of facilities outside the post, however, this order was not carried out.[75]

But this search and order angered the men of Company A, and they were sullen and insolent when they gathered for the regular Sunday morning inspection. In view of past tension and the emotional state of the enlisted men, Sweet insisted upon discipline. When he found unclean muskets and uniforms, he ordered punishment for some of the men, forcing them to stand for a time on water kegs in the middle of the parade ground.[76] The accusation against Mattie Merritt, the ordered expulsion despite no evidence against her, and the presumed

indignity of unfair punishment combined to cause the men openly to
revolt.

The first signs of overt insubordination appeared about two o'clock
that afternoon, when some of the men of the company, obviously angry,
assembled at the post's flagstaff. Among them was the sergeant of the
guard, Thornton Reeves. Returning from an errand to Sweet's quarters,
1st Sgt. William Yeatman saw the crowd, stopped, and asked what was
happening. When Reeves responded evasively, Yeatman ordered him
and the other men to go to their quarters. They reluctantly obeyed only
after Captain Clarke arrived on the scene. Egged on by Pvt. John Holt,
the men continued angry and restless, secretly gathering and whisper-
ing in small groups.[77]

On the next morning Sergeant Reeves announced that Lieutenant
Sweet had threatened to kill him. With a revolver in his hand Reeves
stated that he planned to kill the lieutenant.[78] That night Sgt. Samuel
Allen and a corporal named Grant told Yeatman that an unknown
person or persons had stuck two revolvers in Allen's face.[79] Sergeant
Allen declared to Yeatman that he knew who had pointed the pistols
at him: "It was them two damned sons of bitches, . . . Leggett and
Sweet!" Then Allen got a shotgun and began to load it.[80] At that point
Cpl. Robert Davis and Sergeant Reeves entered the room. Yeatman
attempted to convince Reeves and Davis that further actions would
result in serious consequences for them. Arguments followed.

Shortly afterward, the men of Company A gathered in front of their
quarters. Allen had a loaded double-barrel shotgun, Davis and Reeves
had revolvers, and the remaining men had their muskets. Allen told
Yeatman to find Captain Clarke. When Yeatman set out, Davis accompanied him. Finding Clarke's quarters empty, Yeatman and Davis went
to the sutler's store just outside the walls of the post. There they found
the captain. Yeatman told Clarke that he could not control the men of
the company, but fearful of Davis, he said no more. Davis admitted
nothing about the possible mutiny of himself or his friends. At this time
Clarke heard about the two revolvers allegedly pointed at Allen.[81]

Not understanding the seriousness of the situation, Clarke instructed Yeatman to order the men to their quarters. The men refused
to obey, instead loading their guns and raising them to their shoulders.
At one point Sergeant Reeves shouted that the men ought to kill

Yeatman and then "go up and kill every damned thing in the garrison that wore shoulder straps."[82] When Yeatman left the men and joined Clarke, whom the men apparently respected, the men dispersed, perhaps fearing direct reprisal from the captain.

Realizing the gravity of the situation, Clarke arrested and preferred charges against nine men of the company.[83] In early December Clarke and Sweet escorted the accused men and some witnesses to Fort Selden for trial by general court-martial. As the first trial got underway, testimony about the mutiny revealed new information, and Cpl. James Francis, who was at Selden to testify, was arrested and charged.[84]

While the trials proceeded at Selden, important developments occurred at Cummings. In Clarke's absence, Lieutenant Leggett ordered the post guard again to expel Mattie Merritt from the garrison. In response, twenty to forty men armed with muskets charged the three-man guard, insisting that the black maid not be driven from the post. Lt. James N. Morgan, commander of Cummings while Clarke was away, ordered the men to desist, to return to their quarters, and to put aside their arms. After he repeated his orders several times, Morgan, with Leggett's assistance, finally got most of the men to obey. But when Pvts. Henry Watkins, George Stratton, and George Newton continued to conduct themselves in a contemptuous and disrespectful manner, the officers arrested them, placed them in the guardhouse, and preferred charges against them.[85] A few days later a government train loaded with these additional prisoners and several more witnesses traveled from Cummings to Selden. When the Department of the Missouri headquarters directed that the court-martial proceedings be transferred from Selden to Fort Bayard, twenty-two witnesses and all but one of the accused men were transferred there.[86]

As Cpl. Robert Davis already had been arraigned, his trial was held at Fort Selden in January 1868.[87] Davis was charged with violating the 7th Article of War, which prohibited a soldier from participating in a mutiny, and the 8th Article of War, which provided that a soldier report to his superiors any knowledge of a possible mutiny. Either charge could incur the death penalty.

The prosecution in Davis's trial leaned heavily on the testimony of Sgt. William Yeatman, whose statements that the prisoner was armed and had made threats against Sweet and Leggett were especially damaging. The defense argued that the officers' search of and orders to expel

Mattie Merritt were cruel and unnecessary actions and that the punishment meted out to the men for dirty guns and clothing was unduly severe. The judge advocate replied that both actions were clearly within the authority of army officers, and such punishments were common throughout the military, being necessary for the maintenance of discipline.[88] The defense relied on the testimony of a number of enlisted men of Company A, but because Yeatman was an eyewitness and these men had not seen or heard certain incidents, Yeatman's testimony was more persuasive. The court found Davis guilty on all charges and specifications except for one technicality, sentencing the corporal to be reduced to the ranks, to forfeit all pay and allowances, to be dishonorably discharged, and to be confined in a penitentiary for ten years. In April Maj. Gen. Philip H. Sheridan, commanding the headquarters of the Department of the Missouri at Fort Leavenworth, Kansas, approved the proceedings, findings, and sentence, designating the penitentiary at Jefferson City, Missouri, as Davis's place of confinement.[89]

Charges against six of the alleged mutineers were dropped, but the trials of six men implicated in the events of December 1867 were held at Fort Bayard. Sgt. Samuel Allen was charged with violating the article of war forbidding mutiny, with failing to advise his superiors of an intended mutiny, and with failing to attempt to suppress the mutiny. Among the specifications supporting these general charges were one alleging that he had armed himself with a shotgun, that he had gone in search of his superior officers with ill intent, and that he had alluded to Lieutenants Sweet and Leggett with foul language and had threatened to kill them. Furthermore, he was charged with cursing Capt. Edward Bloodgood at Fort Selden for putting Sergeant Reeves in the guardhouse. Finally, he was charged with two violations of army regulations that had occurred before the mutiny: conduct prejudicial to good order and military discipline for stealing an infantry greatcoat belonging to Pvt. John Hughes, and a violation of the 38th Article of War for selling two greatcoats to an unknown Hispanic woman.

After surprisingly brief testimony, the court acquitted Allen of all the charges relating to mutiny. It returned a verdict of guilty on the two pre-mutiny charges of stealing greatcoats. Allen was reduced to the ranks, required to forfeit $8 pay per month for three months, and restored to duty.[90]

Sgt. Thornton Reeves was charged with mutiny, including threatening to kill Sergeant Yeatman, breaking arrest, and arming himself to resist military authority. He was found not guilty and returned to duty.[91]

Pvts. Henry Watkins and George Stratton were tried for mutiny. The defense readily admitted that they had committed acts of mutiny but maintained that the written charges and specifications were improperly worded. On the basis of these legal loopholes, both men were found not guilty.[92] Pvt. John Holt and Cpl. James Francis were charged with mutinous acts but were found not guilty on all counts and restored to duty.[93]

In summary, of the thirteen men charged with mutiny, seven were tried. One was found guilty of mutiny and was imprisoned, one was acquitted of the more serious charge but found guilty of theft unrelated to mutinous acts, and five were acquitted of all charges.[94] The history of mutiny in the army on the western frontier has yet to be written, but when that is done, it cannot omit this story of black infantrymen at Fort Cummings in post–Civil War New Mexico Territory.

III. The Cavalry and the Indians, 1875–1878

When 488 enlisted men of the Thirty-eighth Infantry marched out of New Mexico in October 1869, the territory was without black soldiers for six years. Later that year the U.S. Army transferred all companies of the white Thirty-seventh Infantry from New Mexico, replacing them with nine (later ten) companies of the white Fifteenth Infantry, most of which remained in New Mexico until late 1881 (one company did not leave until late 1882). The white Third Cavalry, which had moved into New Mexico in full force in 1866, left the territory in 1870, at which time all twelve companies of the white Eighth Cavalry replaced it.[1]

While these troop movements occurred, the Indians of the territory were fairly well under control. In October 1869 Indian Agent Charles E. Drew and Capt. George Shorkley of Fort McRae held a council with five chiefs representing the Mimbres and Mogollon Apache Indians. These Indian leaders were willing to move their bands to a reservation, promising to stay near a hot springs area on the west bank of the Rio Grande not far from Fort McRae. They also agreed to encourage other tribal chiefs to engage in similar talks. Drew and Shorkley believed these Indians earnestly desired peace, and they requested that no military scouting parties disturb the hot springs area.[2] Clearly, the army hoped to maintain into the 1870s the relative calm existing in New Mexico at the end of the 1860s.

Upon becoming president in 1869, Ulysses S. Grant launched his famous peace policy. As a result, in 1871 and 1872 a number of government commissioners went to the Apache country in Arizona and New Mexico territories to further insure a pacified Indian population.

Their primary purpose was to see that the Indians remained on or accepted transfer to various reservations scattered across the Southwest; yet several groups of Indians were not inclined to accept these transfer assignments. By the fall of 1872, in fact, some Apache leaders were clearly encouraging their people to resist transference. At the same time, Apache depredations were increasing. In response, Gen. George Crook, head of the army's Department of Arizona, began a concerted campaign to subdue the Apaches and force them to move to the assigned reservations. Crook's operation ended in 1873, when some of the hostile Apaches in Arizona surrendered. At about the same time, most of the Mescalero Apaches in New Mexico acquiesced to military pressures and settled on a reservation near Fort Stanton.[3]

In 1873 the prospects for a lasting solution to the Indian problem appeared good, even though a few renegade bands continued to make isolated raids on both the military and private citizens. Those prospects were dashed, however, when the government decided to concentrate the Apaches of eastern Arizona and western New Mexico on one large reservation instead of several smaller ones. The Apaches in western New Mexico might have been amenable to the new policy had the government not desired to relocate them at San Carlos, Arizona, a desolate, excessively hot area on the upper Gila River that they detested and which was inhabited by Indian tribes with whom they were not friendly. An uneasy quiet prevailed in the Apache country until the spring of 1875, when a group of warriors attacked white settlements on the San Pedro River, killing at least one rancher and stealing a herd of horses. In view of these attacks, which followed stepped-up depredations, the army assumed a major Indian outbreak was about to occur. Anticipating that event, in the summer of 1875 the army sent additional soldiers to the area encompassing the Arizona–New Mexico border.[4]

As soldiers and various bands of Indians came into conflict more and more often, the army decided to send fresh men into New Mexico. Although it retained nine companies of the Fifteenth Infantry at Forts Wingate, Craig, Union, Bayard, Selden, Stanton, and Marcy, in late 1875 it ordered out of New Mexico the Eighth Cavalry, which had been in the territory for five and a half years,[5] replacing it with the entire Ninth Cavalry, under the command of Col. Edward Hatch.

Col. Edward Hatch. (Courtesy National Archives, Washington, D.C.)

Edward Hatch was a native of Maine. After a time at sea and a stint in the lumber business in Pennsylvania, he moved to Iowa, where he was living when the Civil War broke out. In August 1861 he was appointed a captain in the Second Iowa Cavalry, taking command of that unit less than a year later. He was in several engagements in the war, including the Battles of Franklin and Nashville, for which the army awarded him citations for gallantry and meritorious service. In 1866 Hatch organized the Ninth Cavalry and served as its commander for many years. Racially unprejudiced, this able military leader was an ideal choice to lead black soldiers.[6]

Previously stationed in Texas, the Ninth Cavalry arrived in New Mexico in the winter and spring of 1875–1876, ultimately scattering to nine forts and one camp.[7] All twelve companies of the regiment were stationed in New Mexico between December 1875 and December 1881, with almost always ten — and usually eleven — companies serving there concurrently.

Throughout these half-dozen years almost 22 percent of the army's total black personnel was in New Mexico. Over 670 black enlisted cavalrymen of this regiment served in New Mexico during this period, the number perhaps exceeding eight hundred, counting new enlistments. The companies averaged about 56 men each, but because one or two companies were often out of the territory and three companies were absent for a part of the time, the average monthly number of cavalrymen present in the territory during this seventy-three-month period was 447.[8] Thus, although the regiment had an authorized strength of 840 men, in any given month Colonel Hatch normally had slightly more than half that number available in New Mexico. This shortage of manpower was not unusual for the units serving on the western frontier; most companies and regiments of the army in the 1870s and 1880s operated at about half strength most of the time.

An undermanned regiment was only one of the serious obstacles Hatch and his men faced when they took up their posts in New Mexico. Another obstacle was that the companies were stationed at forts considerably distant from each other, causing problems when communication or assistance was needed. A third obstacle was that most of the enlisted men were unfamiliar with the New Mexico terrain and environment, both of which must have appeared strange, if not downright hostile, to them as they rode to their initial posts. A final problem arose from Bureau of Indian Affairs policy and army orders: the bureau had failed to provide adequate food for its Indian wards, forcing Indians to acquire food wherever it could be found. The army had thus placed the regiment in the undesirable position of starving the Indians by forcing them to remain on their reservations or punishing them if they strayed from their assigned lands.

Despite these obstacles, Colonel Hatch and his men wasted no time pursuing their objectives. Company L had hardly arrived at Fort Stanton in December 1875 when it was involved with a survey of Indian reservations in that vicinity, and at the same time two companies at Fort Union helped move some Jicarilla Apaches from Cimarron to the Mescalero Reservation near Fort Stanton.[9]

In 1876 many men of the Ninth spent long and arduous hours pursuing small raiding parties from the bands of the Chiricahua Apache Indian leaders Juh and Geronimo, as well as groups of other Apaches who often searched for food and animals off their reservations. These several patrols limited raids and depredations, even though the soldiers and the Indians seldom actually came into contact with each other. During 1876 companies and detachments of the Ninth Cavalry reportedly marched a total recorded distance of 8,813 miles.[10]

Because the Apaches of western New Mexico had objected to the government's plan to transfer them to San Carlos, the government finally had established the Ojo Caliente Reservation, located in a large valley called Cañada Alamosa and bounded by the San Mateo Mountains, the Black Range, and the Rio Grande. Because these so-called Warm Springs Apaches apparently were aiding the rebellious Chiricahuas, whose reservation was about to be abolished, in April 1876 Colonel Hatch traveled by stagecoach from Santa Fe to Fort McRae and then on to Ojo Caliente to talk with Indian leaders, including the potentially dangerous Chief Victorio. Armed with late-model weapons, including Springfield, Winchester, and Sharps rifles and carbines and Smith and Wesson revolvers, the Indians were not receptive — indeed, they were openly defiant — to Hatch's requests that they stop depredating and cease stirring up the Chiricahuas. They told Hatch that the government had acted in bad faith, that no meat had been issued to them for a month, and that it was preferable to depredate or

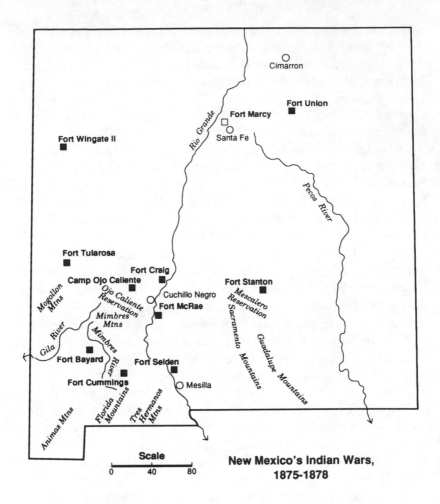

New Mexico's Indian Wars,
1875-1878

even go to war than to starve. These words and attitudes mildly alarmed
Hatch and stimulated him to order constant patrolling in that area of
New Mexico.[11]

In the last half of 1876 the military took a number of actions to
restrict Indian activities. For example, in September Capt. Henry
Carroll and his company scouted the Florida Mountains and surprised
a party of Indians, killing one and wounding three, as well as capturing
eleven ponies. A black private was shot in the arm during the engagement. This command marched a total of 274 miles, returning to Fort

Selden after nine days.[12] A month later Lt. Millard F. Goodwin and twenty-five troopers entered the Florida Mountains looking for Indians. Having gone as far as the Ojo Caliente Reservation, they marched 278 miles in six days.[13] Finally, in November a lieutenant of the Fifteenth Infantry led five men of Company F, Ninth Cavalry, and five Pueblo Indian scouts on a fifty-four-mile journey to seek hostile Indians.[14]

In terms of the future, the most important encounter in 1876 between soldiers and Indians occurred in September. Maj. Albert P. Morrow ordered Lt. Henry H. Wright to help an Anglo named Conwell recover his stolen animals and to destroy a rancheria in the Animas Mountains that was reportedly a rendezvous for stolen animals. Morrow instructed Wright to attack and punish any Indians found off the reservation. On its march, Wright's detachment of fifteen enlisted men and ten Navajo scouts picked up the tracks of a few animals and soon saw some fleeing Apaches. A little later the column came upon Chief Victorio's large camp at Cuchillo Negro. In reporting the skirmish that followed, Victorio complained to Indian Agent J. M. Shaw that without provocation Wright and his men had entered the Ojo Caliente Reservation and charged the camp at full speed, forcing Victorio and his people to flee, the women and children barely escaping being fired upon. Victorio reported that Wright had burned the entire camp and destroyed all provisions, including cornfields, which the soldiers' horses had trampled. He charged that the soldiers had destroyed or carried away cooking utensils and other movables, as well as taking one or two horses. Finally, he said that the Indians fired only one shot during this incident, an alarm at the beginning of the surprise attack.

In conveying Victorio's report to Hatch, Shaw indicated that the Indians had been orderly and peaceable and that Wright's unexpected raid had greatly exasperated them. He suggested that this disregard of the rights of the Indian village and the destruction of the Indians' belongings should be rebuked.

Wright did not agree, and his version of what happened was considerably different from Victorio's. Wright said that he believed that Cuchillo Negro was off the reservation, although he admitted that the reservation boundaries were unclear not only to himself but also to others. He claimed that the Indians fired upon his men first and kept up a lively skirmish, exchanging twenty shots until he drove them away.

He said that his men took nothing from the Indian camp except a few clothing bags, some tin pans, and some bows and arrows as curiosities, all of the items being worth less than $5. He stated that his men did not destroy the cornfields, although they took some of the corn for food. Finally, he acknowledged that he drove away two animals, a colt and a mare, but the latter was sorebacked and not worth anything.

During an investigation of the incident, Morrow found that Conwell, all of the enlisted men, and all of the Navajo scouts supported Wright's report of what had happened. He concluded that Wright's version was substantially correct. Incidentally, the ten Navajo scouts signed X's beside their names at the end of their sworn statements concerning the incident, and ten of the fifteen enlisted men also signed their statements with X's, an indication of total Indian illiteracy and a rather high degree of illiteracy among these particular black soldiers.[15]

While Morrow officially ended the affair with his report to his superiors, the incident worsened relations between the Indians and the military. The stepped-up Indian raids in the next months to some extent were a direct result of the conflict at Cuchillo Negro, as well as the result of white citizens' actions that antagonized the Indians. Exactly one month after the Wright-Victorio encounter, a party of Anglos made a raid upon the Ojo Caliente Reservation, driving away a group of Indian horses.[16] This enraged the Indians, causing them to retaliate with more of their own raids. Finally, in late 1876 Indian raids increased when a part of the Chiricahua tribe refused to move to San Carlos after their reservation was closed and some of those remaining went on the warpath.

In 1877 the hostile Chiricahua Apaches raided along the border of Arizona and New Mexico, and restless braves among the Warm Springs and Mescalero Apaches within New Mexico roamed off reservations more and more frequently to depredate. In late January the commander at Bayard learned that approximately fifty Chiricahuas had a conflict with white troopers of the Sixth Cavalry in Arizona and perhaps were moving into New Mexico. Lieutenant Wright, six enlisted cavalrymen, and three Navajo Indian scouts immediately sought out these Indians, soon finding them encamped in the Florida Mountains. With Wright and his party badly outnumbered, they did not attack but rather tried to convince the Indian band to surrender. After a fruitless half hour Wright broke off the council.

"Saddle Up." (Courtesy Frederic Remington Art Museum, Ogdensburg, New York.)

Completely surrounded by Indians, Wright and his men had to push through the encircled warriors, which resulted in a fight. The troopers used their weapons as both guns and clubs, as the fight occurred at close quarters. By valiant effort Cpl. Clinton Greaves opened a gap through the Indians, and he and his companions were able to escape. In the melee the troopers killed five Indians and wounded others, causing the Indians to flee. After that, the soldiers, who suffered only minor wounds, rounded up six Indian horses and returned to Bayard. For courage in action Corporal Greaves was awarded the Congressional Medal of Honor, and commendations were given to Pvts. Richard Epps, Dick Mackadoo, and John Adams and an Indian scout named Jose Chaves.[17] A few days after this encounter, Capt. Charles D. Beyer and Capt. Michael Cooney, leading Company C and a detachment of Company A, came upon these same Indians and attacked them. The Indians fled but left behind their camp equipage and supplies.[18]

By March it had become apparent that Geronimo and some of his Chiricahua followers were spending time with their Apache friends at Ojo Caliente, no doubt encouraging the latter to be hostile. In response, the commissioner of Indian Affairs ordered John P. Clum, Indian agent at the San Carlos Reservation, to control these renegades and to ask the army for assistance, if necessary. Upon Clum's request, in late April Colonel Hatch sent Maj. James F. Wade and Bayard's three cavalry companies (A, B, and C) to Ojo Caliente to join Clum and his Apache police to make some arrests. Clum had no difficulty making the arrests, but then he made a fateful decision. Clum, a self-assured and totally uninhibited twenty-three-year-old, decided to remove to San Carlos all the Warm Springs Apaches, not just the renegade Chiricahuas. The Apaches both resented and resisted Clum's decision, but in May U.S. soldiers led or drove 453 Indians to San Carlos,[19] leading to a period of considerable conflict between Indians and the army in New Mexico Territory in which the troopers of the Ninth Cavalry played a major role.

Between May 11 and 30, all three Bayard companies scouted for Indians as a group, marching 240 miles. In July Lt. John Conline and his company went to Fort Craig to protect a government supply train. Once that job was completed, Conline and his men proceeded to Ojo Caliente, where they acquired a guide to lead them into the Mimbres Mountains in search of Indians. The command saw no indications of Indians at any time during the scout, and Conline reported: "I believe there have been no Indians in the section of country through which the Co. passed for a considerable period." As he noted, the country itself created problems because it was rough and timbered; near the summit on the eastern side of the range, one of the command's horses fell over a precipice and instantly was killed.[20]

Local whites did not make the soldiers' job any easier. In August 1877 Frederick C. Godfroy of the Mescalero Agency called on Capt. George A. Purington and Company H at Fort Stanton to assist in recovering stock that cattle thieves from Texas had taken from the Indians.[21] At about the same time, Capt. Ambrose E. Hooker's Company E drove away squatters who had moved onto the Ojo Caliente Reservation almost before the Indians had left for San Carlos.[22]

But Indians remained the primary focus of the troopers, and in August Company A made another scout of the Mogollon Mountains. From August 14 to September 23 Captain Beyer and Company C (thirty-one enlisted men) were away from Bayard for field service. Actually they spent the entire five weeks encamped near Mesilla, enjoying a hard-earned rest. While the black soldiers were at Mesilla, the local newspaper editor praised them for having gained "an enviable reputation wherever stationed," as they were "quiet, sober, polite, and unobtrusive" and always under "perfect discipline."[23] This was high praise and well deserved.

While Company C was resting, on September 2 Victorio rudely shattered whatever relative peace had existed between the army and the Indians in the previous months. Leading more than three hundred Warm Springs and Chiricahua followers, Victorio fled the San Carlos Reservation. In response, Hatch ordered into the field every available man. Eight of the eleven companies of the Ninth Cavalry then stationed in New Mexico spent September searching for Victorio and his cohort: four companies (three of which were from Bayard) went deep into the Mogollon Mountains, three others (including one from Union) scouted out of Camp Ojo Caliente, and one remained at Ojo Caliente as a guard. The Indians attacked white settlements along the upper reaches of the Gila River, killing eight people and stealing some horses and mules. During this outbreak the troopers killed thirteen warriors before they forced the Indians to retreat farther into the mountains.[24]

During these confrontations with Victorio's band in late September, the Indians had killed no troopers. However, while in the Mogollon Mountains, Cpl. James Betters of Company C was mortally wounded when his carbine accidentally discharged. Knowing death was near, Betters requested that he be buried in Fort Bayard's cemetery, a request that was honored, but the conditions under which it was carried out displeased Betters's company commander, Captain Beyer. Betters's body was not prepared for interment; even his face was unwashed. Driven by a military convict, a police cart normally used for hauling garbage carried the coffin to the cemetery. Beyer lashed out at this lack of respect for Betters, "a soldier who had served his country honestly and faithfully for eleven years," but who was transported to his gravesite "without a flag covering his coffin, without a formal escort, without a single mourner or friend to follow the poor fellows [sic] remains to their last resting place."[25] Major Wade investigated Beyer's complaints, but because of the condition of the body when it reached Bayard, he charged no one with neglect.[26] Black enlisted men resented the handling of Betters's funeral, and it created warranted tension and resentment in their ranks at a time when all energies were needed to defeat the Indians.

Victorio had not prepared well for his September dash from the reservation nor for what was to come. He had few arms and only small amounts of ammunition, food, and clothing. As the numerous troopers of the Ninth kept up their constant pursuit, the Apaches were in obvious trouble. Soon some were barefoot and naked, and all were hungry. Under such circumstances, in early October 1877 Victorio and nearly two hundred followers showed up at Fort Wingate and surrendered. Soon thereafter seventy more capitulated, leaving only a few others, who fled to Mexico.[27]

Victorio told Wingate commander Col. Peter T. Swain that he and his people despised San Carlos, and he asked that they be returned to Ojo Caliente, a request that Swain fulfilled. On October 31 Capt. Frank T. Bennett and Company I of Wingate and Capt. Francis Moore and Company L of Union led Victorio and 238 Apache Indians without arms and horses toward the Ojo Caliente Reservation. Ojo Caliente, however, proved to be only a stopover, for a few months later the army decided to move these Apaches back to San Carlos. While en route to Arizona, Victorio and eighty followers escaped from their escorts. After being continually chased, some of these escapees arrived at the Mescalero Reservation, where Indian Agent Godfroy permitted them to remain.[28]

In February 1878 Victorio and his remaining followers voluntarily surrendered to Captain Hooker at Ojo Caliente, indicating that they were willing to return to the Ojo Caliente Reservation but under no circumstances would they return to San Carlos. When they were told they could live with the other members of their band at Mescalero but not at Ojo Caliente, they refused and ran into the mountains again. But in June Victorio and his band appeared at Mescalero, where Indian Agent Godfroy promised them good treatment. Shortly thereafter, the Bureau of Indian Affairs transferred the wives and children of this Warm Springs band from San Carlos to Mescalero.[29]

"A Pull at the Canteen." (Courtesy Frederic Remington Art Museum, Ogdensburg, New York.)

This action was designed to make Victorio satisfied at Mescalero, but it did not, for he yearned to lead his people back to the Ojo Caliente area. By the end of the summer he gathered all the warriors and as many of the Indian families as was feasible and fled Mescalero to settle at Ojo Caliente. When he learned that the army was planning to transfer him and his group from Ojo Caliente to San Carlos, in mid-October he and about one hundred followers spirited themselves away from Ojo Caliente, finding safety south of the border.[30]

With Victorio's band in Mexico, the U.S. Army experienced a brief respite from chasing the Warm Springs Apaches, but this did not mean that peace between the settlers and other Indians had come to New Mexico. In the early months of 1878 Hatch received a number of complaints concerning Mescalero raids into West Texas. Godfroy insisted that the Mescaleros were not involved in these raids, laying the blame instead on hostile bands of Indians in the Guadalupe Mountains, whom he recommended be confined to a reservation. Perhaps to confirm the complaints, Captain Purington, at the request of Indian inspector Col. E. C. Watkins, proceeded to the Mescalero Agency with five enlisted men of Company H to be present for a counting of the Indians. In May Lt. Col. N.A.M. Dudley (commander at Fort Stanton), Lt. George W. Smith, and twelve enlisted men of Company H spent three days at the Mescalero Agency, where Dudley held an investigation into the depredations allegedly perpetrated by the Mescaleros. Dudley concluded that a few reservation Indians might be raiding but that renegades, or "cut-offs," also sometimes called "dog Indians," were more likely to be at the root of the problem.[31]

Following this investigation Dudley informed his superiors that a band of about forty "cut-offs" was living and making mescal near Alamo Canyon. He was quoted as saying: "They are bad Indians and . . . should be forced to come into the [Mescalero] Reservation,"[32] and he speculated that if an attempt were made to round them up, they would take shelter in the Guadalupe Mountains. In response to Dudley's report, Hatch ordered Dudley to send a company of cavalry, strengthened to fifty enlisted men from other companies at Stanton, plus some Indian scouts under Lieutenant Wright from Ojo Caliente "to hunt up this band of Indians and compel them to return to the reservation and in the event of resistance to treat them as hostile Indians."[33]

Following Dudley's orders, in July Capt. Henry Carroll led a military party out of Stanton to search for the troublesome Indians. The command, carrying rations for forty days and 150 rounds of ammunition for each man, included Lieutenants Wright and Smith, fifty-two men of Companies F and H, and nineteen Navajo scouts. After searching for the renegades on the reservation, Carroll marched to Pine Spring in the Guadalupes, there meeting Capt. Stevens T. Norvell, who was on a scout with a company of Tenth cavalrymen out of Fort Davis,

Texas. Norvell reported to Carroll that he had seen no Indians or fresh trails along the Pecos River on his march to Pine Spring.[34]

Believing that no Indians were in the Guadalupes, Carroll marched west to the Sacramento Mountains in search of his Indian quarry. Near Dog Canyon he ran into a small party of Apaches. A sharp skirmish occurred, after which the troopers moved into the canyon itself. There the command met a larger party of Indians, who, from a ledge eight hundred feet high, fired at and threw large rocks upon the exposed soldiers. As the soldiers climbed the walls of this especially steep canyon, the almost intolerable summer heat caused some of them to suffer heatstroke. Despite these obstacles, Carroll and his men reached the ledge at nightfall, only to discover that the Indians had fled and scattered. Concluding that pursuing the Indians was futile, Carroll then scouted Alamo Canyon. When he found no more Indians, he returned to Stanton, arriving on August 12 after marching 588 miles.

While on this scout, Carroll had killed three Indians, wounded two others, and captured one Indian child. He also captured twenty-two horses, losing only two of his own. His only casualty was a corporal of Company H, who was accidentally killed. Carroll especially complimented a Corporal Baker of Company H for good conduct while on this march.[35]

While Carroll was exploring the Guadalupes and the Sacramentos, Ninth cavalrymen stationed at Forts Bayard, Wingate, and Stanton were facing the hit-and-run tactics of the Warm Springs remnants and Chiricahua hostiles. Efforts to subdue these Indians were frustrating. The Indians' knowledge of the country, their ability to move to safety beyond the United States–Mexico border when they were in danger, the lag time between the report of a raid and the soldiers' response, and the shortage of military manpower placed the cavalrymen and their leaders at a disadvantage. In view of the manpower shortage at Bayard, Captain Beyer requested and received permission to use the members of the regimental band to chase Indians. By early August these men had traded their musical instruments for carbines and were serving as mounted scouts in both the Hatchet and Florida mountains.[36]

In August a noncommissioned officer and a private from Fort Stanton escorted a U.S. Indian agent to his new location. This nearby agency was far from peaceful, for three days later Lieutenant Goodwin and twelve black cavalrymen and three white men of the Fifteenth Infantry arrived with a Gatling gun to deter Indian violence, to capture the Indian murderers of the agency clerk, and to retrieve the recently stolen stock. A week later three enlisted men arrived at the agency to guard public property.[37]

Of some help to the manpower shortage during the summer of 1878 was the return to Wingate in August of Lt. Charles W. Merritt and a detachment of Company I, which since the previous December had been at a field camp on the La Plata River in conjunction with a massive expedition against the Ute Indians of Colorado. This group had traveled 1,108 miles to perform this service.[38] The increase in manpower afforded by the detachment's arrival was nullified in September and October when Bayard's Company D was detailed to escort the engineers who were surveying the boundary lines between New Mexico and Colorado and between Utah and Colorado.[39]

The shortage of leadership for the Ninth Cavalry was dramatized when Sgt. Henry H.R. Carter led a scout against the Indians. With eleven privates and a guide named Williams, Carter left Bayard at 8:30 P.M. on November 25 with a detachment of Company G in pursuit of a party of Indians said to have stolen horses from settlers on the Mimbres River. Carter and his men quickly found a dead horse, apparently killed for food, as the ribs and other parts of the animal had been cut out. The horse appeared to be one of those reported stolen. Shortly thereafter, another horse mutilated in a similar manner was found. Carter estimated that the party of Indians he was trailing numbered about fifty, and he followed its signs toward Fort Cummings, near which the clues dwindled away. Proceeding from Cummings, he scouted the Florida Mountains, but he did not catch sight of his quarry.[40]

On December 3 Lt. William H. Hugo of the Ninth Cavalry arrived in the Floridas and took command of this scout. Hugo had left Bayard the previous day leading Company B in pursuit of a party of Indians that had been depredating near Hillsboro. This scout was a particularly difficult one; at one point its members struggled through a driving rain, a stock mule died, and Hugo drove away four of his horses and mules because they simply gave out. Its troubles continuing, the main body of the scouting party found a fresh Indian trail and two stray Indian horses, but it was forced to leave the animals in the mountains because they were unable to travel. Evidence indicated that the group of approximately twenty Indians (including women and children) was about thirty hours ahead of Hugo's men. The column discovered an abandoned camp where the Indians had used up all the water. This was unfortunate because thirst plagued this scout, affecting both men and animals; two of this scout's animals died from exhaustion and dehydration while in the Tres Hermanos Mountains.

The command traveled from twenty to forty miles a day on this trip, sometimes moving at night, and at one point even crossing the Mexican border. It found some men's clothing, which the Indians probably had scattered as they fled at full speed. On another occasion it found the skull, spinal column, parts of ribs, and the leg bones of a man whom the Indians had apparently killed. Hugo's men buried the partial remains. This military party returned to Bayard on December 21, having marched 417 miles. At the end of his report on this scout Hugo wrote: "Every effort was made to overtake and punish the Indians, but to no avail."[41] That comment was applicable to many of the scouts in 1878. The field activities of the Ninth in the late 1870s verified what many people were beginning to suspect: that the army's primary method of finding and controlling the Indian enemy was not effective.

IV. Soldiers and Civil Disturbances, 1875–1879

Even though the U.S. Army was located in the American West primarily to protect people and property from hostile Indians, on occasion it was used to quell civil disturbances. While stationed in New Mexico, black soldiers were involved in both the Colfax County War and the Lincoln County War, two of the most famous events in the history of the territory.

The background of the Colfax County War began in 1843 when Mexican Gov. Manuel Armijo, on the recommendation of his government's quasi-legislative body, granted to Charles Beaubien and Guadalupe Miranda a vast tract of land in present-day northeastern New Mexico and southeastern Colorado. When the United States took over this area in 1848 following the Mexican War, it validated the Beaubien-Miranda grant.[1] Lucien B. Maxwell, who married the daughter of Beaubien, obtained control of the land grant, and in 1860 the U.S. Congress confirmed that Maxwell was the legal owner of the land, although its exact boundaries had not been surveyed.[2] Maxwell allowed ranchers and miners to settle and prospect on his land, charging them nominal rents. When some people moved onto his land without authority, he did not object and often paid little or no attention to them.

Interested in land speculation and railroad construction, British investors desired to buy the Maxwell Land Grant. Because foreigners were not authorized to hold real estate in New Mexico, a British syndicate financed a group of Colorado businessmen and some officials of the Territory of New Mexico to purchase it. In early 1870 the Maxwell Land Grant and Railway Company bought out Lucien Maxwell.[3]

Although the company possessed Maxwell's deed for nearly two million acres, Secretary of the Interior Jacob Cox ruled that the deed should have been for slightly less than one hundred thousand acres. The General Land Office extended its public land surveys over much of the original grant, declared it open for settlement, and began to issue deeds to homesteaders and ranchers.[4]

In the meantime, miners had found gold in the area. In September 1870 the company notified miners on the grant immediately to give full statements of their claims to the company office in Cimarron or be evicted. Ranchers who had squatted in the area supported the miners. For several months tension prevailed and some riots occurred. Gov. William A. Pile used military force to quash the violence.[5] Colfax County court dockets became filled with eviction cases.

The unofficial interlocking directorate of Maxwell Land Grant and Railway Company leaders and territorial officials made many settlers suspicious. Three of the company's prominent leaders were Governor Pile; T. Rush Spencer, surveyor general of the territory; and John S. Watts, former territorial chief justice. Stephen B. Elkins, New Mexico's territorial delegate to Congress and attorney for the company, and Thomas B. Catron, U.S. district attorney, both became involved in the ejectment suits. These men and their associates in New Mexico politics came to be known as the Santa Fe Ring, a political group with no fixed membership or formal organization that had considerable political and economic influence throughout the territory. Litigation over the Maxwell Land Grant first launched the Santa Fe Ring into notoriety.[6]

Citizens freely criticized the Maxwell Land Grant and Railway Company's policies and actions, as well as the territory's political leadership and its involvement with the company. A vocal and persistent critic was the Reverend F. J. Tolby, an itinerant Methodist preacher who served Colfax County for several years. Reviving anti-company sentiment in many emotional speeches, the reverend gave public notice by the summer of 1875 that he intended to clean up Colfax County and break the stranglehold of the Santa Fe Ring. In September Tolby was attacked and killed and New Mexicans widely assumed that the company had hired someone to silence one of its most vocal and increasingly influential critics.[7] Tolby's death inaugurated a series of events that brought tensions to an exploding point in Colfax County.

Another Cimarron minister, the Reverend Oscar P. McMains, began a personal crusade to find his friend's murderer.[8] McMains devoted nearly twenty years to this search and to the larger task of opposing the Maxwell Land Grant and Railway Company's claim to the vast tract of land. His speeches and writings inflamed the passions of partisans on both sides. He made trips to Washington, he wrote letters, and he led settlers in direct defiance of land grant officials.

A group of McMains's friends, including Clay Allison, a respected but hot-tempered Colfax County rancher, brutally tortured and then killed Cruz Vega, a Cimarron law officer they suspected of having been involved in Tolby's murder. At Vega's funeral Francisco Griego swore to revenge his nephew's death by killing Allison, but when Griego later attempted to carry out his threat, Allison shot and killed him. Before dying, Vega had indicated that Manuel Cardenas, a Mexican who lived in Taos, was responsible for Tolby's death. Cardenas was arrested and confessed to the murder, but no trial was held, because while he was being transferred from a courtroom to a jail, a group of armed men attacked and killed him.[9]

McMains was not satisfied. He and his friends began to accuse almost anyone who supported the British company of complicity in the Tolby crime. Tolby's death, McMains' agitation, and the resulting bloodshed had created apparent anarchy in Colfax County. Later McMains was tried for the murder of Vega, but on a technicality the judge set aside a guilty verdict for fifth-degree murder and McMains was never incarcerated. Legally the murders of Tolby, Vega, and Cardenas went unsolved.[10]

In the midst of the Colfax County disturbances, the army made Col. Edward Hatch commander of the District of New Mexico and moved his Ninth Cavalry into the territory. Although the Ninth's primary mission in New Mexico was to bring about the final subjugation of the Apaches, Hatch wanted to strengthen Fort Union for other reasons as well. He notified the War Department that "the Post of Fort Union requires two companies of Infantry owing to the details required at the Post, the large Quartermaster Depot . . . and guard duty." He proposed that the fort be kept as strong as possible, especially in view of the civil problems in and around Cimarron.[11] During the height of the Colfax County disturbances, Ninth Companies D, E, K, and L were stationed at Fort Union.

Soon after the Maxwell Land Grant and Railway Company had purchased the Maxwell grant, it established a weekly paper, the *Cimarron News*, primarily for the purpose of promoting land sales and advertising the wealth on its property. Editors of the paper were William R. Morley, a railroad engineer and manager of the company, and Frank Springer, whom Morley had enticed from Iowa to Colfax County to be attorney for the company. Soon Will Dawson, editor of the Elizabethtown, New Mexico, *Railway Press and Telegraph*, joined Springer and Morley to print and publish a successor to the *Cimarron News* renamed the *Cimarron News and Press*.[12]

Unlike the *Cimarron News*, its successor was not the property of the company, and the new paper's owners were soon expressing reservations about the company. Morley's and Springer's increasingly critical comments evolved into open opposition to company policies, and in May 1875 the two men ended their association with the company. This action led to bitter antipathy between them and members of the Santa Fe Ring, especially Elkins and Catron. At the same time, the newspaper's editorials began to express favorable opinions about Tolby's views and McMain's efforts. In January 1876 under cover of darkness a mob stormed the office and destroyed the equipment of the *Cimarron News and Press*. Responsibility for this destruction of private property was never established, but it probably was not attributable to company supporters. More likely, the attack was ordered by Clay Allison, who was not convinced of the editors' change of heart but who was no company man either. He had a long-running feud with Morley and may simply have been carrying out his own agenda.[13]

Authorities took steps to assure that those responsible for violence would be brought to justice. Territorial officials concluded that fair trials could not be held in Cimarron, so they introduced a bill into the legislature that combined Colfax and Taos counties for judicial purposes. Thus, Colfax's accused criminals could be indicted and tried in Taos amid cooler conditions.[14] In addition, volatile suits involving land sales and grant partitions could be handled outside Colfax County. Opponents argued that conditions in Colfax County were not as bad as they were being depicted, fearing that justice would not be served by such a move. Santa Fe politicians were happy to have the court in a less convenient place for their Cimarron opponents and in a more sympathetic atmosphere towards themselves. Despite the protests of area residents, the bill passed. In February Morley and other prominent businessmen of Cimarron asked Springer to go to Santa Fe to request Gov. Samuel B. Axtell to veto the bill. After his trip Springer reported that the governor was quite bitter toward the people of Colfax County, and especially toward Allison, whom he denounced as a murderer.[15]

After this hostile reception from the governor, Morley, Springer, and their associates sent a formal invitation to Axtell to visit Colfax County. The governor did not immediately reply, but in the middle of March, District Attorney Ben Stevens arrived in Cimarron, carrying from Governor Axtell a letter of secret instructions as to what he was to accomplish.[16] At the same time Stevens arrived in Cimarron, thirty enlisted men of Company L, Ninth Cavalry, under the command of Capt. Francis Moore also arrived from Fort Union by order of the president of the United States.[17] Captain Moore indicated that he was to follow the instructions of Stevens.

In the middle of the third week in March, Stevens told Morley that Axtell planned to arrive in Cimarron on the coach due on Saturday but that Axtell did not want this fact generally known. Stevens indicated that the governor desired to talk with those who had petitioned him to come to Colfax County, but he did not wish to have a large crowd meet him. Morley somehow acquired information about the letter of instructions Stevens carried, and he concluded that the governor was not really interested in talking to Cimarron's citizens or in arresting law violators but rather was a willing participant in a dark plot to kill his political opponents, including Morley. As a result, none of the signers of the invitation to Governor Axtell was present when the Saturday coach arrived. Nor was the governor on the coach; he had not left Santa Fe.[18]

Conditions had deteriorated so much in both Colfax and, as we shall see, Lincoln counties that in May 1878 the U.S. Departments of Justice and the Interior sent special investigator Frank W. Angel to look into the violence and the accusations that territorial officials were involved with mismanagement, fraud, and corruption. After four months of intensive investigation Angel concluded that Axtell was inept and that the governor's own actions had discredited him and made him powerless. In his final report, based upon interviews with dozens of people representing all sides of the opposing forces in the two counties, Angel severely criticized Axtell on a number of counts and blamed him for keeping New Mexico in a state of turmoil and confusion. Included among the charges was one that Axtell had no intention of visiting Colfax County to talk with his detractors, but rather that he was at the heart of a plot to have U.S. cavalrymen kill leaders of the opposition, including Allison, Morley, Springer, and Henry Porter, a Cimarron merchant and banker.

Because of continued instability in New Mexico and the damaging accusations in Angel's report, President Rutherford B. Hayes removed Axtell from office in September 1878 amid criticism from Axtell's supporters that Angel had been influenced by the governor's detractors. A continuing debate among modern-day historians has not resolved the question of whether a governor of a U.S. territory actually plotted to have U.S. troops shoot political opponents. The circumstantial evidence is strong that he did.[19]

After ten days in Cimarron in March 1876, half the troopers under the command of Captain Moore were ordered to Fort Union, where the captain was to witness the payment of his company. Before this order could be executed, Colonel Hatch rescinded it because of rumors of renewed disorder in Cimarron. Shortly thereafter, the troopers accompanied the county sheriff to Allison's ranch, where they surrounded the house and arrested the owner. The politicians who asked Hatch to send black soldiers to arrest Allison, an unrepentant and unreconstructed former southern Confederate, may have been trying deliberately to provoke him, hoping his resistance would result in his death. But Allison outsmarted them. He offered no resistance, quietly accompanying the soldiers to their headquarters in Cimarron. The military, however, did not detain him.[20] These events indicated that reports of lawlessness in the county may have been exaggerated.

A few days later another incident involving black troopers proved much less pleasant. The company had established its quarters in a feed yard and livery stable behind the St. James Hotel. Captain Moore had asked the owner of the hotel not to serve liquor to the soldiers, and he had ordered his men to stay out of all saloons in Cimarron,[21] a precaution justified by the tense situation in the town. Nevertheless, two enlisted men made an afternoon visit to Schwenck's saloon, where they became involved in an argument with Texas cowboys Gus Hefron, Henry Goodman, and David Crockett.[22] At one point during the dispute, Crockett held a pistol to the head of one of the soldiers and threatened to shoot. Returning to camp, the men reported the event to their captain.

Moore ordered the two soldiers to remain in camp that evening, but, joined by a third man, they left the encampment after taps and "threw themselves in the way of trouble."[23] When Pvts. George Small, Anthony Harvey, and John Hanson found Hefron and Crockett in Henry Lambert's bar at the St. James Hotel, the five men exchanged fifteen to twenty shots, the soldiers firing at least four rounds. The shootout resulted in the deaths of the three troopers, while the herders were not wounded.[24] Despite an extensive hunt by both military and civilian authorities, Hefron and Crockett escaped, and Captain Moore complained that local citizens had rendered no significant assistance in attempts to locate or capture the killers. Moore sent the dead soldiers' bodies to Fort Union for interment. After the funeral Maj. James F. Wade, Union's commander, ordered the remainder of Company L to rejoin the men at Cimarron,[25] where the entire company remained until the middle of April.[26] Six months later Crockett and Hefron rode into Cimarron and became drunkenly boisterous. A sheriff's posse chased them out of town, killing Crockett and badly wounding and capturing Hefron,[27] but this was little consolation to the friends and comrades of the slain soldiers.

The deaths of the three troopers were seemingly unrelated to the political troubles in Colfax County. Because Crockett had earlier expressed his dislike of the presence of black soldiers in Cimarron, the incident was more likely related to racial prejudice than to politics.

The violence in Cimarron was far from over. The next disturber of the peace was Pvt. William Breckenridge, who had not been permitted to go to Fort Union with the bodies of his murdered comrades and consequently did not receive his military pay. Finding himself short of cash, Breckenridge robbed and killed William Maxwell and his son Emmett, an act netting him $58.50. A Taos court indicted Breckenridge for murder and he was speedily tried, convicted, and hanged. In May 1877 over four hundred curiosity seekers witnessed his public execution at Cimarron.[28]

Axtell's removal from office in September 1878 went a long way toward ending armed conflict in Colfax County. Apparently no troopers were used to quell civil disturbances there after that time. Because the Ninth Cavalry moved out of New Mexico in 1881, certainly no black soldiers were involved after that date. Because army involvement in the disputes had ended, the remainder of the Colfax County War story is not relevant here, but it should be noted that lawsuits gradually replaced the violence. Legally the major dispute was finally settled when in April 1887 the U.S. Supreme Court handed down its decision in the case of *United States v. the Maxwell Land Grant Company*, in which the court fully confirmed the rights of the company to the huge tract of land. By that time the British investors had sold their rights to a Dutch company, which thus benefited from the favorable ruling.

Disheartening as the Supreme Court decision was to the squatters in northeastern New Mexico, it did not suddenly end the Colfax County War or entirely dampen the spirits of the anti-company leaders. Oscar McMains continued his agitation, denouncing the company and pledging to continue to defy its demands that the settlers sell or leave. He suggested that as legal means had failed to secure the settlers' lands, violence against the foreign company might be justified. Rumors circulated throughout the area that a civil war was possible. Threats of mob action and occasional shots at company sympathizers occurred. When President Grover Cleveland refused to support the settlers, however, many of them began to abandon their strong anti-company stands.[29] Slowly, almost imperceptibly, open opposition to the Maxwell Land Grant Company declined. The Colfax County War was over.

To some extent intertwined with the Colfax County War was the better-known Lincoln County War. In the 1870s New Mexico's Lincoln County constituted all of the southeastern quadrant of the territory, a vast area about the size of the state of Pennsylvania. Its county seat, the town of Lincoln, normally had a population of about four hundred. Like other regions of the partly settled West, the county and town of Lincoln attracted not only legitimate settlers but also a sizeable share of undesirable ones. Desperadoes, outlaws, and rustlers constituted a significant proportion of the population, and killings and shootouts therefore occurred more often than respectable citizens cared to recall. Hollywood movies and television series could hardly exaggerate the cast of shady characters and the list of unlawful acts committed in historic Lincoln.

Situated about nine miles west and slightly north of the town of Lincoln was Fort Stanton. The primary purpose of the soldiers stationed at Stanton was to control the regional Indian population, but in view of Lincoln's diverse civilian population, the soldiers sometimes assisted with civil disturbances as well. An early example of this occurred in 1877 after a well-known desperado, Frank Freeman, formerly of Alabama, appeared in Lincoln County. When Freeman became involved in a dispute over a land claim, he had a shootout with a prominent Lincoln citizen. Shortly thereafter, he entered a restaurant and for no apparent reason other than racial prejudice he shot and wounded a black noncommissioned officer from Fort Stanton. The sheriff and a posse arrested Freeman and turned him over to soldiers from the fort. While under military escort to Stanton, Freeman managed to escape, and later joined a band of cattle rustlers and thieves located on the Ruidoso River. When a sheriff's posse and a detachment of fifteen black cavalrymen led by Lt. George W. Smith surrounded the gang's hideout, exchanges of gunfire occurred, after which most of the group surrendered, except for Freeman, who was killed while attempting to escape.[30]

It was not only the lowest underside of Lincoln County society who created problems. Sometimes socially prominent citizens allowed conditions to overwhelm their morals. Secret business agreements, including land and mercantile schemes, were commonplace, often involving greed, graft, corruption, fraud, deceit, manipulation, and embezzlement. Commonly, the emotional response was anger, hostility, hatred, and vengeance. In addition, supposedly law-abiding citizens were not above using desperadoes for their benefit. These factors combined to create a number of turbulent years in the history of Lincoln County.

In the mid-1870s Lawrence G. Murphy and James J. Dolan dominated the economic and political life of Lincoln County. Murphy and Dolan were business associates of Thomas B. Catron, who was not only U.S. district attorney but also president of the First National Bank of Santa Fe, a rancher and land speculator, and a powerful scion in territorial politics and business.[31] Operating a general store named L. G. Murphy & Co. in the town of Lincoln, the Murphy-Dolan combine, or "the House" as the business was called, held the contract to supply the Mescalero Agency with beef and flour. The lucrative legal contract became even more advantageous when "the House," unashamedly and systematically cheated the Indians on the quality and quantities of their delivered goods. Because Murphy and Dolan supplied large amounts of beef, grains, and vegetables to Fort

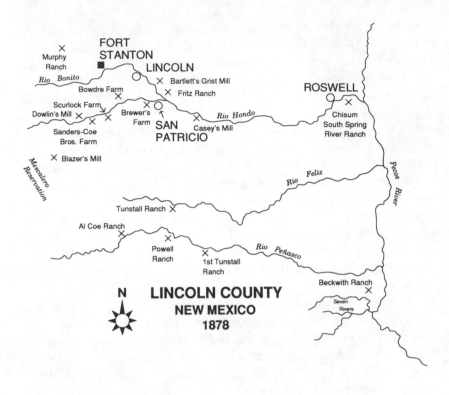

N

LINCOLN COUNTY
NEW MEXICO
1878

Stanton, they were on intimate terms with the officers at Fort Stanton and with Frederick C. Godfroy, the Indian agent on the reservation.[32]

Problems began to arise for "the House" and its profitable enterprises when John S. Chisum, a former Texas cowman, expanded his ranching operation in southeastern New Mexico. After laying claim to approximately one hundred miles of fertile land along the banks of the Pecos River, Chisum presented formidable competition to the Murphy-Dolan business enterprises. After competitive bidding on Indian supplies began, "the House" was no longer assured of its previous contractual arrangements. Soon Chisum was being awarded contracts to supply beef to the Mescaleros. This development plus his alliance with a Lincoln lawyer, Alexander A. McSween, began to cause "the House" anxiety,[33] as Murphy and Dolan were already at odds with McSween over legal matters.

In 1877 events took an ominous turn when John H. Tunstall arrived in Lincoln. A young Englishman with access to family funds abroad, Tunstall allied himself with Chisum and McSween and promptly began to compete with "the House" on all fronts. Indeed, his goal was to replace "the House" as the dominant economic and political power center in Lincoln County.[34]

The competition between the Murphy-Dolan combine and the McSween-Tunstall group resulted in each side stealing or damaging the property of the other, occasional personal injuries to supporters of each group, and the use of force or the threat of force to accomplish each group's objectives. By early 1878 civil law was difficult to maintain, especially since law enforcement officers were not, or found it difficult to remain, neutral. Inevitably federal troops became involved. At that time Companies F, H, and M of the Ninth Cavalry (about one hundred men) and Company H of the Fifteenth Infantry (about fifty men) were located at Fort Stanton.[35] In early February Deputy U.S. Marshall Robert Widenmann, a close friend of Tunstall, applied to Capt. George A. Purington, commander at Fort Stanton, for troop support for maintaining civil law. Purington assigned a detachment of cavalrymen to Widenmann, who used the soldiers to assist him in serving arrest warrants to members of the Murphy-Dolan group. This was not pleasant duty. On a trip to an outlying ranch, three of the soldiers were frostbitten and had to be hospitalized.

A few days later Stanton cavalrymen helped Widenmann and some citizens surround a Dolan residence in Lincoln. Widenmann searched the house but did not find the men for whom he was looking. The citizens then ransacked the house, examined drawers and pockets of clothing, and took jewelry and private letters. On the same day, with troopers assisting, Widenmann entered the Tunstall store and confronted an armed posse organized by Lincoln County Sheriff William Brady. Widenmann arrested some of the members of the posse, dispersed the others, and confiscated property that had been in the custody of the sheriff. Soon thereafter, a group of Widenmann's men arrested and killed two opponents, riddling their bodies with bullets. Upon learning that Widenmann's appointment as deputy marshall had been annulled and "firmly believing that if troops are given him [Widenmann] they will be used to serve his own purpose," Purington questioned the role of federal troops in the Lincoln affray.[36]

In late February 1878 the situation reached a crisis when members of Sheriff Brady's Lincoln County posse killed Tunstall. Passions ran high over this murder and the lack of any apparent attempt by Brady (who was considered a "House" man) to apprehend the killers. The county was near anarchy and widespread bloodshed was a distinct possibility. Governor Axtell, concerned about maintaining law and order and protecting life and property (which in turn would protect his and "the House's" economic interests), sent a telegram to Colonel Hatch requesting the assistance of U.S. troops stationed at Fort Stanton and making it clear that he believed McSween to be the major source of the trouble.[37]

Hatch hurriedly approved Axtell's request, and Captain Purington dispatched a detachment of twenty-five troopers of Company H, Ninth Cavalry, to the town of Lincoln to preserve the peace and prevent bloodshed. Two days later a lieutenant and a detachment of white infantrymen joined the black cavalrymen in Lincoln.[38] Stanton's soldiers found that McSween had organized a party of twenty-five or thirty armed men who were defying the sheriff and his posse and at one point even firing on the soldiers, wounding a horse.[39]

Purington and his men found that the situation in Lincoln remained extremely unstable. Justice of the Peace John B. Wilson had issued warrants for the arrest of members of Sheriff Brady's posse for the killing of Tunstall, while Brady demanded assistance in rounding up law-violating members of the McSween faction. Understandably, Purington was perplexed as to his role in Lincoln.[40] Hatch eased Purington's dilemma by directing the captain to assist the county sheriff, as Brady was the recognized authority in the region.[41]

In March Sheriff Brady, Lieutenant Smith, and a detachment of the Ninth's Company H traveled to the Chisum Ranch, where they attempted to serve McSween with a warrant for his arrest.[42] McSween went into hiding, escaping arrest, but his wife informed Brady and Smith that her husband, who she said did not intend to be a fugitive from the law, was planning to return to Lincoln on April 1. Because Lieutenant Smith was under orders to keep the peace, both he and Brady guaranteed McSween's safety. Smith and his soldiers returned to Stanton, while Brady and his men returned to Lincoln to await the arrival of McSween.[43]

On April 1, when Brady and two of his deputies, George Hindman and Jacob B. Mathews, were walking along Lincoln's main street, someone fired upon them from behind an adobe wall. Brady and Hindman instantly fell dead. Blamed for these killings were William "Billy the Kid" Bonney and other members of the McSween faction. Upon learning of these deaths, Purington, Smith, and the Ninth's Company H returned to Lincoln, assisted in making numerous arrests (without warrants), and searched the McSween house. Finding no weapons, Purington and his men returned to Fort Stanton.[44]

On April 5 Lt. Col. N.A.M. Dudley assumed command of Fort Stanton. Dudley's military career had begun in 1843, when he entered the Massachusetts Militia. After joining the Tenth U.S. Infantry in 1855, he was stationed in the West, where he fought against the Cheyenne and the Sioux Indians. During the Civil War he served without distinction in the Department of the Gulf and in western Virginia and eastern Tennessee. At the end of the war he was an officer in the Fifteenth Infantry, and in the postwar years served mostly in the Southwest. After brief service in the black Twenty-fourth Infantry and the white Third Cavalry, Dudley was assigned to the Ninth Cavalry in 1876. For drunkenness and conduct unbecoming an officer, Dudley was court-martialed and found guilty in Arizona in 1871. At Fort Union six years later, following a bitter dispute with Hatch, he was court-martialed a second time. Although Dudley was found guilty of vilifying Hatch, President Rutherford B. Hayes ordered his sentence remitted. Eccentric, contentious, and petty, Dudley constantly quarreled with his superiors. Despite his vanity and limited intellect, he had no qualms about leading black troopers. Even so, a man with his temperament and inclination to alcoholism was not a proper choice to command Fort Stanton, especially at that time.[45]

Within three hours after taking command of Stanton, Dudley received a confidential note from Lawrence G. Murphy reporting the rumor that fourteen men were on their way to intercept and probably kill Judge Warren Bristol and other members of the Third Judicial District Court. Dudley ordered Lt. Millard F. Goodwin and ten enlisted men of the Ninth's Company H to find the Bristol party and escort it to Stanton. Under the black soldiers' protection, the judge arrived safely and remained as Dudley's guest during the session of the court,

Lt. Col. N.A.M. Dudley. (Courtesy Massachusetts Commandery of the Military Order of the Loyal Legion and the U.S. Army Military History Institute, Carlisle, Pennsylvania.)

traveling between Stanton and Lincoln almost daily by government transportation under a military escort varying from five to twenty-five officers and men.[46]

Shortly after Dudley took command of Stanton, the Board of County Commissioners appointed John Copeland as sheriff. Although Copeland was a McSween sympathizer, the commissioners were willing to try anybody who might bring peace to Lincoln. Copeland immediately requested Dudley to supply three troopers to act as sentinels for prisoners confined in the county jail by order of Judge Bristol.[47]

On April 20 Bristol asked Dudley to station twenty men in the town of Lincoln to aid the sheriff in maintaining public order while the court met.[48] Dudley complied with this request, and when the court's session ended, he assigned Cpl. Thomas Dale and three privates from the Ninth's Company H to the town of Lincoln to help the sheriff keep peace and serve warrants.[49] Copeland quickly made use of this corporal's guard. The soldiers attended an evening gathering in the courthouse to prevent anyone from interfering with the meeting. The event ended without violence. On the next day, on Copeland's orders the soldiers accompanied the sheriff to search the McSween residence, where they found not fewer than five armed men in each room of this ten-room residence. Copeland did not attempt to arrest anyone, although he believed he had found the men for whom he was looking. Two days later Copeland ordered Corporal Dale to visit Murphy's house. Dale found three men, but he did not arrest them. Although the corporal's guard thoroughly searched Lincoln for concealed outlaws, it found none. Dale, however, did assist in serving an arrest warrant to George Coe, a McSween ally.

But generally Copeland was too inclined to be friendly with the McSween crowd, for which Dale faulted him. Furthermore, Dale lost confidence in Copeland because he often was too drunk to lead soldiers. Finally, Dale questioned Copeland's abilities because the sheriff was such a highly excitable person. Although Dale was under Dudley's orders to do the sheriff's bidding, the black corporal did not hesitate to write in excellent English a long, well-organized, and frank letter about Copeland's shortcomings.[50]

In late April, Hatch ordered Dudley to provide soldiers to guard life and property in Lincoln and to assist the sheriff in serving arrest warrants

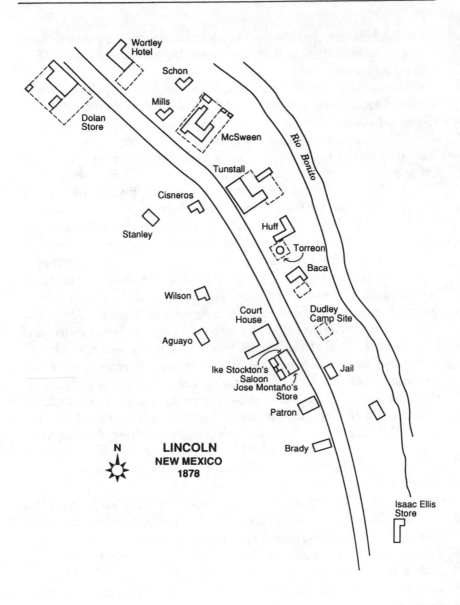

Wortley Hotel

Schon

Mills

Dolan Store

McSween

Rio Bonito

Tunstall

Cisneros

Stanley

Huff

Torreon

Baca

Wilson

Court House

Dudley Camp Site

Aguayo

Ike Stockton's Saloon
Jose Montaño's Store

Jail

Patron

N

LINCOLN
NEW MEXICO
1878

Brady

Isaac Ellis Store

issued by the courts.[51] During succeeding days, Dudley received and filled a number of requests for the use of soldiers.[52]

At the same time, a new force in the Lincoln County War appeared. Men from the Seven Rivers area of the Pecos Valley entered the conflict, committed to supporting the Murphy-Dolan element. The Pecos men agreed to Murphy's suggestion that they make a surprise attack upon the Isaac Ellis store, rendezvous and supply depot for the McSween crowd. When the Pecos men entered Lincoln, they found that the McSween men at the Ellis store were ready for them, foiling the planned attack.[53]

On April 30 Sheriff Copeland wrote Dudley, stating that a band of outlaws had killed three men and wounded another near the town of Lincoln and asking Dudley to assign twenty soldiers there.[54] Before Dudley could respond, hostilities broke out in the town itself when men of the McSween group fired at and wounded a Pecos man. Members of the opposing groups were hidden on adobe roofs and behind buildings, where occasionally they shot at each other. Lincoln appeared to be on the verge of a bloody battle. In response to Copeland's request, Dudley hurriedly dispatched Lieutenant Smith and a detachment of twenty cavalrymen of Company H to aid the sheriff in saving life, protecting property, and preserving the peace. As Smith and his troopers approached Lincoln they heard a number of shots, but upon their arrival hostilities ceased.

Copeland then told Smith about a party of men outside the town limits whom he desired to arrest but could not. Covered by the carbines of the men in his detachment, Smith rode within earshot of the men, who were on a bluff above a river bank, and asked some of them to meet with him. When they complied, Copeland wanted to arrest them, but they insisted on keeping their guns and said that they were afraid the sheriff would turn them over to their enemies to be murdered. They contended they were in the custody of Smith and were willing to go with him to Fort Stanton. To avoid conflict Smith led twenty-three men around the town of Lincoln to the fort.[55] Dudley reported that Smith's good judgment, courage, and ability and the conduct of the cavalrymen under his command deserved commendation.[56] Although Copeland continued to request and use federal troops and apparently made some effort to enforce the laws,[57] Governor Axtell removed him from office at the urging of Murphy and Dolan and appointed in his place George Peppin, a "House" tool.

On May 30 Axtell requested Colonel Hatch to send soldiers to Roswell to help curtail large-scale rustling. At the same time, Axtell asked that troopers be sent to Lincoln to disarm all bands of men there, including those claiming to be the sheriff's posse. Hatch honored the request by sending the Ninth Cavalry's Captain Purington and Company H to Roswell and Capt. Henry Carroll and Company F to Lincoln. Hatch also asked Dudley to cooperate with Sheriff Peppin and to furnish soldierly escorts for contractors' cattle being driven to the Mescalero Reservation.[58]

On June 18 Peppin rode to Fort Stanton requesting trooper assistance in making arrests in Lincoln, a request that Dudley granted, sending Lieutenant Goodwin and twenty-seven cavalrymen to accompany the sheriff on his return trip to Lincoln. When a group of twenty heavily armed civilians, including a notorious gunman, joined the soldiers, Goodwin refused to enter Lincoln in such company, remaining on the edge of the town with his men while Peppin and the others searched Lincoln. When Peppin did not find the men he sought, Goodwin and his men returned to Stanton.[59]

About a week later, in response to another request from Peppin, Dudley sent a posse comprised of Goodwin and Carroll with thirty-five cavalrymen from Companies H and F to assist in making arrests near Ruidoso. They traveled several miles during a forty-eight-hour period but were unable to apprehend the men being pursued. Carroll praised Goodwin and commented on "the cheerful manner and alacrity of the men in performing the most disagreeable duty that can be assigned either officer or soldier."[60]

In the meantime, Hatch had written department headquarters at Fort Leavenworth requesting clarification of the military's participation in the Lincoln County dispute. Ironically, for some time the U.S. Congress had been concerned about the legalities involved in the use of federal troops as a posse comitatus — a body of people summoned to help preserve the public peace in civil disorders. In June 1878 — at the very time Hatch asked for clarification — Congress passed the Posse Comitatus Act, designed to clarify the president's powers to use military force to repress internal disturbances. The law was not clearly written, however, and the real meaning of the provisions of the Posse Comitatus Act were the subject of dispute in the future.[61]

Despite the vagueness of the law, at that time the secretary of war ruled that the use of the army as a posse comitatus, was unauthorized. Department headquarters relayed this information to Hatch, who in turn informed the commanding officer at Fort Stanton, telling Dudley that U.S. troops could no longer assist the civil authorities of Lincoln County.[62] Dudley ignored Hatch's directive. His unauthorized involvement of himself and his men in the conflict in the town of Lincoln from July 15 through 20 tipped the balance in the so-called Battle of Lincoln and greatly influenced the outcome of the Lincoln County War.

By the middle of July members of both the Murphy-Dolan and McSween forces were determined to have a showdown. On the morning of July 15 nearly sixty McSween men entered Lincoln and took positions in the McSween home, the Jose Montaño store, and the Isaac Ellis store. A few hours later Sheriff Peppin, Dolan, and about thirty men took positions where they could observe and fire directly on the McSween-occupied buildings. Peppin sent his deputy, John Long, to the McSween house to serve outstanding arrest warrants against some of the men inside. When the McSween men fired upon the deputy, the five-day battle of Lincoln began.[63]

On July 16 Peppin wrote to Dudley at Fort Stanton requesting to borrow a Howitzer, the presence of which he believed would frighten his opponents into surrendering. Dudley denied this request, but he assured Peppin that he was sympathetic to him and his cause, writing: "Were I not so circumscribed by laws and orders, I would most gladly give you every man and material at my post to sustain you in your present position, believing it to be strictly legal."[64]

Later that evening Dudley sent Pvt. Berry Robinson of the Ninth's Company H to Lincoln to deliver his note. As Robinson approached Lincoln just before sundown, he saw four men mounted on horses and painted like Indians at a crossing of a creek near the town. These men stopped the courier, asking him where he was going, to which Robinson replied that he was on government business. The men said, "You talk damn 'saucy,' " and surrounded the enlisted man with drawn six-shooters. In response, Robinson put a cartridge in his carbine, brought it to

"Dismounted Negro, 10th Cavalry." (Courtesy Frederic Remington Art Museum, Ogdensburg, New York.)

advance position, and rode on. As the courier entered Lincoln, McSween's men fired about four times, the bullets tearing up the earth near him. The shots were so close that Robinson's frightened horse reared and fell, but Robinson was able to get off the animal, hold onto the bridle, and remount. James Dolan quickly motioned to Robinson to ride to the Wortley Hotel, which he did, placing the building between himself and the gunfire. He reached Sheriff Peppin's position safely.[65] Although McSween claimed that the shots fired near Private Robinson were random and not directed toward the soldier, Dudley chose to believe the soldier's report of the incident.

Many people, including a delegation of twenty-seven Hispanic women from San Patricio, a small community southeast of Lincoln, previously had traveled to Stanton to ask Dudley "in the name of God and the Constitution" to protect private property and the lives of women and children. This pressure plus the relatively harmless episode involving trooper Robinson allowed Dudley, after consulting with his officers, to justify military intervention in Lincoln.[66]

When Dudley — contrary to direct orders — made his decision to take bold action in regard to Lincoln's civil disturbances, half his troopers were scouting for Indians in the Guadalupe and Sacramento mountains, and some personnel had to remain at Stanton as guards. Nevertheless, on July 19 Dudley saddled up the remainder of his command and headed for Lincoln. To fit the image he wished to portray, the troopers were required to wear full-dress uniforms, including swords. The movement of this column toward Lincoln was an impressive spectacle — five officers (including Dudley), eleven black cavalrymen, twenty-four white infantrymen, one rapid-firing Gatling gun, one twelve-pounder brass mountain Howitzer, ample supplies of arms, two thousand rounds of ammunition, and three days' rations.[67]

Upon reaching Lincoln, Dudley met with Sheriff Peppin and the deputy marshall, stating that he and his command were in Lincoln to protect women and children — not to take sides in the dispute. Despite Dudley's statements of neutrality, however, he clearly did not favor the McSween group. Dudley said that if anyone fired on his camp or any of his men, he would request that person be turned over to him. If his request was not met, he said he would evacuate the women and children from the houses of the guilty, which would then be fired upon by his Howitzer.[68]

Dudley set up camp in the middle of town on the north side of the main street across from the Montaño store. The enlisted men pitched tents for themselves and their officers and strung a picket line for their horses, and at Dudley's request pointed the Howitzer directly at the front door of the Montaño store, where the McSween contingent was hiding. In response to this show of force, the McSween men fled to the Ellis store down the street. When Dudley aimed the cannon there, the men abandoned that hiding place as well. Susan McSween, fearing for her husband's life, visited Dudley's camp to urge the lieutenant colonel to allow McSween to surrender to him, a request that Dudley refused, telling the woman that he had no control over the sheriff or his posse.[69]

As his next move, Dudley forced frightened Justice of the Peace John B. Wilson to issue warrants against McSween, Billy the Kid, and several of their associates, sending his troopers to assist Peppin in serving the warrants. Dudley then ordered the judge to take affidavits from Captain Purington, Capt. Thomas Blair, and assistant surgeon Daniel M. Appel, who had accused McSween and others of firing on Robinson.[70]

On the evening of July 19 Peppin demanded that his opponents surrender. When they would not, he ordered the McSween house set on fire. As the house began to burn, under cover of darkness Billy the Kid and about two-thirds of the McSween men escaped from the rear of the house across a ravine. The following morning, the fire, which had moved slowly through the wooden and adobe structure, finally drove the remaining men from the house. The posse shot and killed McSween and three of his associates as they exited the burning building. One deputy sheriff was killed,[71] and the Battle of Lincoln was over.

Unquestionably, the presence of federal troops in Lincoln turned the tide of the battle. Although Dudley did not give his verbal consent to the torching of the McSween house, and his soldiers fired no shots and were not actively involved in the fighting, the commander's tacit approval and the presence of the troopers gave Peppin the courage to set the house ablaze. Because the fire drove many of the McSween faction into the woods, it no longer had a two-to-one numerical advantage, and Peppin's newfound comparative numerical strength, plus the presence of the not-so-neutral Dudley and his troopers, placed the sheriff in command of the situation. The McSween faction had neither the numbers nor the audacity to return to Lincoln to continue a battle that it could not win.

On July 21 Dudley and a detachment of enlisted men visited the smoldering ruins of the McSween house. McSween's body lay where it had fallen, chickens pecking at the dead man's face and eyes until two of Dudley's troopers chased them away. A dazed Susan McSween refused Dudley's belated offer of assistance, angrily ordering the commander and his men off her property. Satisfied that he had done his duty, Dudley led his command back to Fort Stanton.[72]

At district headquarters in Santa Fe, Colonel Hatch reviewed the reports coming out of Lincoln, after which he sent a telegram to Dudley telling him that his actions had been illegal and that he should cease them at once. Thereafter, Dudley generally limited the use of his troopers to protecting the Mescalero Agency from attacks by roving bands of outlaws.[73]

Lawlessness did not disappear from Lincoln County, even though the battle of Lincoln had ended. The killing, stealing, and unstable conditions continued to plague not only the reservation Indians but also the inhabitants of Lincoln County. Faithfully reporting incidents showing that the Lincoln County War continued,[74] Dudley virtually begged his superior to give him more soldiers.[75] However, frustrated with Dudley for involving troopers in the battle of Lincoln against explicit orders, Dudley's superiors not only rejected these requests but also continued to remind him that he must not disobey orders.[76] Dudley's actions were not forgotten: when the army occasionally authorized civil officials to use soldiers, it carefully circumscribed the conditions under which they could participate.[77]

After Governor Axtell was removed from office, Civil War hero Gen. Lew Wallace replaced him,[78] appealing to Colonel Hatch to restore law and order in Lincoln County. On October 8 Wallace received and immediately publicized a presidential proclamation ordering those responsible for the lawlessness in Lincoln County to disperse peaceably before noon on October 13, or face military force as long as resistance lasted. By the end of October violence had subsided to the point that Wallace issued a general amnesty, which applied to everyone except the officers at Fort Stanton. Dudley took exception to this exclusion and openly criticized the governor's decision.[79] In response,

Wallace requested that Hatch relieve Dudley as commanding officer of Fort Stanton, pointing out that Dudley had "excited the animosity of parties in Lincoln to such a degree as to embarrass the administration of affairs in that locality." After Hatch had forwarded the request through proper channels, Gens. John Pope and Philip H. Sheridan approved it, but Gen. William T. Sherman did not.[80]

Following their escape from the McSween house, Billy the Kid and his companions continued to roam the streets of Lincoln, terrorizing local inhabitants. In February 1879 the remaining members of the Murphy-Dolan faction shot and killed Mrs. McSween's unarmed lawyer, Huston Chapman, without provocation on the streets of Lincoln. At that very moment, George Kimbrell, who had succeeded Peppin as sheriff, was at Fort Stanton asking Dudley for assistance in arresting Billy the Kid and his gang. In response, Dudley sent to Lincoln Lt. Byron Dawson and a detachment of twenty men drawn from Ninth Companies F, H, and M. They came across the badly burned body of Chapman, but when they were unable to find Billy the Kid, they returned to Stanton.[81]

The sheriff and frightened citizens pleaded with Dudley to station a force of soldiers in Lincoln to protect lives and property. In response, Dudley ordered Lieutenant Goodwin, an assistant surgeon, eighteen black cavalrymen, and three white infantrymen to take a Gatling gun and three days' rations and forage to Lincoln, where Goodwin was to report to Kimbrell and offer assistance in keeping the peace.

Due to public fear, Kimbrell was unable to man a civilian posse, setting out instead with six black soldiers to arrest Billy the Kid. The mission was unsuccessful, but the detachment remained in Lincoln for several days, committed to impartiality and to keeping the peace. In late February another posse composed of the Fifteenth Infantry's Lt. Charles E. Garst, five white infantrymen, and six black cavalrymen, went on a similar — and equally unsuccessful — mission.[82]

After Chapman's murder, Governor Wallace became personally involved in the continuing dispute, asking Hatch to send soldiers to the Carrizozo Ranch to arrest William Campbell, William Mathews, and Jesse Evans, whom he believed had killed the lawyer. Lieutenant Goodwin and fifteen men carried out this assignment, capturing the three men and taking them to Stanton, where they were placed in the guardhouse.[83]

Because of the troubled conditions, in March Wallace went to Lincoln; following this visit, the soldiers there were ordered to carry out his directives.[84] For example, Wallace approved a request from Kimbrell that a detachment of men accompany the sheriff to arrest J. G. Scurlock and Charles Bowdre, who had been indicted for murder.[85] In addition, at Wallace's request Hatch went to Fort Stanton, where he removed Dudley from command and ordered him to Fort Union to await the formal charges that Wallace intended to press.[86] Hatch then elevated Captain Carroll to post commander at Stanton. In April a Lincoln grand jury indicted Dudley, charging that he had set fire to the house of Alexander A. McSween.[87] A jury in Mesilla acquitted him.

A military court of inquiry convened at Fort Stanton to review a host of charges against Dudley growing out of his actions during the Battle of Lincoln. Among the charges reviewed were the allegations that Dudley had aided in the killing of McSween, assisted with the burning of the McSween home, slandered McSween's wife, and badgered Justice of the Peace Wilson. After seven weeks of testimony from more than sixty witnesses, including several black enlisted men, the court of inquiry cleared Dudley of all charges.[88]

Interestingly, two black civilians were among the parade of witnesses who testified at Dudley's court-martial. The first was George Washington, possibly an ex-cavalryman who had worked as a civilian laborer at Fort Stanton in the early 1870s and was an employee of McSween during the 1878 disturbances in Lincoln. Whenever McSween gathered his gunshooters, Washington was often a member of the group. The second, Sebrian Bates, was a servant in the McSween household at the time of the Lincoln fight. He had served in the Ninth Cavalry from its inception in 1866 until his discharge at Fort Stanton in January 1877. An able musician, for part of that time Bates had served in the regimental band. During the battle of Lincoln, McSween had sent Bates to learn the intent of Dudley's soldiers. Sheriff Peppin had detained him and forced him to help burn the McSween house. On the next day Bates helped bury the bodies of McSween and one of his slain associates. For a time Susan McSween continued to employ him after her husband's death.

The testimony of Washington and Bates was direct and detailed. Generally, it supplemented the testimony of others. Each was emphatic in portraying Dudley as domineering and rude and as an unsympathetic partisan who failed to halt the destruction of private property.[89]

Dudley's dismissal as commander of Fort Stanton did not retard the army's efforts to bring peace to Lincoln County. For the remainder of 1879 detachments of cavalrymen continued to protect the citizens of Lincoln and to aid civil authorities in tracking down desperadoes, outlaws, and thieves.[90] The work was tedious, more so because the local population was uncooperative with the black soldiers. Hatch's statement made a year earlier still applied: "Unquestionably the troops find this duty disagreeable, as it must expose them to more or less odium and obloquy from the community."[91] Despite these unpleasant conditions, the troopers continued to search for lawbreakers. Occasionally they captured horse or cattle thieves, but generally they were unsuccessful in rounding up the participants in the Lincoln County War. Gradually an uneasy peace settled over southeastern New Mexico.

For years historians have sorted contradictory information and attempted to make valid interpretations of the turbulent events in Lincoln County in the late 1870s. Whatever else they have decided, they correctly have concluded that Lieutenant Colonel Dudley directly affected the outcome, which he could not have done without the support of his soldiers. The enlisted men of the Ninth Cavalry therefore were major contributors to the final outcome of one of the most famous episodes in the history of the American West.

V. Cavalrymen Versus Victorio, 1879–1881

The attention New Mexico's black soldiers gave to civil disturbances did not keep them from their primary objective as the U.S. Army continued its relentless pursuit of recalcitrant Indians. In early 1879 Chief Victorio and his band returned to the United States from Mexico. Shortly thereafter, Victorio surrendered to Lt. Charles W. Merritt at Ojo Caliente, but within a few weeks he was on the move again, still opposed to the policy of Apache concentration at San Carlos.[1]

Throughout 1879 Ninth cavalrymen spent hours searching for both Victorio's band and other Indians refusing to cooperate with the policies of the U.S. government and army. In late January 1879 Capt. Charles D. Beyer led Companies C and G out of Fort Bayard into Arizona to the headwaters of the Prieta River looking for a band of renegade Chiricahua Indians. Beyer went as far west as the eastern boundary line of the San Carlos Reservation, "over country never before travelled by troops." He found no Indians, but before he returned to Bayard in February he marched eight miles in a blinding snowstorm and abandoned one pack mule because of exhaustion. He and his men had traveled 256 miles.[2]

In May Lt. William H. Hugo led a scout composed of all the mounted men of his Company B and sixteen enlisted men of Company G, all fully armed and equipped for field service and with thirty days' rations. Hugo traveled from Bayard toward Ojo Caliente via the North Star Road. While camped at Willow Spring, Hugo's command encountered a forest fire that raged with such force that for a time Hugo and his men could move in neither direction along the road. Established in the dense forest, Hugo's camp was saved from the fire only by the utmost exertion of the troopers. After surviving the fire, Hugo traveled north, where he found many signs of Indian pony tracks, but they were several days old. He saw no Indians.[3]

The day after Hugo returned to Bayard, Maj. Albert P. Morrow learned that a band of Indians was crossing the Mogollon Mountains. Believing that the band was Victorio's, he ordered Bayard's Companies C (led by Captain Beyer) and G (led by Lt. Patrick Cusack and guided by a Mr. Keller) immediately to proceed separately to the area and to intercept it. With five Navajo Indian scouts, Lt. Robert T. Emmet of the Ninth Cavalry also joined this expedition, as did a lieutenant of the Fifteenth Infantry. After finding no Apaches, Cusack reported that white men and Navajo scouts were not useful guides and recommended that Apache scouts be hired to search Apache country for Apache Indians, arguing that they were better adapted for the service and would be less expensive.[4]

Following Morrow's orders, Captain Beyer, Lt. Henry H. Wright, thirty-one men of Company C, a detachment of fifteen men of Company I out of Fort Wingate, two Navajo scouts, and a volunteer guide named John R. Foster moved quickly out of Bayard, crossing the Mimbres River and marching north into the mountains. The entire country to the Gila River was on fire, and this command had difficulty getting through the burning forest to establish a camp. Soon, however, Foster struck a two-day-old trail of about twenty Indians, convinced it was the trail of the Indians they had been sent to intercept. As the soldiers neared, the Indians began deliberately to set the underbrush and the forest afire to cover their trail.

At last this expedition came upon the Indians, who were busily engaged building breastworks on a rocky peak near the Continental Divide. It was indeed Victorio and his band. Victorio signaled that he wanted to talk and suggested Beyer come to his camp unarmed. Wary, Beyer agreed to meet Victorio halfway, an offer that Victorio rejected, expressing considerable anger at Beyer's reluctance. He informed Beyer that he and his people were poor, that they did not want to fight the soldiers, that they simply wanted to be left alone.

While Victorio raved, both sides prepared for a fight. Beyer sent Sgt. Delaware Penn and a few men of Company I forward and to the right in order to flank the Indians. When Beyer gave the order to advance, the troopers and the Indians fired many rounds of ammunition at each other, during which exchange Penn and his men were able to get behind the Indians. After about thirty minutes of sharp firing the Indians abandoned their works and camp, retreated down a ridge, and scattered, two of their number seriously, if not mortally, wounded. At the camp, the Indians left much plunder — blankets, skins, hides, baskets, meat, and mescal — which Beyer ordered burned.

In this engagement, Pvt. Frank Dorsey (Company C) was killed, Pvt. George H. Moore (Company C) was seriously wounded, and Pvt. John Scott (Company I) was slightly wounded. Beyer saw that Private Dorsey was buried near where he fell, in a well-marked grave. In his report, Beyer indicated the following men displayed gallantry and bravery: Lieutenant Wright, Mr. Foster, Sergeant Penn, Sgt. George Lyman, Sgt. Thomas Boyne, Pvt. Isam Malry, a private named Ridgely, and a Navajo scout named Hostensorze.[5] Later Boyne was awarded a Medal of Honor for bravely rescuing Lieutenant Wright when the lieutenant was surrounded by Indians after his horse was killed.[6]

On June 30, about two weeks after the encounter with Beyer, Victorio voluntarily surrendered at the Mescalero Agency. But as he had done previously, he bolted from the reservation, this time in August. Once again, the Ninth Cavalry sought him. On September 4, 1879, in a lightning-fast surprise attack, Victorio and about sixty warriors swooped down upon the horse herd of Capt. Ambrose E. Hooker's Company E at Camp Ojo Caliente, killing the five black troopers and three civilians guarding the herd and capturing eighteen mules and fifty horses, including Hooker's and three other officers' personal mounts. The dead troopers were Sgt. S. Chapman and four privates, whose names were Graddon, Hoke, Murphy, and Percival.[7] Because the army had been chasing Victorio for a number of years, in view of this brazen and successful raid it resolved that it must give new vigor to subduing the chief. Of this resolve to check Victorio, Gen. John Pope said: "The capture is not very probable, but the killing (cruel as it will be) can, I suppose, be done in time."[8] The Victorio War had begun.

Immediately following Victorio's embarrassing attack at Camp Ojo Caliente, Col. Edward Hatch put all of his regiment's companies into the field, beginning a concerted effort that lasted more than a year to finally subdue the Apache chieftain. Victorio killed nine citizens

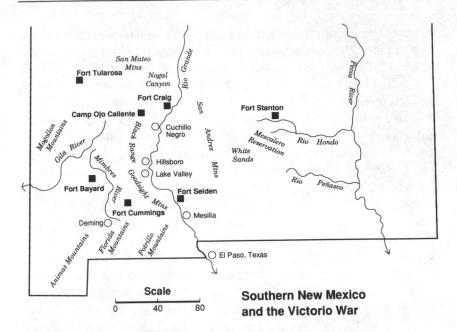

Scale
0   40   80

**Southern New Mexico
and the Victorio War**

during the week after his daring and profitable raid at Ojo Caliente; he, too, appeared to be ready for a showdown.

During late 1879 and 1880 the average number of enlisted men of the Ninth Cavalry in New Mexico was about 550. Occasionally detachments of mounted enlisted men from the Fifteenth Infantry were also used in the fight against Victorio, and often a number of Navajo scouts were in service. Sometimes men of the Sixth Cavalry from Arizona and the Tenth Cavalry of Texas were brought to New Mexico to fight the Apaches, and in addition, in July and August 1880 five companies of the white Thirteenth Infantry were stationed at Fort Wingate to assist the anti-Victorio efforts. The total number of pursuers was over one thousand. Victorio's band of warriors, by contrast, numbered from twenty to one hundred.[9]

On September 16, 1879, scouts from a column led by Lt. Col. N.A.M. Dudley consisting of Lt. Byron Dawson's Company B and Captain Hooker's Company E found Victorio's trail. Two days later this column caught up with Victorio in the canyons at the head of Las Animas Creek, where a battle occurred between the strongly entrenched Apache band and the troopers who found themselves at a disadvantage and under withering fire. Fortunately for Dudley's men, Captain Beyer and Lieutenant Hugo and Companies C and G were not far away and, hearing gunshots, they rushed to the scene.

Despite superior numbers, the four companies were unable to overpower the Apaches before darkness, which compelled Dudley to order a withdrawal. At the end of the day, Dudley counted five dead troopers, three dead Indian scouts, and thirty-two fallen horses.[10] Lt. Matthias W. Day and Sgt. John Denny of the Ninth Cavalry received Medals of Honor for their heroism during the Battle of Las Animas, Denny being cited for most conspicuous gallantry when, in the face of heavy Indian fire, he rescued a wounded private named Freeland.[11]

The direct but unsuccessful encounter with Victorio at Las Animas Creek was a portent of months of frustration for the army. On September 28 Victorio's band of fifty to seventy warriors, most mounted on stolen cavalry horses, attacked Sgt. Henry Robinson and four privates of Company E as they escorted mail through a canyon about two miles from Ojo Caliente. A brisk engagement ensued. In a four-mule escort wagon, the mail party rapidly retreated and narrowly escaped capture, their escape ensured by the arrival of Company E's Sgt. James Williams and a small hunting party.[12]

On the next day, Morrow, now in command of all military operations in southern New Mexico, and detachments from Companies B, C, and G and a group of Apache scouts — who had been searching for Victorio for eleven days — caught up with the Indian leader near Cuchillo Negro Creek. The two groups fought from mid-afternoon until ten o'clock in the evening, when each side rested both men and firearms. Morrow had lost no men, but he had killed three Indians and captured fifteen horses (saddled and packed) and some assorted stock.

Early the next morning while the troopers were eating breakfast, an Apache Indian shot and killed an army sentinel. The general fighting resumed, and the black troopers, with the help of some white soldiers from the Sixth Cavalry, finally drove the Indians away in a two-hour running fight. The soldiers finally abandoned the chase when they had to return to Cuchillo Negro Creek for water for their animals. Morrow lost two soldiers and a number of horses, killed three of the enemy, and believed that he had wounded a number of Indians, including Victorio's son, Washington.

Two days later Morrow again was in pursuit of Victorio when, near sundown, his scouts found the chief encamped about four miles away. In the moonlight after midnight Morrow moved his men closer in order to attack at sunup, later observing: "Our scouts on the west side advanced with cat like stealth and were shortly in the presence of the [Indians'] works." But when he ordered the attack, he found that "the slippery enemy had again eluded us." Morrow volunteered that if Victorio had held his position, nothing but artillery could have dislodged him, except at a fearful sacrifice of life. He speculated further that Victorio would certainly have killed half of the military command before it could have taken his position.

On October 4 Morrow marched to Camp Ojo Caliente and then asked Fort Bayard to send replacements to relieve his tired and dismounted soldiers. He soon marched out of Ojo Caliente and shortly thereafter was joined by Capt. George A. Purington and Company H, Captain Beyer with a detachment of Company C, a detachment of Company A, Sixth Cavalry, and twenty-five San Carlos Indian scouts, a total of 113 men. Three weeks of tough pursuit followed, including marches through drenching rain and over rough terrain. Morrow, in fact, had to order some of the enlisted men and Indian scouts back to Bayard to replace their worn-out horses. Even so, he lost five horses and one mule. At one point Morrow led his command into Fort Cummings, where he acquired more rations, reshod his horses, cut out unserviceable mounts, and rested pack mules. Able to carry only fifteen days' rations, he established a supply camp at McEvert's Ranch.

But mainly, Morrow kept after the Indians. On one occasion he caught up with them and had no trouble dislodging them from their camp, but they retreated to a high place on a mountain, and Morrow and his men had difficulty pursuing them because they found they had to concentrate on climbing rather than fighting. But they continued, and a moonlit battle occurred. Rolling rocks down upon the soldiers, the Indians were able to stop the advance.

After this encounter was over, Morrow's horses were in such need of water that he was tempted to take his command back to Bayard on foot. The men, too, were suffering. Morrow marched them twelve miles to a river, arriving at 5 A.M. He wrote: "I unsaddled and put the Command into Camp, where in a few minutes all but the guard were asleep, completely worn out."

By this time Morrow's command had been reduced to eighty-one enlisted men and eighteen Indian scouts, his stock had broken down, and he had ammunition for no more than three hours of fighting. Although he had not captured or killed Victorio, he said he had accomplished his objective: to punish Victorio severely and to drive him from the country that he declared he would never leave. With that, on November 2 Morrow led his worn-out and battle-weary column into Fort Bayard. Morrow praised his officers and men who "all behaved gallantly through the entire campaign," singling out five of the black soldiers: Sgts. Thomas Fredericks (Company H) and David Badie (Company B), Cpl. Charles Parker (Company G), and Pvts. Isaac Holbrook (Company H) and William Jones (Company I).[13]

After Victorio and Morrow parted, the Apache chief went into the Candelaria Mountains in northern Mexico. His departure, however, did not tempt the army to become complacent. Throughout November several detachments of black cavalrymen out of Bayard did picket duty at ranches such as McEvert's, Mason's, and Knight's. The army's caution proved well founded: when Victorio's men killed some Mexican citizens, the Mexican government ordered soldiers into the field to dispose of him, and Victorio again moved north of the border.[14]

When Victorio made a raid in New Mexico in January 1880, Hatch once again ordered the Ninth Cavalry into the field to fight him. From early January through August the regiment's companies in the territory were almost constantly searching for the elusive Apache chieftain. Under the leadership of Morrow, in January and February one or more of these companies was involved in a half-dozen engagements or near engagements as Morrow and Victorio fought and fenced with each other. Near the Rio Puerco, two cavalrymen were slain.[15]

Hoping to catch and defeat Victorio in a pincers movement, Hatch organized his men in late February into three battalions under Morrow, Hooker, and Capt. Henry Carroll, all experienced commanders. Morrow took charge of Companies H, L, and M of the Ninth Cavalry (seventy-five men), a detachment of the Fifteenth Infantry, and some San Carlos Indian scouts. Later he was joined by reinforcements from Arizona: eighty-five troopers of the Sixth Cavalry and about forty Indian scouts. Hooker had detachments from Ninth Cavalry Companies E, I, and K, as well as some Navajo scouts and twenty men of the Fifteenth Infantry.

Carroll had about one hundred men from Ninth Cavalry Companies A, D, F, and G. While Carroll was to cover the northeast and east side of the San Andres Mountains, Hooker was to scout the west side and try to assure that Victorio, once flushed out, did not cross the Rio Grande to the safety of the Black Range. Hatch and Morrow were to move into the mountains and force Victorio into what they hoped would be a climactic battle.[16]

Hatch's ambitious plan failed. In April, Carroll's men were in the San Andres Mountains searching for both Victorio and good water, the latter sometimes as important a goal as the former. After having drunk gypsum-laden water and becoming quite ill, Carroll's men finally arrived at a spring in Hembrillo Canyon, only to discover that Victorio's band was already there. In an all-night conflict on April 8 the Apaches and Carroll's sick troops fought, the latter rescued only after a detachment of Morrow's men arrived, driving the Indians from the water hole. Carroll and several of his men were wounded, two mortally. As Victorio's band dispersed, some of its members, including the chief himself, went east toward the Mescalero Reservation, while the others went west to the more familiar area beyond the Rio Grande.

After this near disaster, Hatch took command of Morrow's and Carroll's forces, resolving to deal with that portion of the Indian band remaining east of the Rio Grande. With a force of four hundred cavalrymen, sixty infantrymen, and seventy-five Navajo scouts, Hatch moved toward the Mescalero Reservation to disarm and dismount not only the remnant of Victorio's band, but also hostile Mescalero Indians.[17]

In the meantime, following orders from Gen. E.O.C. Ord, Col. Benjamin Grierson and a force composed of Tenth cavalrymen and Twenty-fifth infantrymen had set out from Texas for the Mescalero Reservation. As Grierson moved north, his forces skirmished with resisting Indians. On April 16 the commands of Hatch and Grierson fought a group of nearly three hundred Indians, capturing about 250 of them.[18]

Still Victorio remained active. In late April 1880 he moved into the Mogollon Mountains, and throughout May he killed whoever came across his path: ranchers, sheepherders, cattle drivers, and miners. In response, Morrow moved from the Mescalero Reservation to the Ojo Caliente Reservation to search for him, and Hatch, now also in charge

Victorio. (Photo #19705, Courtesy Arizona Historical Society, Tucson.)

of Hooker's battalion, personally pursued the renegade chief and his band into Arizona and back into New Mexico.[19]

In May Sgt. George Jordan and a detachment of twenty-five men of Company K stationed at the Barlow and Sanderson stage station learned that Victorio was in the vicinity of then-abandoned Fort Tularosa, about fifty miles northwest of Camp Ojo Caliente, probably attacking a small settlement there. Jordan and his detachment rode through the night to reach Tularosa, where they set about building a stockade. After Jordan had moved the frightened civilians into the stockade, Victorio and his band advanced, but Jordan's men withstood two separate attacks. In the face of withering fire and the considerable courage of the black soldiers, Victorio abandoned the Fort Tularosa region to Jordan and moved south toward Mexico.[20]

Shortly after the Jordan-Victorio engagement, Hatch took up the chase. While Hatch and his men paused at Camp Ojo Caliente, Morrow's command joined them there. Supplies were low, and the two groups were weary, both men and mounts badly run down. While these groups briefly rested, Capt. Henry K. Parker and his large detachment of Indian scouts continued to trail Victorio. On May 23 Parker located the chief's camp in the Black Range near the head of the Palomas River. The following daybreak, Parker attacked, capturing seventy-four head of cattle and killing about thirty men, women, and children, and perhaps wounding Victorio himself. But he was unable to overwhelm the Indians, and, running out of ammunition and water, he had to withdraw.[21]

Upon receiving word of Parker's encounter with Victorio, Hatch sent Morrow into the field after the chief. Morrow caught up with Victorio's rear guard, killing three warriors and wounding others, but the main body of Victorio's band reached the Mexican border, again safe from the Ninth Cavalry. On June 5 Morrow and four troopers found a smaller body of Indians in Cooke's Canyon, not far from Fort Cummings. Apparently the group was making its way to Mexico. Morrow and his men wounded three Indians and killed ten of them, one of the fatalities being Victorio's son. Whatever consolation his death may have been to the U.S. Army, though, most of Victorio's followers made it safely across the border, and the army remained frustrated in its attempt to conquer them and their leader.[22]

In late July Victorio reentered the United States, crossing into the area of Texas under the military responsibility of Colonel Grierson and the Tenth Cavalry. For the first two weeks in August, Grierson and his troopers prevented Victorio from using watering holes and mountain passes and continually hounded the chief and his supply lines and camps. Under these circumstances Victorio returned to Mexico.

On this and earlier occasions, crossing the international border had assured Victorio sanctuary, because U.S. troops legally could not pursue the Indians beyond the line. For several years the American and Mexican governments had negotiated over the lack of a united campaign to annihilate Victorio.[23] When Colonel Hatch misinterpreted a diplomatic communique written by the Mexican war minister to mean that American soldiers could search for Victorio on Mexican soil, Gen. John Pope ordered Col. George P. Buell and men of the Fifteenth Infantry to move from New Mexico into Mexico, and he directed Col. Eugene Carr to move south of the border from Arizona. These American troopers did not capture or kill Victorio, but their presence helped a Mexican force corner the heretofore elusive chief. On October 15, 1880, these Mexican soldiers found and attacked Victorio's band in the Tres Castillos Mountains, killing Victorio.[24] Although Mexican soldiers had ended Victorio's life, the soldiers of the Ninth Cavalry in New Mexico and the Tenth Cavalry in Texas had set the stage and played an important role in Victorio's demise.[25]

Not surprisingly, American citizens in New Mexico were relieved when they heard of Victorio's death. As the editor of one newspaper wrote: "The news was received in Silver City with a great rejoicing, the people feeling a great relief had come to them. . . . As Victorio is killed, his band nearly destroyed, we can only look to the future and feel comparatively safe." But the editor cautioned: "The Indian warfare as far as Victorio's band is concerned is ended, but we must not forget one principle in evolution, the survival of the fittest, the few that are left will be more treacherous, more ugly than ever before known."[26]

The editor was a perceptive prophet: the death of the chief did not completely halt Indian resistance in New Mexico. Some of Victorio's followers, or those who agreed with his actions, had remained in the territory, requiring the army's attention. With word of Victorio's death being slow to reach all commanders and soldiers in the territory, some of them continued to search for the Apache leader for months after his demise.

In September, attempting to capture some army mules, a force of twenty-five or thirty Indians, on foot but well armed, attacked a detachment of Company G, Ninth Cavalry, in Agua Chiquita Canyon. Sgt. James Robinson and ten privates charged the Indians under heavy

fire, driving them away, but all the mules they were protecting were
wounded, three of them later dying. More importantly, the Indians
killed two privates. Company G's lieutenant praised Robinson for his
gallant conduct, although the officer reported that all the men behaved
remarkably well.

Especial credit was due Pvt. Alonzo Drake, "who carried the
dispatch [about the encounter] on a wounded mule, bare back and
alone, leaving Agua Chiquita at 7 o'clock P.M. and arriving here [South
Fork] at 4 P.M. the following evening, a distance of over 70 miles, the
Indians at the time supposed to be in the mountains and all around
him." Making Drake's journey even more difficult was an Anglo named
Martin who lived near the Peñasco River and who refused to lend
Drake a saddle for the mule.[27] Whether the color of Drake's skin made
Martin uncooperative or whether he would have treated a white soldier
the same way under such circumstances is uncertain. But because the
soldiers were there primarily to protect people like him, it is likely
Martin normally would have been more cooperative. The open and
latent racism of the late nineteenth century had curious ways of
expressing itself.

For several weeks following Victorio's death but unaware of that
event, Lieutenant Colonel Dudley, commanding officer at Fort Cummings, directed a great deal of attention to Victorio or his bands,[28]
sending scouting parties to patrol between Fort Cummings and the
Florida, Potrillo, and Goodsight mountains. White commissioned officers were in charge of most of these parties, but black noncommissioned officers led some of them. Sgt. Thomas Bills, for example,
headed a detachment of enlisted men stationed at Mason's Ranch in
southern New Mexico. When Lt. Stephen R. Stafford and a small
contingent of Fifteenth infantrymen passed by the ranch on patrol,
Stafford ordered Bills and his men to return to Fort Cummings. Not
sure he should follow the order, Bills wrote to Dudley: "I shil remain
here For further orders from The General as I have no way to fetch my
rations. Say I will remain here Tell I hare from The Genaral."[29]

In November, after Mexican herders reported seeing Victorio near
Palomas, Dudley dispatched Lt. Charles W. Taylor, Company F, ten
Indian scouts, three packers, one guide, and one courier as a precaution,
even though he gave no credence to the reports. Dudley was guarding
the Southern Pacific Railroad line from the Potrillo Mountains to

Shakespeare.[30] After two days of searching, Taylor reported seeing no Indians, convinced that the supposed sighting of Indians was "the idle talk of a lying Mexican sheep herder."[31]

When unknown persons stole the stage stock at Mason's Ranch near Shakespeare, Dudley dispatched two separate groups of soldiers under Lts. Millard F. Goodwin and Thomas C. Davenport to look for the animals. A Private Parker of Company H had a hand severely frostbitten while on one of these scouts. Dudley recommended that all citizens be vigilant in watching stock because of starving tramps in the area. He stated that railroad contractors had furnished transportation to these tramps but that the construction engineers were not ready for their labor and therefore the men were destitute. He pointed out that these hungry men, rather than the Indians, could have done much of the stealing.[32] Lieutenant Davenport reported that the country around the Florida Mountains was covered with miners and with railroad camps related to the construction of the Southern Pacific Railroad from Cummings to the Floridas. He reasoned that because of this large population, Indians would avoid that land.[33]

Dudley never failed to respond to a report or rumor. When he heard that Indians who had defeated the Mexicans in a fight just across the border were headed to New Mexico, he sent a cavalry company to protect the Southern Pacific Railroad graders who were working near where the Indians would likely cross the border,[34] despite a lack of evidence for the advance.

When Dudley heard that Indians had corralled some sheepherders at Cuchillo Negro, he sent a force under Lt. Ballard S. Humphrey composed of Company C, reinforced to a total of forty men from Company H, and fifteen scouts.[35] Humphrey and his command arrived at Hillsboro at daylight on November 22, but they found no Indians. In fact, Humphrey learned nothing that would warrant any suspicion that hostile Indians were, or had been, there recently. Humphrey concluded that Hispanic sheepherders had seen a few miners and had reported they were Indians. This conclusion agreed with Dudley's original assessment: "I do not give the slightest evidence to the rumor that Indians are in the vicinity of Cuchillo Negro. Me and my colored troops and Indian scouts have scouted that region from Knight's Ranch to Mason's Ranch and we have not seen any Indians in that vicinity."[36]

When construction crews for the Atchison, Topeka and Santa Fe and the Southern Pacific railroads met at a common junction in the vicinity of Fort Cummings in November 1880, Dudley sent one non-commissioned officer and nine privates of Company K, Ninth Cavalry, to a camp occupied by the railroad graders to protect them against Indians and other stock thieves. The detachment took one hundred rounds of ammunition per man, three A-tents, rations for two weeks, and two barrels for holding drinking water.[37] Grain forage for the ten horses was transported by a six-mule team and wagon. Soon Lt. Frank B. Taylor and his entire company joined in protecting railroad contractors and their stock not only against Indians but also against gangs of white horse thieves and outlaws. Taylor kept patrols out at night along the line of the railroad because that region was infested with these undesirables.[38] The black soldiers in southwestern New Mexico performed similar duty when they protected miners at Silver Camp west of McEvert's Ranch, and when they watched over telegraph construction workers, including those who strung telegraph lines between Mesilla, New Mexico, and El Paso, Texas.[39]

The exact moment when Dudley and other New Mexico field commanders learned of the death of Victorio is uncertain. But whether Victorio was still in the field was relatively unimportant, for the task of Dudley and the other military leaders was to continue to search for and subdue all hostile Indians. They did not waver from that commitment. For those who believed the Indian menace had ended, January 1881 was a stark reminder that it had not.

On January 14, 1881, a band of thirty-five to fifty mounted Indians, probably from Mexico, attacked and killed two Hispanos and an Anglo named Omery Jackson as they were traveling in a wagon loaded with fish about twelve miles east of Fort Cummings at the foot of the Goodsight Mountains. The Indians burned the bodies and disfigured the heads of the men.[40] At sundown two hours later near the same place, the same band attacked a mail stagecoach, killing two mules in harness, the stage driver named James Sweeney, and a passenger named Thomas White, the only people on the stage. The Indians cut open mail bags, scattering the contents over an acre, and stole or destroyed nearly all the express matter, including musical instruments of the Twelfth Infantry band. Only a keg of butter remained. The Indians captured a total of four mules in the two attacks. These massacres were discovered by the driver of a second mail stage, who reported them to Lieutenant Colonel Dudley at Cummings.[41]

Dudley took two companies of cavalry to the scene of the events. When he discovered that the Indians had fled in the direction of Macho or McEvert's Ranch, immediately he dispatched Lieutenants Humphrey and Charles W. Taylor and Companies C and F with ten pack mules to search for them.[42] They began their scout at 3 A.M., even though a hazy sky obscured the moon. A week later Dudley arranged to have 2,500 rations available for Humphrey at Hillsboro, as both the colonel and the lieutenant were intent on punishing the Indians for these massacres.[43] These attacks so offended Dudley that he asked that the troopers and all transportation at Fort Bayard be placed under his command so that he could run down these "hell hounds." He suggested that the Ninth Cavalry company at Colorado, New Mexico, be sent to support Humphrey's command.[44]

Ordered to follow the Indian trail to its end, Humphrey and Taylor were diligent in their pursuit. From January 14 to 30 they were in the Floridas as well as near Hillsboro. When these two companies and another returned to Cummings, they reported leaving the Indian trail as it headed toward the Black Range. Companies C and F went out again to see if the trail went as they presumed, but heavy snow in the mountains made their task especially difficult, their trail leading over precipitous and mountainous country. Both men and horses suffered from cold and exposure, being three days and nights in the snow. Two horses suffering from exhaustion were abandoned.[45]

During the same week, just east of the San Mateo Mountains, Indians attacked Madison Ingorman and six other privates of Company D while they were escorting wagon trains from Fort Craig to Camp Ojo Caliente. They severely wounded Pvt. William Jones, who died the next day in the camp hospital. Even as they were being chased, the Indians continued to depredate, stealing two horses near Hillsboro and a buckboard near Cuchillo Negro.[46]

In late January 1881, Indians with sixteen animals jumped Ninth Cavalry Lt. John F. McBlain and an ambulance driver, a trooper named Armstead, burning a spring wagon, killing a mule and wounding another, and driving two mules away. McBlain and his driver were fortunate to reach Mason's Ranch unharmed. Then six Indians attacked a stage near Santa Barbara, although they killed no one. Their raid was unsuccessful because two soldiers of the Ninth Cavalry were riding the stage as guards.[47]

The massacres, the conflicts, and the sightings did not instill a sense of peace in the minds of the citizens in southwestern New Mexico. Rather, the whole section was alarmed. When several railroad workers indicated that they might leave the area because of the Indian danger, Dudley requested that an infantry company be distributed for a few days along the railroad between the Goodsight Mountains and a proposed railroad junction. He assumed authority to lend captured Indian guns to railroad contractors to defend the grading camps, taking such action to build confidence and to prevent a human stampede out of the region. He established a station of twelve mounted men at Macho with instructions to patrol twelve miles east and southwest on the railroad on a daily basis. Finally, he suggested that the stage running from Fort Cummings to Mesilla be removed, doing away with the necessity of stationing Company M at Mason's Ranch.[48] When on January 23 Companies C, D, E, F, and M reached Camp Ojo Caliente to rest from one of the busiest weeks in their existence, Dudley suggested that Companies E and M and some of Lt. James A. Maney's Indian scouts be placed under his command, because he was "ready to take the field and do all I can to capture these devils."[49]

All of these efforts did not halt Indian activities, however. In early February, Sgt. Stewart Albert and a detachment of Company D made a scout on which they saw no Indians, but they did see evidence of another massacre about forty-five miles from Fort Craig, where they found a burned wagon, a dead horse, burned articles (including pieces of women's clothing), and a bloody gray hat with a bullet hole near the crown. The sergeant reported: "A suspicious looking Mexican was picking through the debris but I cannot state who he is." He reasoned that the massacred family came from Monica in the San Mateo Mountains, because recent white inhabitants of that place apparently had left in a great hurry. There he saw many signs of both mounted and dismounted Indians. While in camp, during the night, this detachment heard several Indians yell not more than four hundred yards away, but a group that went out into the night found nothing. On the next morning they saw signs of Indian ponies near their encampment. When this group's mule forage ran out, it returned to Camp Ojo Caliente to await orders.[50]

In February Lieutenant Maney and his Indian scouts and a detachment of Company K under Lt. Charles Parker struck the trail of retreating Indians about twelve miles south of Deming and followed this trail into Mexico about 150 miles. When Maney's scouts discovered the teepees of the enemy in some small mountains southwest of the Candelaria Mountains, the lieutenant planned an attack, but he was foiled when the Indians' scouts alerted their leaders to the presence of the American troopers. The Indian party — consisting of twenty men, three women, and one child — escaped, but they left their camp equipage, including blankets and thirty-three animals, all of which Maney acquired. Maney followed the retreating Indians for thirty miles, but, finding it impossible to overtake them, he returned to New Mexico, some of his men sick from drinking alkali water. While he was not succcessful, Maney received the praise of Colonel Dudley: "Lt Maney is entitled to great credit for the indomitable perserverances and energy he exhibited in continuing the pursuit of this band across the most barren plains of northern old Mexico."[51]

From January through May 1881, Indian raids had frustrated the leaders and men of the Ninth Cavalry, and their responses to them had been largely unfruitful. But worse was yet to come. One of Victorio's followers named Nana (pronounced Nan-ey) continued the resistance of his fallen leader. Even though Nana was more than seventy years old, partially crippled, and almost blind, he was an able and bitter foe of the U.S. Army. After gathering men, arms, and ammunition, in July he and fifteen warriors, some of whom had survived the deadly October 1880 battle in the Tres Castillos, rode north out of Mexico to cause the kinds of problems Victorio earlier had created.[52]

In July he and his band, enlarged by twenty-five Mescalero warriors, attacked the supply train of Company L, which was stationed in Texas and which was scouting the New Mexico–Texas border area. The supply wagons were loaded with provisions from Fort Stanton when they were attacked near the entrance to Alamo Canyon. The Indians instantly killed two pack animals, which two black troopers were riding, and the troopers used the bodies of the dead animals as shields behind which they fired at the Indians. After wounding one black soldier and capturing three mules, Nana and his warriors fled.

"A Study of Action." (Courtesy Frederic Remington Art Museum, Ogdensburg, New York.)

This ambush stimulated Lt. John F. Guilfoyle, twenty troopers of
Company L, and some Apache Indian scouts to pursue Nana's band
through Dog Canyon and along the edge of the White Sands, a
forty-mile chase across the blistering desert. When the Indians paused
in the San Andres Mountains, Guilfoyle's men caught up with them,

forcing them to abandon two horses and twelve mules and to continue their flight. Guilfoyle reportedly killed or wounded two of the Indians.[53]

Leaving the San Andres with Guilfoyle in pursuit, Nana moved westward across the Rio Grande, killing three civilians before turning north toward the San Mateos. Guilfoyle continued his relentless pursuit, but the desperate condition of his men and animals (men without boots and animals without shoes) compelled him temporarily to give up the chase while he stopped at Fort Craig for rest and supplies. In three raids in three days, Nana killed ten citizens and burned one ranch, while Guilfoyle rested only eight miles from the site of some of the killings.[54]

After his brief rest, on August 3 Guilfoyle again engaged Nana's band, this time at Monica Springs. He captured eleven of the Indians' horses and probably wounded two Indians before Nana and his braves disappeared again. After this brief encounter, Guilfoyle's column gradually fell behind in its pursuit of the Indians, even though the old chief left an obvious path of death and destruction wherever he went.[55]

Working out of Fort Bayard, in August a detachment of fourteen privates of Company B, led by Sgt. David Badie, and some Indian scouts fought a detachment of Indians in Nogal Canyon east of the San Mateos. Three days later the remainder of Company B, under the direction of Lt. George W. Smith, engaged another band of Indians in Gabaldon Canyon. Saddler Thomas Golding and Pvts. James Brown and Monroe Overstreet were killed and William A. Hollins was badly wounded in this engagement.[56]

On August 12, 1881, under the leadership of Lt. Charles Parker, a detachment of nineteen men of Company K engaged Nana's band at Carrizo Canyon, about twenty-five miles west of Sabinal. Even though they were outnumbered more than two to one, Parker and his men fought the Indians for an hour and a half before Nana and his band fled. This engagement resulted in the loss of two men, farrier Guy Temple and Pvt. Charles Perry, and nine horses; three other troopers were wounded and one was captured. Parker claimed one Indian killed and three wounded. For extraordinary courage in action during this engagement, Sgt. Thomas Shaw was given a Medal of Honor. Sgt. George Jordan also received the coveted award for his bravery in action at Carrizo Canyon and for his fearlessness at Tularosa a year and a half earlier.[57]

On August 16 an overwrought Hispanic rancher informed Lt. Gustavus Valois and Company I, who were camped in Cañada Alamosa, that Nana had attacked and killed his family. Valois sent Lt. George R. Burnett and a detachment of fifteen enlisted men to the ranch, where they found the mutilated bodies of the rancher's wife and three children. Burnett was able to follow the Indians' trail rather easily, and he overtook the Indians, encumbered by stolen stock and other plunder, in the foothills of the Cuchillo Negro Mountains, where they had taken strong positions among the rocks. When Burnett had difficulty dislodging them, trumpeter John Rogers volunteered to carry a message to Valois, whom Burnett knew was in the vicinity. Even though Indian guns wounded Rogers's horse, the trooper was able to obtain assistance. Valois and the remainder of the company reinforced Burnett, but even the united command was unable to defeat the Indians. When four enlisted men were cut off from the others, Burnett and two volunteers, Sgt. Moses Williams and Pvt. Augustus Walley, rescued them, even though the Indians fired many rounds at them. When nightfall came, Nana and his men escaped to the hills. For their courage during the successful rescue, Burnett, Williams, and Walley were awarded Medals of Honor.[58]

As Nana moved southward, Capt. Michael Cooney and Company A and Valois and Company I followed. In an attempt to prevent Nana from escaping to Mexico, Hatch ordered Lieutenant Smith and a detachment of forty-six men from Companies B and H to march from Cummings to intercept him. Despite his orders, Smith took only twenty men on this scout, although twenty cowboys led by rancher George Daly joined him on the Goodwin Trail somewhere between Lake Valley and Georgetown. As the trail led into Gavilan Canyon near the Mimbres River, Smith slowed down, fearing an ambush. When the inexperienced cowboys rushed into the canyon, however, Smith followed to protect them. Shortly after that, as the lieutenant had feared, the Indians ambushed the group, quickly killing Smith and Daly and injuring some of the cowboys. The remaining cowboys fled, leaving the handful of remaining soldiers to carry on the battle by themselves.

Sgt. Brent Woods of Company B took command and fought the Indians to a standstill until Sergeant Anderson and a detachment of Company H arrived. The combined command forced the Apaches to run, and Anderson pursued them, "carrying his dead and wounded with him." Besides Smith and Daly, two soldiers and one civilian were killed, and eight men were wounded, one of whom later died. Capt. Byron Dawson was dispatched to direct Smith's officially leaderless column, although Woods, who received a Medal of Honor for his actions, and Anderson had obviously provided the necessary leadership in the emergency.[59] A few years later, Lieutenant Smith's widow praised her husband's black troopers, writing that "a braver set of men never lived."[60]

Nana and most of his band went into the Sierra Madres in Mexico, although some members of the group stayed in the vicinity of the recent fight. In October Capt. Henry Carroll, Lt. Charles Parker, and Companies F and K found the trail of the remaining Indians on the eastern slopes of the Dragoon Mountains, where a fifteen-mile running fight ensued before the Indians dispersed and dashed to the Mexican border. Three enlisted men and a horse were wounded in this battle.[61] By this time five more companies of the Thirteenth Infantry had arrived at Forts Cummings, Selden, and Stanton to support the cavalry in the field.[62]

To combat Nana's band, Colonel Hatch had assumed personal command of his forces and had placed every available fighting man in the field. For more than six weeks nearly twelve hundred enlisted men and their officers (eight companies of black cavalry, eight companies of white infantry, and two companies of Navajo scouts) had spent almost all of their time attempting to defeat Nana.[63] Although Ninth cavalrymen never won a decisive battle against Nana and his warriors, they had gradually pushed these hostile bands farther south until they fled into permanent hiding in the mountains of Mexico.

With Nana in Mexico, the army had many fewer problems with Indians in New Mexico Territory, and the need for soldiers in the territory decreased. During the last two months of 1881 all black troopers in New Mexico were relocated, most of them transferred to posts in Kansas. When regimental headquarters were transferred from Santa Fe to Fort Riley, Kansas, the Ninth Cavalry Regiment left New Mexico Territory for a well-deserved rest.[64]

If the reaction of a Las Cruces newspaper editor represented the attitude of the general population, the people of New Mexico were sorry to see the soldiers go. Shortly after the black troopers left Fort Selden, four white replacements got drunk and created disturbances in

Las Cruces, causing the editor to write that "this part of the country has lost rather than gained by the change of troops." He concluded: "The negro troops . . . were vastly more respectable and in every way a credit [compared] to the fellows who disgraced their uniform here last Thursday."[65]

Because of feats of heroism during the Indian Wars of the late nineteenth century, eighteen black enlisted men, eleven of whom were members of the Ninth Cavalry, received Congressional Medals of Honor. Eight of these men performed their deeds of valor in New Mexico,[66] where, along with others who pursued Victorio and Nana, they experienced some of the most grueling ordeals in the history of the Indian Wars. In the face of great dangers, they fought — and died — to make New Mexico and the West safer for civilians of all races.

VI. Cavalry Garrison Life, 1875–1881

When most Americans think of soldiers on the western frontier in the last quarter of the nineteenth century, they usually visualize the cavalry either mounting long scouts to search for Indians, or battling these hostile Indians, or providing general defense measures against Indian depredations. Hollywood movies and a heavy dose of television programming have indelibly printed such images upon the American mind. To be sure, the army's cavalrymen did engage in these and related activities — and the enlisted men of the Ninth Cavalry Regiment were no exception — but as busy as the men of the Ninth were chasing and fighting Indians, there was another side to their army experience: the soldiers' less than glamous garrison life. Although collectively the cavalrymen rode thousands of miles and spent countless hours chasing Indians, camp life occupied most of their time.

When the men of the Ninth Cavalry arrived in New Mexico between December 1875 and October 1876, each of the posts to which they were assigned had a number of assorted buildings normally associated with a frontier post. This was true not only for the forts established before or during the Civil War but also for Forts Bayard and Selden, founded immediately upon the end of that conflict. Inevitably some older buildings were in perpetual need of repair, and occasionally a commander erected a new building to serve a special need. Although some of this renovation and new construction was contracted to civilians, soldiers often did a share of the work. For example, in late 1876 black troopers at Fort Stanton helped erect new quarters for the post's laundresses, and about six months later they hauled the material necessary for the erection of a new hospital.[1]

While some of these soldiers were constructing new buildings or renovating old ones, others spent time fighting fires to save existing buildings or other wooden structures. At 2 A.M. on February 13, 1876, a fire broke out in Fort Union's lumber-planing mill, located at the post depot. The fire destroyed not only the mill but also the machine shop and engine house adjoining it, as well as about thirty thousand feet of lumber. Fortunately the soldiers were able to save the nearby coal sheds and their contents and most of the finished lumber stored in the yard. Fort Union's quartermaster assumed the fire was the work of an incendiary because there had been no previous fires in the mill, and he requested an investigation, hoping to assign responsibility for the loss of public property.[2] If, however, the fire was the result of arson, that fact was never established.

When a fire occurred in the officers' quarters at Fort Wingate on December 15, 1876, enlisted men of the Ninth Cavalry and the Fifteenth Infantry scurried to extinguish it. As with all the fires, extremely dry wood and lack of adequate firefighting equipment caused a serious conflagration, which the enlisted men — both black and white — fought with little regard for their clothing and not much more for their lives. These black enlisted men whose apparel had burned were two corporals and four privates, namely John Rogers, Richard Thompson, William M. Coleman, Stephen Flake, Seth Jones, and Marshall Phillips. They lost items such as boots, trousers, blouses, and forage capes. Not all the items were lost to the fire, however. For example, when Rogers and Flake removed their boots before climbing on the roof to fight the fire, someone stole the footgear. Rogers especially felt the loss because his was a good pair of brass-screwed boots. The blouse that Phillips had hung on a fence before he began fighting the fire was stolen, too.[3]

On April 16, 1878, a fire at Fort Stanton destroyed a shed, stables, and part of the quartermaster corral, where one government horse was so badly burned that it had to be killed. The men of Company F, Ninth Cavalry, helped rebuild the burned structures, but exactly one month later fire destroyed the new corral. Capt. Henry Carroll was injured during this second fire. The men of Company F helped fight both of these blazes.[4]

Although Camp Ojo Caliente was never elevated to the status of a fort, it was a relatively permanent camp, located near the traditional home of the Warm Springs Apaches and used as a base in the army's efforts to compel the members and leaders of that tribe to remain on their designated reservation lands. Ojo Caliente's wooden and adobe structures were as vulnerable to fire as the buildings at the permanent posts. At 10 A.M. on April 22, 1879, a fire broke out in the camp's animal grain room, situated at the southwest corner of the corral. Upon discovering the blaze, a sergeant immediately gave the alarm at the guardhouse, which was connected to the corral. A general fire alarm was sounded, and the men of Company E, who had just arrived for temporary duty from Fort Union, rushed to extinguish the blaze, tearing down part of the roof connecting the grain room to the guardhouse, under the instructions of Lt. Charles W. Merritt. After putting out the fire, the men stayed in the corral until all sparks had been extinguished and the adobes had cooled, at which point Merritt had the troopers saturate the ground around the burned part of the grain room and ordered the sergeant in charge to inspect the whole corral every five minutes.

Needless to say, such care was not adequate, for at 3 P.M. flames appeared in a small haystack situated at the northwest corner of the corral, which was outside the wall of the fort. The enlisted men again rushed to the scene, and according to their lieutenant they did all that men could do under the circumstances to save the corral. From the beginning, they were fighting a losing battle. Merritt reported: "There was a fearful wind blowing from the West, greater than we have had here at any time before," which blew the fire directly into the corral. Because the mangers were full of hay and the roofing and a large portion of the walls of the corral were composed of dry pine poles, the fire was impossible to control. Along with the corral structures and thirty-five tons of hay, much government property was burned or otherwise damaged, including twenty-one currycombs, seven spurs, twenty-four horse brushes, four camp kettles, two shovels, two pickaxes, five water buckets, sixty-four pounds of rope, four sets of horse harnesses, two wagon tongues, and three wagon whips. Merritt talked to everyone who might know anything about the beginning of the fire, but he was unable to ascertain its origin.[5]

Finally, on November 26, 1879, at 8 P.M., a fire was discovered at

"A Trooper and the Wind." (Courtesy Jose Cisneros.)

Fort Wingate in a stable behind the quarters occupied by the families of two officers. The fire alarm was sounded and the men of the garrison rushed to the scene. By almost superhuman efforts, the men kept the fire from spreading, although it destroyed the stable and an adjacent privy. Reporting the fire to his superiors, Capt. Frank T. Bennett wrote: "The wind had been blowing a perfect gale for the previous 24 hours, and fortunately had partially subsided when the sun went down," otherwise the men could not have prevented the officers' quarters and probably the hospital from being destroyed. An ash pile in the rear of one of the officer's quarters probably caused the fire. Bennett wrote: "We have given explicit instructions about fires and hot ashes, but . . . it is impossible for me to see that the instructions are always carried out." The captain, however, praised officers, soldiers, and citizens for containing the fire.[6]

About a year after arriving in New Mexico, Lt. Clarence A. Stedman led a group of ten people, including five privates and one noncommissioned officer of the Ninth Cavalry, over the North Star Road to ascertain what improvements the road needed. The North Star Road extended from Fort Bayard in a northeasterly direction to and through the Mimbres Mountains, a total of at least 126 miles over generally rough terrain that was, in places, more than 9,500 feet high. Beyond the Mimbres Mountains, it joined the old Fort Tularosa and Ojo Caliente roads. After a tough, fifteen-day reconnaissance, Stedman reported that improving the road would require much grading of badly washed-out sections, excavating rocks, leveling steep grades on many hills, and building some bridges. He estimated that this job would cost $25,700 in labor and materials, noting that the cost would be greater if not for the good prime timber along the route that could be used for building materials. He further noted that the costs could be reduced to $19,800 if the road were rerouted in a few places.[7]

Other jobs were rather more humble, if no less important. While at Fort Cummings, Captain Bennett ordered an army surgeon, one noncommissioned officer, and six privates of Company M to visit ranches on the upper Mimbres River to purchase as many potatoes as their two wagons would carry, at a price not to exceed three cents per pound. The captain hoped, in this manner, to acquire twelve thousand pounds of potatoes, a vital commodity. When Capt. Ambrose E. Hooker requisitioned ten thousand pounds of potatoes for his company stationed at Camp Ojo Caliente, he ordered his enlisted men to prepare a cellar to protect them from the frost.

The acquisition of supplies and maintenance of the post often involved a welcome break from the monotony of routine. For example, when Lt. Charles Parker and his Company K were at Sabinal, he was able to procure only 1,480 pounds of corn, and he sent his troopers to forage for feed. At Fort Cummings, Cpl. Forester Surgeon of Company C led a small detachment of fully armed, equipped, and rationed men to accompany the post butcher to get some beef cattle. When a lieutenant and some privates of the Fifteenth Infantry were ordered to drive all the unserviceable mules at Fort Cummings to Fort Craig, a sergeant named Baker and two privates of Company H, Ninth Cavalry, were ordered to accompany them as a guard. After ox trains carried ten coils of military telegraph wire to Fort Bayard, enlisted men of the Ninth Cavalry helped string it.[8]

Near the end of the Ninth Cavalry's stay in New Mexico, a minor brouhaha resulted from the assignment of an unusual task. When Lt. Patrick Cusack led Company G out of Fort Stanton to serve at a temporary field camp at La Luz Canyon, he left Sgt. Bush Johnson and two privates at the post in charge of the company's garden and other property, instructing the men to harvest the vegetables and to make sauerkraut from the cabbages. He requested that the post adjutant relieve Johnson and his helpers of guard duty so they could devote all their time to the garden.[9]

When the post commander ignored the request and ordered the men to serve guard duty on alternate days, they believed they were unable to tend the garden properly. The situation worsened when cattle broke into the garden and destroyed a quantity of vegetables. Johnson wrote to Cusack:

> Sir I have the honor to inform you the reason is because I have bin so Order by the Comdy Officer it is More than I can do to Do Guard Duty & the Other Duty i have to Perform i am not able to Do both Dutys Which I am not able to give the Company Property the Whright attention as it Should have. The reason is because men is very Scarce for Duty at the Presant that is the reason that i have to Do Duty I believe
> Your Obedient Servant Bush Johnson Sergeant Co G 9th Cav.[10]

When Cusack received Johnson's note, he complained to the post commander, who was not sympathetic.[11] The dispute finally had to be settled by the district commander, who ruled that post commanders should relieve men from ordinary post duties in order to carry out the instructions of their company commanders.[12] The post commander accepted the ruling, but he was not happy about it, pointing out that other men had been able to do guard duty as well as assigned chores such as caring for vegetable gardens. Furthermore, he charged that

Johnson and his men had been absent from the post much of the time because of "certain attractions known to exist at a Ranche [*sic*] 4 miles distant." His sarcasm showed when he wrote: "I am unable to say whether these men were making Kraut at this Ranche or not." The "ranch" to which the commander referred was a house of prostitution. He concluded: "Considering myself competent to command a garrison composed of a Band, 7 men in C Co[mpany] for duty, and a few Cavalry[men] left behind to pick vegetables and make Kraut, I did not deem it advisable to consult a Field Office 4 days march from the Post."[13] Even so, Johnson and his men were able to give full attention to their assigned task.

At the small southwestern forts the formalities of the army were not always observed. But some commanders insisted upon enforcing all military regulations, particularly during those times when the pursuit of Indians was nil or limited and the men consequently spent most of their time at the posts. In October 1880, Lt. Col. N.A.M. Dudley ordered the troopers at Fort Cummings to observe the following calls:

Reveille, 1st call	5:50 A.M.
Reveille	6:00
Reveille, Assembly	6:05
Stable Call	immediately thereafter
Breakfast Call	6:30
Fatigue Call	7:00
Sick Call	7:30
Water Call	8:00
Guard Mounting, 1st Call	9:00
Guard Mounting, Assembly	9:10
Drill Call	10:00
Recall from Drill	11:00
Recall from Fatigue	11:00
1st Sergeants Call	11:00
Dinner Call	11:30
Fatigue Call	1:00 P.M.
Drill Call, 1st Call	1:55
Drill Call, Assembly	2:00
Recall from Drill	3:00
Recall from Fatigue	3:15

Water and Stable Calls	3:00
Parade, 1st Call	25 minutes before sunset
Parade Assembly	20 minutes before sunset
Adjutants Call	15 minutes before sunset
Retreat, 1st Call	10 minutes before sunset
Retreat, when there is no parade	sunset
Tattoo, 1st Call	7:45
Tattoo	7:55
Tattoo, Assembly	8:00
Taps	8:15
Sunday morning inspection, 1st Call	9:00 A.M.
Sunday morning inspection, Assembly	9:10

Guard mounting on Sundays, immediately after inspection

Herd to go out immediately after Water Call in the morning and to come in at 1:00 P.M. and then to be taken to water[14]

Special events called for special ceremonies or schedules, as when, in late October 1880, a large party led by President Rutherford B. Hayes traveling by rail and bound for California stopped overnight at Fort Cummings for twelve and one half hours. Unfortunately the ceremony was not as successful as Dudley would have liked, because three men of the Fifteenth Infantry, all members of a singing group, were in the guardhouse, preventing the group from serenading the president and his cohort. Perhaps as a result of Dudley's embarrassment, a few weeks later trumpeter George Washington of Company M, Ninth Cavalry, was borrowed from Fort Bayard and placed in charge of music at Cummings.[15]

A year later, in respect for the memory of President James A. Garfield, who had just died, the commanding officer at Fort Cummings ordered all drills and unnecessary work to be suspended on the day the news of the president's death reached the post. When Garfield was buried a few days later, the commander again suspended all drills and unnecessary fatigue duty at Cummings.[16]

If a regimental band was available, it added a special flavor to both formal ceremonies and informal events. Being in the band had advantages over being a regular cavalryman: an enlisted man who could play a musical instrument enjoyed the diversions afforded by military ceremonies, Fourth of July celebrations, weddings, parties, grand openings, serenades, and political rallies. Some of these events even gave the musician an opportunity to make trips away from the post, providing an escape from some monotonous garrison life.[17]

When two companies of the Ninth Cavalry arrived at Fort Union in early 1876, the regimental band, composed of about twenty musicians, accompanied them. In June the music committee of the city of Santa Fe invited the band to its Fourth of July celebration, announcing that it had appropriated $100 for its services for that occasion. After military leaders expressed no objection to the proposed visit, they ordered the band members to travel as lightly as possible, taking only their instruments, fatigue suits, caps, ornaments, and rations for five days. They left behind extra baggage, weapons, and women (these women were perhaps wives, but more likely laundresses). Traveling in two ten-men wagons, the band was in Santa Fe on temporary duty from June 28 to July 13, after which it returned to Fort Union.[18]

The band impressed the residents of Santa Fe. "Recognizing the humanizing influence of music upon the New Mexican people," twenty-one leading Santa Feans, including the acting governor, postmaster, surveyor general, and U.S. attorney, as well as merchants, bankers, and a druggist, requested Maj. Gen. John Pope, commander of the Department of the Missouri, to assign the band to Santa Fe's nearby Fort Marcy. They reminded Pope that Fort Marcy was the headquarters of both the Ninth Cavalry and the Military District in New Mexico and that Santa Fe was the largest and most important city in New Mexico, as well as the commercial and ecclesiastical center and capital.[19]

Pope rejected this request. He acknowledged that military regulations provided that when a regiment occupied several locations (as was true of the Ninth in New Mexico), the band was to be located at regimental headquarters, but he reminded the Santa Feans that the rules required that one or more companies of troopers must also be serving wherever the band was stationed. Because Fort Marcy had no companies of the Ninth Cavalry, the regimental band, therefore, could not be stationed there.[20]

The citizens of Santa Fe were not the only people who wanted or enjoyed the services of the band. In March 1877 Col. Edward Hatch requested permission for the band to make limited visits to the different posts where the troopers of the regiment were serving. He believed that the various companies should have the benefit of the band for a portion of the year.[21] The band's subsequent movements attest to the granting of Hatch's request.

In May 1877 the seventeen members of the band traveled from Fort Union to Fort Stanton, remaining there until the following March. Between March 20 and April 12, 1878, they made their way to Fort Bayard, traveling 512 miles.[22] Because Bayard and Stanton were only 230 miles apart by regularly traveled routes, the band probably made detours to Forts Craig, Selden, and Cummings on the way to Bayard, its new temporary post.

Shortly after the band settled in at Bayard, it was ordered to Santa Fe to perform during reception ceremonies for Gen. Philip H. Sheridan. Band members took all their music and necessary instruments, as well as their fatigue and full dress uniforms. They traveled as lightly as possible, taking no women, extra baggage, or property of any kind. Before beginning this assignment the men's leader was admonished that "every feature of good conduct will be expected and exacted from them while on the March and in Santa Fe, and every indication on their part otherwise will meet with *prompt and severe* Punishment. . . . [G]ood sense will doubtless point out to them the necessity and advantage of securing by their good behavior and perfect discipline while [in Santa Fe] the praise of their immediate officers and the satisfactory appreciation of the Citizens generally."[23]

Soon after this brief visit to Santa Fe, the band left Bayard and marched back to Stanton, arriving there on May 21, 1879. In October the band officially was relieved from duty at Fort Union and was assigned to Fort Stanton until further orders. On the previous June 3 and 4 the band had traveled from Stanton to Santa Fe to temporarily serve at the headquarters of the District of New Mexico. It remained on detached service in Santa Fe until the end of October 1880.[24]

During that time the band entertained frequently in and around Santa Fe. The highlight of its performances occurred in October 1880, when it played for President Rutherford B. Hayes during his visit to New Mexico's capital city. On his transcontinental journey, Hayes became the first U.S. president to visit New Mexico. As the president's train stopped at the south end of the city, Colonel Hatch was among the official reception party that would escort the chief executive and his entourage to the city. As Hayes stepped from the train, the crowd

Ninth Cavalry Band, Santa Fe Plaza, July 1880. (Photo by Ben Wittick, Courtesy School of American Research Collections, Museum of New Mexico, Santa Fe, Neg. #50887.)

of people lining the platform of the depot gave three cheers and the band struck up "Hail to the Chief." Then the marching band led the large carriage procession into Santa Fe.

Acting Governor W. C. Ritch received the president at the Santa Fe Plaza pagoda across the street from the historic Palace of the Governors, the band playing "Hail Columbia" as the president and the governor met. A newspaper editor was enthusiastic: "The firing of the guns, cheers and shouts of the people, and the music of the band mingled in chaotic harmony, and betokened a warmth of welcome that could not fail to impress its recipient." After the governor's welcoming address, the president responded. At the close of his remarks while the crowd loudly cheered, the band struck up a national air.

Prior to and during a reception for the presidential party that evening, the band, under the direction of Professor Charles Spiegel, gave a concert in the pagoda. It rendered "beautiful and appropriate selections, specially noteworthy among which was a potpourri of national melodies of different nations, arranged by Prof. Spiegel." Following an exceedingly well-performed introduction of "Hail Columbia," the band played "What is the German Fatherland," the Russian national anthem, the "Marseillaise," and "America." This part of the program ended with "Yankee Doodle" with variations. The evening's remaining selections were "made with a taste, and rendered in a manner reflecting greatly to the credit of the Professor and all members of his band."[25] Playing for the president of the United States no doubt was a once-in-a-lifetime experience for the members of the Ninth Cavalry band.

In all likelihood the band remained in Santa Fe until November 1881, when two of the Ninth's companies left Stanton as a part of the regiment's general exodus from New Mexico. Thus, the Ninth's band spent its last two and a half New Mexico years at Santa Fe, much to the pleasure of the regiment's leaders and the citizens of Santa Fe. By remaining officially stationed at either Fort Union or Stanton, the band observed the regulation that it be at a post with regular cavalrymen, while at the same time being in Santa Fe on detached service.

The men of the Ninth Cavalry not in the regimental band were required to provide escort services, revealing much about military life and its relationship to general conditions in the West. Fear of Indian attacks provided the impetus for some of the escorts, such as when ten enlisted men of Company G out of Fort Bayard escorted the mail from Silver City to Ralston for a week in 1877 and when later they spent a month escorting the mail from Silver City to Camp Bowie, Arizona Territory.[26]

Generally paid every other month, enlisted men perhaps were happy to provide an escort for army paymasters. But Indians and others recognized the potential gain from attacking and overcoming a paymaster and his guard, making such duty dangerous. In any event, black soldiers were used for this duty: a small group of them relayed Maj. Albert S. Towar and his money bags from Fort Stanton to Roswell, and men of Company G, then of Stanton escorted paymaster Maj. J.C.H. Smith for about ninety miles.[27]

From time to time soldiers were called as witnesses at civil or criminal court trials. In 1877 six enlisted men of Company G testified at a court-martial of Lt. John Conline, their company commander. They were Sgts. Joseph Broadus, Joseph Blew, and Robert Johnson; Cpls. Samuel Kirkley and Henry H.B. Carter; and trumpeter Charles Johnson. Events leading to Conline's court-martial are worth recounting because they involved these black enlisted soldiers.

Shortly after Company G transferred from Fort Garland, Colorado, to Fort Bayard in July 1877, Col. Edward Hatch brought a number of charges against Conline, charges so serious that the colonel suggested the lieutenant immediately resign from the army. After interviewing a number of people at Fort Garland and Del Norte, Colorado, Hatch reported that the following events had occurred, warranting charges against Conline. In June 1877 Conline and Company G were traveling from the Uncompahgre Indian Agency to Fort Garland when they camped near the town of Del Norte, due west of Fort Garland and a few miles north of the New Mexico–Colorado boundary. That evening Conline went to the dance house in Del Norte, where he proceeded to get drunk. Remaining in a drunken state for two days, the lieutenant entered a private gambling room, where he was badly hurt in a fight. After having been removed from the premises, he reentered the gambling room while still inebriated and reportedly conducted himself in a disgraceful manner. He interfered with a game in progress and used insulting and abusive language that provoked a second altercation, in which he was knocked down and after which he was forcibly ejected from the gambling room.

At this point Conline ordered an enlisted man to go to his command's camp outside Del Norte and tell the sergeant to bring up the company and to "clear out the house or burn it down," saying, "I have been struck by a damned Rebel." Fearing that these orders might be carried out, some of the town's citizens began arming themselves. Conline's behavior attracted the attention of a Del Norte policeman, who with the assistance of an enlisted soldier and a hotel keeper put the intoxicated lieutenant on a wagon, which carried him back to his camp.[28] Conline's embarrassing actions attracted the attention of a Denver newspaper, which recounted "the antics of one of Uncle Sam's

Lieutenants."[29] The unfavorable newspaper report spurred Hatch to action.

To strengthen his case against Conline, Hatch alleged that while at Fort Garland in February 1876, Conline had behaved himself in an ungentlemanly manner when he had become drunk and attempted to enter the room of Kate Holland, a laundress for Company G who was at that time employed by and lived in the quarters occupied by Lt. David J. Gibbon, also of the Ninth Cavalry. Hatch added more charges of drunkenness, stating that Conline had been drunk on duty from June 10 through 13, 1877, in Del Norte and Saguache, Colorado, as well as on July 7 at Belen, New Mexico.[30]

When Hatch informed Conline by letter that he was bringing charges, Conline stated that "Col. Hatch did me gross injustice by listening to statements of known enemies of mine, officers and officers' wives, and probably enlisted men at Garland." He called Hatch's letter "the most insulting communication I ever received from anybody during sixteen years of honorable service in the Army of the United States during the late rebellion, and since." Conline reported that he had contacted every available man of Company G (including those who had recently spoken against him?) and "obtained their sworn statements relative to said allegations in the presence of four officers showing their gross falsehood in all important matter[s] and in everything worthy the notice of a gentleman." Then the lieutenant telegraphed Hatch that he had important official business to attend to immediately before he could attend to this personal matter. Hatch responded by placing Conline under arrest and relieving him from command of Company G.[31]

Conline then sent telegrams and wrote letters to some of Hatch's military superiors, to which Hatch responded that Conline had written "a disrespectful and scandalous telegram, reflecting on the official conduct of his Commanding Officer." Conline's telegrams and letters caused Hatch to charge that the lieutenant had disregarded the army's proper channels concerning such matters.[32]

But Hatch was not finished. Responding to Conline's counterattacks, he brought forward even more allegations, charging that in March 1877 Conline borrowed $100 from Sgt. Joseph Broadus, promising to pay back the money at the expiration of Broadus's term of enlistment but returning only $70. Hatch also charged that in April

1877 Conline had received $13 from Cpl. Samuel Kirkley but that he had failed to deposit that amount to the credit of Kirkley and instead had appropriated the money for his own benefit. Conline again was charged with cheating Kirkley in July 1877 of $70. Hatch further alleged that in November 1877 Robert Johnson, a private at that time, gave Conline $25 to hire a lawyer for the private's defense at a general court-martial but that Conline failed to procure the requested services and appropriated the $25 for his own use. Broadus, Kirkley, and Johnson each signed official statements verifying Hatch's charges.[33]

Hatch's evidence against Conline was irrefutable, despite the lieutenant's protestations. The various witnesses at the court-marial — commissioned officers of the Ninth Cavalry, an enlisted man of the Fifteenth Infantry, and the six enlisted men of Company G — generally coroborated the charges. Their testimony was straightforward, factual, and undramatic, but damaging. Conline was relieved of his command and lost several months' pay. Over ten years passed before he was promoted to captain. Having taken seven years to complete the regular four-year course at West Point, ranking low in his class, and having been in continual trouble throughout his military career, Conline was hardly a credit to West Point or the army's officer corps.[34]

While the commissioned officers of the post–Civil War army were generally competent, a few of them were the caliber of Conline, creating various problems for enlisted men. Although the men were inconvenienced by such leaders, the problems those officers caused them were inconsequential compared to the hazards of disease. In the early summer of 1877 a smallpox outbreak occurred at Fort Union. This contagious disease was allegedly introduced by J. A. Davis, the post trader's black servant, who had contracted it from his concubine, Lulu, who in turn had brought it from nearby Loma Parda.[35] However, soldiers themselves may have carried the disease to Fort Union, since many of them frequented Loma Parda's saloons, dance halls, gambling rooms, and houses of prostitution. The epidemic did not discriminate between enlisted men and officers, blacks and whites, males and females, or young and old.[36] The quarantine that followed was only partially responsible for keeping the deadly disease from spreading. In due course the outbreak subsided and temporarily disappeared.

The army's experience with disease at Fort Cummings was relatively typical, illustrating the problems the military had with a variety of diseases and health conditions. In 1880 when the army was making a major effort to wipe out Chief Victorio and his band, it used Cummings as a central rendezvous. Between June and September many soldiers were moved to Cummings, a number of scouting parties operating directly out of that post during the troop buildup. Because of these movements the number of men at Cummings varied greatly. In October the numbers reached their peak, with twenty-eight officers and 461 enlisted men, both black and white, although the yearly numbers averaged considerably less than these figures. But whatever the numbers, an increase in sickness occurred.

In July when the command had about 450 men, over 40 men were on sick report for several days in a row, a relatively high incidence of sickness. The prime factor in this increase was the post's not altogether satisfactory drinking water: water from the surrounding countryside drained into the post's spring, near which the ground was thoroughly saturated with the excrement of cattle, sheep, and horses, as well as the polluting filth of a large number of parties who camped nearby as they hauled supplies to Silver City and Mexico. Not all sickness, however, was necessarily related to a contaminated water supply, and in August and September the post hospital treated the following numbers of cases: acute diarrhea (85), remittent fever (23), rheumatism (19), conjunctivitis (11), acute dysentery (9), neuralgia (8), intermittent fever (5), typhoid fever (4, two of whom died), typho-malarial fever (1). Fort Cummings's commander reported that when the command left Cummings in search of Victorio in late September, many of the men were experiencing either diarrhea or dysentery or both, the problems gradually diminishing as the command got farther from Cummings and the sanitary conditions improved. Three cases of typhoid fever developed on this march, however, and the sick men were sent to Fort Bliss for treatment.

Because of the increased threat of sickness and death, the commander recommended that the companies stationed at Cummings be sent to their respective posts before winter set in and that Cummings be abandoned as headquarters for soldiers operating against the Indians.[37] The army chose not to accept that recommendation, but when more men became ill, some of them being sent to Fort Bayard for treatment, military authorities ordered direct actions to rid Cummings of some of its worst unsanitary conditions. Black soldiers were a part of the work detail fulfilling orders that "hereafter all manure from picket lines, both from cavalry battalion, corral, and pack train, also all dumping from police wagons, will be hauled to the south side of the old stone corral . . . on the southeast side of this camp." Before digging new sinks, black enlisted men frequently helped cover the old company sinks with fresh earth as a health safety measure. Other filth was cleared away, and the spring was cleaned again.

In view of inadequate shelter and a limited supply of firewood, the commander anticipated pneumonia, pleurisy, and more rheumatism in the coming winter. In fact, as the winter came on the number of cases of sore throats, catarrhs, and similar problems brought on by cold and exposure increased, although diarrhea and dysentery diminished during the cold months.[38] Circumstances made duty at Fort Cummings through the winter of 1880–1881 less than pleasant.

During the last year that black troopers served at Cummings, problems with sanitation continued. In May 1881, Company E, Ninth Cavalry, was informed that its privy was too close to its tents, and the latrine was ordered to be removed at least fifty yards farther away. The company also got low marks for its general lack of cleanliness, and for two days the soldiers were suspended from drills so they could devote full time to a thorough cleaning of their camp and its immediate vicinity.[39] No doubt the troops were happy to be moved out of Cummings before the worst weather of the winter of 1881–1882 appeared.

Disease, poor sanitation, and generally unhealthful conditions were only some of the hardships with which the soldiers had to cope. Life on the military frontier in New Mexico was filled with additional difficulties. From May to October the weather in southern New Mexico was often extremely hot, and the clothing the army issued to its soldiers sometimes was not satisfactory in such extreme heat. According to one army surgeon writing from Fort Selden in 1877, the ordinary forage cap was wholly inefficient: "Men wearing the forage cap under the brassy sky and blazing sun of a midsummer day in this country are subjected to a positive torture." He pointed out that "the meagre covering for the head afforded by the 'repo' [was] an absolute torture for the men." Indeed, besides the discomfort, the surgeon believed the "repo" was a "very great peril to life." He contended that the men should be issued felt hats or cork helmets, the latter combining qualities of light weight, durability, light color to reflect the sun, strength, and uniformity of appearance. But felt hats and cork helmets were unavailable. The surgeon concluded his report by admitting that the blouses and shirts were light enough for New Mexico's heat, but that soldiers needed trousers made of a light material such as linen or cotton duck.[40]

Despite the searing summer heat, New Mexico was sometimes subject to quite cold winters, and soldiers not prepared for bitter cold could suffer as much or more than those not prepared for hot weather. In the summer of 1879 Company E of the Ninth Cavalry was temporarily stationed at Camp Ojo Caliente. In September the captain of the company began to sense that he and his men might spend the winter there, which in fact they did, and he requested that officers' baggage, company property, extra clothing, and other articles then stored at Fort Union be sent to him. He made the request because the camp was poorly prepared to endure the severe inclemency of the approaching season.[41]

Undesirable conditions at Fort Cummings during the last fifteen months of the Ninth's presence in New Mexico related not only to disease but also to other hardships. As cold weather appeared in late 1880, Lieutenant Colonel Dudley requested a dozen stoves from Fort Bayard because sick soldiers were suffering from lack of heat, and a few days later he announced that he needed fifty-seven stoves for three companies of infantry and six companies of cavalry, pointing out that clerks and officers could not write in such cold weather without them. When the commander at Bayard offered stoves if Dudley would pick them up, Dudley reported that he had no transportation to do that job.[42]

This lack of transportation also prevented the soldiers from gathering sufficient wood to heat either hospital tents or the quarters of healthy troops. Wood-gathering expeditions resulted in only enough fuel for cooking purposes. If the troopers hoped to burn lumber instead of wood, they were disappointed because such lumber was not available.[43] Referring to the enlisted men in his command, Dudley wrote: "It is painful to me to visit their camp as I did last night and found them shivering." When the temperature was quite low at night and did not rise above freezing at noon, the troopers all suffered.[44] To illustrate the extreme severity of the weather in November 1880, Dudley reported that while on a scout in the Florida Mountains, Pvt. Richard Parker, Company H, Ninth Cavalry, had three fingers of his left hand so severely frozen that he had to be sent back to Cummings for surgical treatment. Dudley admitted that although the injury was probably not sufficiently severe to cost the soldier his fingers, it did demonstrate that the whole command to which Parker was then attached suffered considerably from the cold.[45]

Part of the men's suffering resulted from lack of adequate clothing. With six companies of black cavalrymen and three companies of white infantrymen at Cummings, Dudley reported that eight of these companies were "nearly all destitute of proper clothing." Later discovering that the men of the Ninth's Company K were almost entirely without overcoats, Dudley noted that the men would suffer severely if they were ordered to make a scout and immediately requisitioned the needed coats.[46]

The men suffered even further inconveniences. In October 1880 the cavalry companies at Cummings counted more than one hundred horses unfit for service, which sharply limited the cavalrymen's contributions to the army's fighting efforts. When twenty-five mules were delivered to Dudley, he contended that "they are old, vicious, and wild mules, unbroken and unfit for immediate use." A few days later he pointed out that nearly every mule in his command required reshoeing but that he had no coal for the fire necessary to the shoeing process. Such conditions obviously prevented him from sending men into the field against the Indians. But that was not all. Dudley complained that his cavalry command needed currycombs, brushes, and proper horse equipment, and he feared that if a stampede occurred, the men would be unable to control the animals because they had no lariats.[47]

Before one expedition, Dudley inspected and sent to auction thirty-five unserviceable cavalry horses, recommending that a number of these horses be shot.[48] Three or four had already died of natural causes. If Dudley, who admittedly was inclined to exaggeration, was describing conditions even reasonably accurately, such unsatisfactory mounts worsened the oftentimes wretched conditions endured by both black and white cavalrymen and infantrymen, adding frustration and difficulty to their jobs.

In late 1881, a few weeks before the Ninth's withdrawal from New Mexico, the troopers were struggling with the same basic problems confronting them a year before: inclement weather, lack of fuel, and lack of transportation, which interfered with gathering wood and baking bread at Fort Cummings. Fortunately, when two inches of snow fell and the weather turned quite cold and disagreeable, Dudley's replacement at Cummings ordered eight thousand feet of lumber, which both officers and enlisted men used to floor their tents against wind, snow, and cold.[49]

Perhaps general hardships contributed to the soldiers' fighting with, and sometimes killing, each other. In 1878 at Fort Bayard a member of Company C, Ninth Cavalry, was knifed by a fellow soldier and later died. And in another incident in 1881 at Fort Craig, Pvt. John R. Matchett of Company D died in the post hospital from a gunshot wound received in a personal altercation.[50]

When Fort Cummings was going through its troubled times in November 1880, a shooting affray occurred involving Pvts. Phillip Henry and William H. Holloway, both of Company F, Ninth Cavalry. At about 8:30 A.M. on November 2, Holloway entered Henry's tent while the latter was cleaning his carbine for guard duty. After an exchange of heated words, including Henry's "God damn it," Henry shot Holloway, who fell backward out of the tent. As Holloway fell he drew his pistol and shot Henry in the mouth, the latter falling forward out of his tent. Both men were carried to the post hospital, where Henry died within ten minutes of being hit. Shot through both legs above the knees, Holloway survived. The officer reporting the incident indicated that there seemed to have been no quarrel existing between the men, concluding his report with: "Henry was a good soldier and Holloway is a very poor one."[51]

Sometimes enlisted men were killed while they were on duty. In 1877 Sgt. John Pearm shot and killed Cpl. James Billions when the former's pistol accidentally discharged. Both men of Company C were on detached service out of Fort Bayard when the mishap occurred.[52]

In 1880 two white privates murdered two black privates on official guard duty. When white Pvt. Ernest Manhart of Company E, Fifteenth Infantry, became disorderly in his quarters at Fort Craig, white Cpl. Charles N. Klein ordered him to be quiet. Manhart persisted and Klein ordered him placed under guard, whereupon Manhart attacked the corporal. When Klein asked a white private named Carrier to assist him in taking charge of Manhart, Carrier refused. Charged with disorderly conduct and refusal to obey orders, Manhart and Carrier were placed in the post corral and tied to logs. Because Corporal Klein could not control his detachment with Manhart and Carrier present, Craig's commanding officer, Lt. Satterlee C. Plummer of the Fifteenth Infantry, decided to send the men to Camp Ojo Caliente. Corporal Klein, a driver, and two Ninth Cavalry privates were detailed to escort the rebellious men.

Knowing the party would travel through Cañada Alamosa, a large canyon traversed by Indian trails and often containing hostile Indians, Plummer instructed Klein to allow the prisoners to carry arms when going through the canyon. Just before the party entered the canyon the prisoners, with guns in hand, shouted "Indians," firing upon and killing the two black guards sitting near them. Then they turned their guns on the corporal and the driver, but they missed. Despite a chase, the driver got away, and Klein hid in some bushes, his gun becoming black from repeated shooting as he used all his ammunition. Although Plummer sent a detachment to search for the prisoners, they were never captured.[53] Plummer's report carried implied racism, for he mentioned the names of all the participants in this event except those of the black cavalrymen.

During most of the Indian Wars period, the army paid enlisted men on a basic salary scale ranging from $13 a month for privates to $34 for an ordnance sergeant. Corporals received $15 a month, duty sergeants $17, and first sergeants $22.[54] Enlisted men used much of their money for entertainment — drinking, visiting prostitutes, and gambling. The first few days after payday saw a rise in the number of soldiers frequenting post sutler's facilities and visiting off post establishments providing alcohol, sex, and gambling facilities. Both black and white soldiers stationed at New Mexico's forts visited these businesses, which inevitably sprang up just outside the posts' gates, or rode to a nearby town to spend their money.

Gambling had been a pastime for soldiers for centuries. Although the army officially forbad gambling, the men engaged in it both on and off the posts. Some gambling was done with dice, but most was done with cards, poker being the favorite game. When cash was in short supply in the weeks just before payday, in barrack-room poker games the men sometimes gambled with socks, drawers, trousers, and other items drawn from the quartermaster.[55] Men of the Ninth Cavalry developed the custom of cutting their monthly tobacco allowances into eight- or ten-ounce pieces for gambling purposes. When Victorio's raid of September 1879 resulted in the loss of a Ninth Cavalry company's entire horse and mule herd, the captain of the company charged that the men assigned to watch the herd were gambling instead of being diligent while on guard duty.[56]

The combination of liquor and racial prejudice created problems for the soldiers. One night in June 1876 the telegraph operator at Fort Selden became drunk and noisy, and when the guards attempted to control him, he called them "niggers" and attempted to assert his presumed superiority as a white man. The commanding officer, to his credit, arrested the troublemaker.[57] A few months after this incident the post commander ordered the sutler's store on the Selden military reservation closed to soldiers because the operator had been selling liquor to enlisted men who were already drunk.[58]

Besides drunkenness, thievery was also common among the enlisted men of the frontier army. When a theft was discovered, the soldier was usually court-martialed and often punished, sometimes severely. When Pvt. Paul Hamilton of Company F, Ninth Cavalry, was found guilty of this crime at Fort Cummings, he was fined and imprisoned for a month, during which he was required to do hard labor, carrying on his back a board imprinted with the word "thief." When Pvt. Charles Cole of Company C was convicted of stealing, he, too, forfeited his military pay for a month and was confined to hard labor. At the same time, he carried on his back a board with "overcoat thief" printed on it.[59]

Often when soldiers stole government property, they planned to sell it to civilians. In 1881 at Fort Cummings a civilian named Johnson induced a black soldier named Brown (known as a bad man) to steal a government gun from a fellow soldier, paying Brown $8 for his trouble through an intermediary, a civilian named John Duncan. Sergeant Lyons and Privates Bradley and Jacob N. Tyler, all of the Ninth Cavalry, observed the transaction. After receiving the gun, Johnson wrapped it in a sack and buried it in the post's stable yard. Duncan helped a deputy sheriff find the gun and then agreed to testify against Johnson. Black soldiers served as witnesses in Johnson's subsequent trial.[60]

One of the most serious crimes a soldier could commit was desertion. While statistics reveal that in the post–Civil War era black soldiers had a lower rate of desertion than whites, the records are rich in detail concerning many of those blacks who chose to flee military service. Sometimes desertion involved stealing. In June 1880 Pvt. Floyd Quinn of Company B stole a government horse and deserted. After Quinn was captured, tried, found guilty, and incarcerated, the army took $20 of his pay, which was the cost of recovering the army horse that he had taken when he deserted.[61] In November 1881 at Fort Cummings, Pvt. Thomas White, Company M, broke into Lt. John F. McBlain's trunk and stole $140 belonging to Pvt. George Brown of Company M, who had deposited it with McBlain. White also allowed Otto Ansel, an employee of a beef contractor, to take from his tent one carbine, one cartridge belt, sixty rounds of ammunition, and several blankets. Ansel then sold White a civilian overcoat for $10, after which White deserted. Both Ansel and White were apprehended, the former being tried in a civilian court and the latter being court-martialed.[62]

In November 1881 at Fort Craig, Pvt. William Richardson of Company D deserted after breaking into his sergeant's locker and stealing $550 belonging to the men of the company. Two search parties were sent in pursuit. Sergeant Dickerson and two privates learned Richardson was near San Marcial, where he had purchased two revolvers. They tracked the deserter three miles beyond San Marcial and were searching some underbrush when Pvt. Edward Kelsey discovered him. Richardson shot and instantly killed Kelsey and then swam the Rio Grande, after which the other search party, composed of Sergeant Stewart and Private West, found him in a house, where they disarmed him. Later that day when the deserter broke away from his captors and ran, both men fired at and killed him. They found $180 of the stolen money on his body. After an investigation, the commanding officer at Fort Craig concluded that no other official action was necessary in this case.[63]

When three Ninth cavalrymen, James Nelson, William Burns, and Henry Burks, deserted at Forts Cummings and Union in late 1880, they teamed up to make their escape. Because one of them had shot the captain of Company K just before he fled, the army called upon civil authorities to help apprehend the deserters. The sheriff at Trinidad, Colorado, arrested the men, after which a military guard composed of Fifteenth infantrymen retrieved them and returned them to Fort Marcy for trial.[64]

Sometimes New Mexico's black soldiers, as well as white soldiers and Navajo scouts, were sent in pursuit of deserters, using not only horses but also the railroads. On occasion they traveled as far as El Paso, Texas, and the Mexican border in search of their quarry.[65] In late 1880 Lt. Matthias W. Day and his detachment of troopers traveled to Las Vegas, New Mexico, to pursue deserters. They found their task difficult. Day wrote: "The whole colored population here seem to be in league with them and spy around to find out everything I do." At that time San Miguel County counted ninety blacks among its civilian population, nearly 10 percent of the territory's total black population. The majority of the county's blacks lived in or near Las Vegas. Referring to this rather sizable group, Day wrote: "They make reports and lead me on a wild goose chase all over town. While I believe that there are plenty of deserters in this vicinity I do not believe that my stay here is beneficial to the service as my errand is too generally known." Sgt. Thomas Ford of Company A was with Day at this time and was dutiful in inspecting all trains at Watrous, although he discovered nothing. Even with the help of this black noncommissioned officer, Day was not successful in pursuing black deserters.[66]

Although the enlisted men of the Ninth Cavalry were in New Mexico from 1875 to 1881 primarily to subdue the Indians, during their stay in the territory they were involved in many other activities related both directly and indirectly to that main job. These activities had to do with life both on and off the various military reservations. Clearly they interacted with the civilian society while serving as the major military presence in New Mexico.

VII. Soldiers at Work: Fort Bayard, 1887–1896

After the death of Victorio in 1880 and the flight of Nana across the southern border in 1881, major Indian resistance in New Mexico essentially ended, causing the army to move the Ninth Cavalry Regiment out of the territory. At the same time the Indians in New Mexico were being subdued, their neighbors in Texas also were being quieted. However, when the Tenth Cavalry Regiment was no longer needed in the Lone Star State, in April 1885 its headquarters and entire command of twelve troops[1] were transferred to five forts in Arizona Territory, where some Indian resistance remained. In making this move, thirty-eight officers and 696 enlisted men marched across New Mexico Territory along the tracks of the Southern Pacific Railroad. For the next eighteen months these soldiers assisted in pacifying the Apaches of Arizona, a job that was essentially finished by the end of 1886.[2]

In 1887 the regimental headquarters and band of the Tenth Cavalry were moved from Wipple Barracks, Arizona, to Santa Fe, New Mexico.[3] Soon four troops of the Tenth were stationed at Fort Bayard. The arrival of these groups ended a period of nearly six years during which no black soldiers had been stationed in New Mexico. Units of the Tenth remained in New Mexico until 1892.[4]

Concurrently at Fort Bayard with the Tenth Cavalry were black enlisted men of the Twenty-fourth Infantry, several companies of which were reassigned from Indian Territory and Texas to three forts and an Indian agency in Arizona and to Fort Bayard, New Mexico, in 1888. Regimental headquarters and the regimental band were settled at

Col. Zenas R. Bliss. (Courtesy Massachusetts Commandery of the Military Order of the Loyal Legion and the U.S. Army Military History Institute, Carlisle, Pennsylvania.)

Bayard, and from 1888 until 1896 eight companies of this regiment served at Bayard.[5]

The Twenty-fourth's leader was Col. Zenas R. Bliss, who upon arrival at Bayard became the post commander. Bliss was a native of Rhode Island and an 1850 graduate of West Point. Serving in the Union army during the Civil War, he was cited for gallantry and meritorious service in the battles of Fredericksburg and the Wilderness in Virginia. He won a Congressional Medal of Honor. In March 1869 he began serving with the Twenty-fifth Infantry, and in April 1886 he became the commander of the Twenty-fourth.[6]

The movements of black soldiers to and from Fort Bayard were related to movements of some white units, namely the First, Sixth, and Seventh Cavalry regiments and the Thirteenth and Fifteenth Infantry regiments. The presence of a considerable number of both black cavalrymen and infantrymen at Fort Bayard at the same time had not previously occurred in the army's history in New Mexico.[7]

While troops of the Tenth Cavalry were at Bayard between October 1887 and April 1892, at least 270 — and perhaps as many as 330 — cavalrymen spent from a few weeks to many months there. While companies of the Twenty-fourth Infantry were there between June 1888 and October 1896, between 470 and 670 black enlisted men served there.[8] Thus, no fewer than 740 and, depending on the number of new recruits, perhaps as many as one thousand black soldiers served at Bayard over this nine-year period. From June 1888 through April 1892, when the Tenth Cavalry and the Twenty-fourth Infantry were at Bayard simultaneously, the monthly average of black enlisted men was 332. After the withdrawal of the Tenth, from May 1892 through October 1896 the average number of black enlisted men at Bayard decreased to 256 per month.[9]

As major Indian resistance had ended earlier and no Indian reservations were adjacent to Fort Bayard, why did the army station such large numbers of men there? There were several reasons. First, even though soldiers were no longer particularly needed in the West, they were needed even less in the East, so the army chose not to transfer its soldiers eastward after the end of the Indian Wars. At the same time, the army was closing down numerous forts in the West. In order to have stations for all the troops and companies, those forts remaining were often filled to capacity. Finally, because a significant portion of the army's enlisted men were black and thus not welcomed by easterners or by the people of many western cities, the army normally chose to station these men in remote frontier areas. Under these circumstances, in the late 1880s and throughout the 1890s Fort Bayard was a natural choice for posting large contingents of black soldiers.

The Ninth Cavalry Regiment had served in New Mexico from 1875 to 1881 to quash the deliberately organized resistance of Apache leaders such as Victorio and Nana. The Tenth Cavalry Regiment, during its years in New Mexico from 1887 to 1892, did not face such overt resistance. Its official mission was not to break the back of Indian military operations but rather to maintain the status quo by keeping the Indians peaceful and subdued. Oftentimes, scouts were deployed as a preventive measure, not necessarily to seek specific Indian parties. With hardly more than a notation, and with no details whatsoever, the military records indicate that such general scouts occurred frequently.[10] Usually these scouts resulted in no Indian contacts; apparently they were designed primarily as a show of force and to keep the soldiers occupied.

But this does not mean that the Tenth had no contact or trouble with Indians, for Indians occasionally wandered off their assigned reservations either deliberately or because they did not understand the concept of boundaries as they searched for food or animals. An example of the army's response to such Indian activities occurred in late 1887, when the Tenth's Capt. Stevens T. Norvell and Troop M, which had just arrived at Fort Bayard, rode 183 miles on a scout in search of three hostile Indians. A similar excursion occurred a year later, when Bayard's Troop M pursued an Indian raiding party, capturing it at Whitewater.[11]

When the sheriff of Deming reported in 1889 that reservation Indians were killing and burning in San Simon, Arizona, close to the New Mexico line, Colonel Bliss concluded that the report was inaccurate, but he held soldiers at the post in readiness just in case.[12] The threat of Indian violence was real. In May 1890 a sergeant, corporal, and ten privates of Troop M left Bayard for three weeks to pursue hostile Indians near Lordsburg; while they were out, Capt. Richard H. Pratt and Troop L traveled to Lordsburg for the same purpose. A month later Lt. Percy E. Trippe and fifteen men searched for hostile Indians in the direction of the Mexican border, marching 204 miles before returning to their post.[13] A year later Tripp, ten men of Troop D, and ten men of

Troop C marched 143 miles scouting for Indians reportedly hiding in the Hatchet Mountains. While on this expedition, the group also searched the Mogollon Mountains.[14]

Wholly dependent upon horses, cavalry units suffered when they lost animals, for whatever reason. During a five-year period encompassing 1890, the Tenth at Bayard appeared to have more than its share of diseased or injured animals. Horses died or were condemned to destruction because of broken legs, broken necks, and gunshot wounds. Some of them had to be shot because they ate locoweed, developed the blind staggers, or were incapacitated by a variety of animal diseases.[15] Losses from disease and accidents required the shipment of a number of replacement animals for the cavalry at Bayard.[16]

Several scouts occurred in the last half of 1890, when the men of the Tenth were enlisted to track down and capture a small band of renegade Apaches led by an Indian named Kid. In July Kid and his band were south of the international border. When the Mexican government began a concerted campaign to wipe out Kid and his followers, it requested the U.S. Army's assistance in the event the Indian group moved north onto American soil. Tenth Cavalry Troop D, some Indian scouts, and a signal detachment, all under the command of Capt. A.S.B. Keyes, were assigned expressly to kill or capture Kid and the members of his band. Lt. Herbert S. Whipple and a detachment were readied to enter the fray.

When the Indians reportedly killed a citizen at Hachita, about fifty miles south of Bayard, Keyes and a detachment of fifteen men and some Indian scouts with ten days' rations immediately rode out of Bayard. At the same time, Whipple and his group moved to the Lordsburg area. Keyes's command found evidence of the fleeing Indians, but it did not catch up with them because rain had washed out the trail. When Keyes learned that Indians had killed prospectors Alf Williams, Carl Coleman, and Peter Riggs, he requested permission to station troopers along the border at Gilbert's Ranch, Hachita, and Long's Ranch. He was authorized to remain in communication with Whipple and to take twenty men with twenty days' rations to Gilbert's Ranch.

When rumor had it that Kid was near San Carlos, Arizona, Keyes was ordered to send a detachment toward Fort Bowie and to intercept the Indian leader before he made his way to Mexico, Colonel Bliss reiterating his orders that Keyes should pursue Kid and his band until

Tenth Cavalrymen in Camp Near Chloride, New Mexico, 1892. (Photo by Henry A. Schmidt, Courtesy Museum of New Mexico, Santa Fe, Neg. #58556.)

they were killed or captured. Keyes, however, was unable to fulfill his orders when Kid's group escaped across the border. After nearly six weeks of intensive operations, Keyes and Whipple were ordered back to Bayard empty-handed.[17]

After Kid's flight south, Keyes and his men had hardly rested when they were ordered out again. Their commanding officer had heard that fifteen Indians had killed two miners and stolen three horses near Chloride in the Black Range and that the Indians appeared to be fleeing southward. Therefore, he sent Keyes, twenty-two men, and two Indian scouts to the Cooke's Peak area to intercept the hostile Indians. When Keyes's search was unsuccessful, he moved north to Hillsboro, but he saw no Indians there either. Keyes concluded that the band he sought was made up of reservation Indians who probably fled north instead of south. Nevertheless, Keyes's superiors ordered him to continue his search. A group of cowboys reported that the Indian band was composed of seventy-five warriors, but the army discounted the report; indeed, it concluded that the Indians committing the murders were considerably fewer than fifteen.[18]

When J. A. Lockhart reported that seven Indians killed a steer and drove away five horses from his ranch thirty miles west of Deming, Colonel Bliss arranged for Lockhart and Captain Keyes to meet at Nutt, at which time Lockhart was to give Keyes more details about this raid. After the meeting, Keyes, another officer, thirty-two enlisted men, and three Indian scouts proceeded to Lockhart's Ranch to pursue the Indians. When other citizens in the region asked for protection from hostile Indians, Bliss had to inform them that he had only Cavalry Troop D available and that it was already in the field.[19]

Following his investigation at Lockhart's Ranch, Keyes reported: "All the Indian reports we have heard since we came out combined do not make up as big a humbug as this one of the Lockhart Ranch." He stated that while his men were on their way to Lockhart's property, they found the reputedly stolen horses exactly where they belonged — four miles from the ranch. Keyes suspected Lockhart's men had lost contact and simply assumed the animals had been stolen. Keyes's group did, however, find signs that Indians, presumably, had killed a calf, and they followed the fresh trail, composed of three burned matches and the prints of a pair of high-heeled boots, to Hachita and the ranch of a man named Doyle. There they found part of the slaughtered calf. Keyes cynically wrote to Bliss that this "was a fine thing to bring a company [troop] over a hundred miles for," frankly stating that he believed that no hostile Indians were in southwestern New Mexico, unless the men on Chloride Creek had been killed by Indians, but he thought even that was doubtful.[20]

Because so many reported Indian sightings were false, military leaders began to resist sending troopers to investigate on hearsay evidence only. When Bliss heard that Indians had killed two Hispanos near Kelly's Ranch, he hesitated to send out his men, pointing out that all his command had been in the field for nearly a month and had been unable to obtain reliable information on any Indians. He concluded: "Since my Cavalry have been out nearly all the time since Aug 1st, they need rest. I don't want to send them out on false rumors."[21] After a party of eight citizens had followed the trail of five Indians into the mountains to the north of Chloride, Bliss belatedly ordered Captain Keyes and a detachment to take up the chase. After a week with no success, Bliss ordered Keyes to return to Bayard, leaving Lt. Lawrence

Tenth Cavalry Troopers and White Miners Near Silver Monument Mine, Chloride, New Mexico, ca. 1892. (Photo by Henry A. Schmidt, Courtesy Museum of New Mexico, Santa Fe, Neg. #12828.)

J. Fleming in command of the detachment with instructions to discover to what tribe and reservation the Indians belonged.[22]

In a summary report to military headquarters about his autumn activities, Bliss reported that apparently no large groups of Indians were in the vicinity of Kelly's Ranch. He discounted the killing of the calf and the reported stealing of horses at Lockhart's Ranch, saying that the calf had been killed by a neighboring ranchman and that the horses had not been interfered with. He corroborated the deaths of the two miners, a blind man and a boy, near Chloride, but he doubted that Indians had killed them, as the bodies had not been robbed or mutilated. If Indians had indeed killed the miners, he believed there were no more than two and they had probably come north from Mexico rather than being reservation Indians. He speculated that Kid, who was still free, may have been responsible for the deaths.[23] The inconclusiveness of Bliss's report emphasized the military's continuing frustration with Indians from Mexico crossing the border, with wandering reservation Indians, and with general problems concerning the control of the Indian population. The situation was further exacerbated by rumors, half-truths, and civilians' unwarranted fears.

Concurrently serving with the cavalry units at Bayard between 1888 and 1896 was the Twenty-fourth Infantry. But unlike the mounted infantry units that helped the Ninth Cavalry rid New Mexico of Victorio and Nana, infantrymen at Bayard in the 1880s and 1890s did not pursue Kid or other Indians, serving primarily as support groups that remained at the post while the cavalry looked for Indians.

On occasion, however, infantrymen were used off the military posts. Between 1892 and 1894 both cavalrymen and infantrymen at Bayard patrolled the southern border. In January 1892 the citizens of Columbus, New Mexico, reported that Mexican revolutionists from northern Chihuahua were in the territory endangering life and property. Military protection was needed. Bayard's commanding officer responded by sending Lt. James W. Watson, three Indian scouts, and twenty enlisted men of Troop C of the Tenth Cavalry to the border town.[24]

Two troops of the First Cavalry, which replaced the Tenth at Bayard in April 1892, and men of the Twenty-fourth Infantry took up the task of patrolling the border as reports of revolutionary activities in northern Mexico increased. In late 1893, when Colonel Bliss heard that from fifty to one hundred revolutionaries had taken possession of Palomas and the surrounding Mexican countryside, he sent an officer and a detachment of men to Columbus, even though the revolutionaries had not moved north of the border. At the same time, he ordered Lt. Charles Dodge, Jr., of the Twenty-fourth Infantry to move by rail from Separ to Silver City to investigate conditions there.

Two weeks later Bliss sent Lt. Henry W. Hovey of the Twenty-fourth to Silver City to inquire about a possible concentration of Mexican revolutionaries. Hovey reported that several weeks previously two different Mexicans had bought a combined total of 350 rounds of ammunition but that in recent weeks the gun stores had sold neither weapons nor ammunition to anybody. Silver City residents reported that they had seen no strangers in the town and that nothing had occurred to indicate unusual activity or excitement among the Hispanic population there. Based on Hovey's information, Bliss concluded that reports indicating that Mexican revoutionaries were concentrating in or near Silver City were without foundation.[25]

In early 1894 Bliss was told that Victor L. Ochoa and his band of marauders, if not revolutionaries, were headed north from Mexico

toward Silver City. As a precaution, Bliss sent Lt. James E. Brett of the
Twenty-fourth with an ambulance and buckboard to the vicinity of
Columbus to inquire about Ochoa's activities and whereabouts. Brett
learned nothing. Bliss asked a U.S. marshall, local sheriffs, and citizens
along the railroad line in the southwest corner of the territory to watch
for Ochoa and his men and immediately to report any sighting of the
group. He promised to send infantrymen to capture the band. In
response to one report, an officer and four men of the Twenty-fourth
were dispatched to the vicinity of Bear Creek, but they found no
evidence of marauders.[26] Like most of the reports of Indian activities
in the 1890s, reports of Mexican revolutionists and marauders north of
the border were unfounded or greatly exaggerated.

Both infantrymen and cavalrymen from border posts in Texas, Fort
Huachuca in Arizona, and Fort Bayard in New Mexico were used for
escort and guard duty for parties of engineers surveying for the United
States–Mexican Boundary Commission. In January 1892 Lt. Arthur C.
Ducat, Jr., and thirty enlisted men of the Twenty-fourth left Bayard to
serve for a few weeks with the boundary commission. A few days later,
Lieutenant Trippe and twenty-one enlisted men of the Tenth Cavalry
left Bayard to serve the commission along the border of Texas, traveling
to Texas in two six-mule wagons and with two pack mules and performing this duty until April, when they returned to Bayard.[27]

Although soldiers in the post–Civil War army were occupied with
the exciting duties of chasing Indians and with their considerably less
exciting duties associated with the routine of garrison life, normally
they were removed from the nation's mainstream of events, their lives
seldom intersecting with those of the civilian population.[28] Important
exceptions, however, occurred in the late nineteenth century, after
large labor unions were organized to advance the laborers' interests
vis-à-vis the giant industrial corporations that sprang up in that era.
Beginning with the great railroad strike of 1877, strike duty became a
part of the army's peacetime functions. One authority, in fact, has
claimed that strike duty was the most conspicuous function of the army
during the last quarter of the nineteenth century.[29] The army's task was
usually to quell widespread disturbances threatening the larger interests
of the national economy or the rights and property of a large group of
people. Sometimes, though, the army intervened in a contest of wills
between well-organized laborers and powerful corporation owners.

Numerous instances of soldiers acting as peacekeepers or strikebreakers occurred from the late 1870s until the end of the century.[30]

The financial panic that struck the country in 1893 set off an economic depression that reached its nadir the following summer. Tough economic conditions caused large numbers of employers to lay off thousands of employees and to cut the wages of those who continued to work, these actions adding to the continuing downward spiral of the economy. Many workers could not tolerate reduced income or unemployment, and they went on strike. The most famous of the 1894 strikes was a large and bitter one against the Pullman Company of Chicago. Quickly joining these protesting factory workers were railroad workers throughout the Midwest. Violence became widespread, moving both eastward and westward like a prairie fire, setting the entire country aflame. The commanders of six of the nation's eight military departments were authorized to act in the national emergency, making some sixteen thousand soldiers available to protect property or to break strikes. Duty related to the railroad strike involved almost two-thirds of the men in the army and brought about the most extensive field service for U.S. soldiers since the Civil War.

From early July through the middle of September 1894, soldiers from the military departments in the West were in the field supporting federal marshals in opening rail traffic, protecting railroad property, and restoring order. When railroad workers in northern New Mexico and southern Colorado protested deteriorating conditions, leaders of the Denver and Gulf Railroad became concerned about protecting their property and nonstriking employees and called upon the army for help. In response, Lt. Gen. John M. Schofield ordered Brig. Gen. Alexander McDowell McCook, Department of the Colorado, to provide troopers to aid federal marshals protecting railroad property in receivership of the U.S. Court at Trinidad, Colorado.[31] As a result of these events and orders, soldiers stationed in New Mexico and Arizona became directly involved in protecting railroad property during a strike. On July 9 the Twenty-fourth Infantry's regimental commander, Col. Zenas R. Bliss, Companies D, E, F, and G, and a detachment of the hospital corps marched two and one half miles from Fort Bayard to Halls Station. They remained there in a heavy rainstorm for a day, after which they boarded a train bound for Trinidad. Already on the train were officers and men of Company H, Twenty-fourth Infantry, from Fort Huachuca.[32]

When it was rumored that strikers had opened switches near Deming in order to wreck the train carrying these 205 enlisted men and nearly a dozen officers, guards were positioned on the front and rear platforms of each car. After passing through Las Vegas, New Mexico, the stock car of the train caught on fire twice, causing delays. At Raton the train ran dangerously low on water. Because Raton's water tank was empty, the cars were unhooked, and under heavy guard the engine of the train continued two more miles to obtain more water for steam power for the remainder of the trip to Trinidad. When the engine did not return after two hours, a group of men in a handcar was sent to find it. They discovered that the engine had run off the track, and another engine had to be obtained to carry the troopers farther.

After overcoming these problems, the train continued its journey north, the men of Company H disembarking at the New Mexico–Colorado border to guard the Raton railroad tunnel against sabotage. The majority of the infantry battalion arrived in Trinidad on July 11 and immediately established a camp, this military presence a visible symbol of the power of the national government. When people along the track in northern New Mexico had learned that the infantrymen en route to troubled Trinidad were black, they said that it "was an insult to send Negro Soldiers up there," but they addressed no adverse remarks to the soldiers themselves. The situation in southern Colorado was volatile; the strikers were in bad humor. They burned or attempted to burn railroad bridges, they applied soap to rails, they put sand in brake boxes, and they assaulted railroad employees. But these events occurred far from the soldiers; clearly the strikers were hesitant to damage railroad property directly under military guard. The only incident involving people or property guarded by the troopers occurred during the night of August 4, when someone threw a coupling link through the window of the Santa Fe freight office. The sentinel fired two shots at a man but missed. After that incident, Bliss purposely left some railroad property defenseless to see whether the strikers would attempt to destroy it, but they did not. The presence of soldiers probably did deter violence, for without the soldiers destruction of depots, bridges, rolling stock, and the Raton tunnel surely would have occurred. During the two months the soldier-guards were at the Raton tunnel, they removed from trains about six hundred tramps, forcing them to walk around or over the hill through which the tunnel ran. Most of these men were simply stealing rides and had no connection with the strikers, but Bliss took no chances.

Because conditions appeared quiet and essentially no violence had occurred, Bliss received orders to pull out. He and his command left Raton and Trinidad on September 4, arriving at Bayard and Huachuca shortly thereafter. The mayor of Trinidad, the chief of police, and other officials and prominent citizens commented upon the exceptional and highly commendable conduct of the enlisted men of the command during their stay in southern Colorado. After this duty had ended, Bliss wrote to his superiors: "I take pleasure in testifying to the excellent and satisfactory conduct and performance of duty by both officers and enlisted men of my command."[33]

The success of the Twenty-fourth Infantry at Raton and Trinidad was part of the larger story: the great railroad strike of 1894 sputtered to an end in late summer. Even though the army in general, and black soldiers in particular, were unable to be fully integrated into American society, they were nevertheless efficient tools of that society. Indeed, despite the reservations, and sometimes hostility, that American citizens expressed toward the military establishment, the army's participation in southern Reconstruction, the patrolling of the U.S.–Mexico border, the subjugation of the Indians, the control of labor violence, and episodes of civil strife such as the Colfax and Lincoln County wars caused it to develop an image as the government's "obedient handyman," performing without question or hesitation the responsibilities assigned to it.[34]

Investigating rumors of Indian activities, guarding survey engineers, and protecting lives and property during labor strikes did not occupy all the time of the soldiers at Fort Bayard. They also played war games. In the fall of 1888 a detachment of Tenth cavalrymen led by Captain Norvell searched for a group of men led by Lt. George H. Paddock who were acting the part of an Indian raiding party. At daybreak on October 18, Norvell's group "captured" the raiding party near Whitewater.[35]

Prior to this military exercise, Norvell and a detachment of soldiers had spent a week examining the country north of Bayard to learn about Indian trails and to find sites for signal stations. Captain Keyes and a detachment spent another week exploring even farther north for the same purpose. Following these investigations, troopers established several signal stations to the north of Bayard, after which Lt. James S. Jouett and his men rode farther north into the Mogollon Mountains to see whether it would be practical to place a heliograph station on the highest peak in the range, in hopes of linking Forts Bayard and Wingate by signal stations. Unfortunately the men at the signal stations were not adept at spotting Paddock's raiders in the subsequent war games. They had little or no experience with heliographs, and defective telescopes prevented them from seeing signal flags except at comparatively short distances. Upon the end of these maneuvers, Bliss ordered additional training for three men of each troop and company at Bayard to improve their effectiveness with the heliographs and signal flags. Bliss concluded that despite the problems with the signal stations, the exercises were instructive, although he admitted they were necessarily hard on animals and riders.[36]

The training in signaling and heliograph work that Bliss ordered for soldiers after the 1888 war games continued as long as the men were at Bayard. In 1889 some men of the Twenty-fourth Infantry worked eight hours a day practicing signaling, three becoming good enough to be stationed at Lordsburg. In April 1894 a lieutenant and seven infantrymen of Companies D and G were on detached service from Bayard to practice heliographing, and later that year two officers and six enlisted infantrymen were on detached service at Cow Springs in order to heliograph with a detachment at Bayard.[37] Some men became relatively good at sending and receiving messages, "but to make experts out of some of these men in a short time would be hard."[38]

The soldiers worked in other areas related to communications. For a time, Corporal Holden of Company A of the Twenty-fourth served as the military telegraph operator at Silver City, and other infantrymen were responsible for keeping the area's military telegraph instruments and lines in good repair.[39] In May 1892 two officers and thirty enlisted men of the Twenty-fourth traveled by rail from Bayard to Separ to help construct a military telegraph line from that point to the international border to the south. Enlisted men out of Bayard also built the important telegraph line from Bayard to Silver City and then operated the line without expense, except for items such as line batteries.[40] Later, men of the Twenty-fourth dismantled the telegraph lines in the vicinity of Bayard. Their leader requested that they receive extra pay for performing this duty, as it was such hard work: some of them carried iron telephone poles on their shoulders for distances of a mile in order to reach the wagons used to haul the poles away. Their leader also requested extra remuneration for them to compensate for wear and tear of their clothing while doing such rough work.[41]

Besides playing war games and working with heliographs and telegraphs, the soldiers at Bayard learned to be better soldiers by attending camps of instruction. In September 1889 Troops D, L, and M of the Tenth took four days to travel 147 miles from Bayard to a site near Fort Grant, Arizona, where they then spent four weeks receiving training.[42] In September 1892 eighteen officers and 199 Twenty-fourth infantrymen at Bayard marched twenty-eight miles to a three-week camp of instruction near Moulten's Ranch on Sapillo Creek.[43] One year later Bayard's infantry battalion returned to Moulten's Ranch for similar duty, even though Colonel Bliss had hinted to his superiors that the 1893 encampment should be called off because the men of the garrison recently had done an unusual amount of fatigue — digging a water well, policing the post, cooking, pitching tents, and practicing for rifle competition.[44]

In addition to attending camps of instruction, the soldiers performed exercises in the field. While the Tenth cavalrymen were returning from Fort Grant in October 1889, Company D, Twenty-fourth Infantry, spent two days performing military exercises just north of Fort Bayard, and one month later Companies A, D, and F repeated these exercises.[45]

While occasional camps of instruction and exercises in the field were held for both cavalrymen and infantrymen at Bayard in the 1880s and 1890s, practice marches formed the major part of the life of the infantrymen during their last year at Bayard. Between September 1895 and September 1896 practice marches occurred almost every month. Some were relatively short, such as those to Santa Rita, Pinos Altos, Lake Valley, Old Saw Mill, Silver City, Horse Mountain, and nearby ranches, but others were longer, such as the one to Camp Maddox, near the Mogollon Mountains, when four companies of 183 infantrymen and their officers traveled a total of 242 miles. On this march the men traveled in two groups of two companies each, the columns arriving at their destination and back at Bayard on different days. Bayard's commander wrote: "It was a good march, but the rough roads wore out half the shoes of the two columns on the march. The route purposely selected for the practice march was a severe test on the endurance of the men and the result shows a very creditable march both in the advance and forced march in return."[46]

Once the Indian threat was removed and soldiers were not badly needed at their posts, they sometimes worked for private businesses. Men on such detached service were usually paid a small wage for their services. Between June 1888, when most of the Twenty-fourth Infantry arrived at Fort Bayard, and July 1893, from three to ten enlisted men, both noncommissioned officers and privates, spent from a few days to several months on detached service at a sawmill not far from the post. At least one of these men was a skilled sawyer.[47] Officially the army frowned on the hiring out of soldiers, but regulations were ignored when soldiers were not needed for serious military duty.

The records indicate that other black soldiers had similar skills, which the army put to use. They were painters, printers, saddlers, machinists, and mechanics, and they used these skills at Bayard.[48] One private of the Twenty-fourth was given the important responsibility of being in charge of the post's ice-making machine, which ran fifteen hours a day.[49]

Because the underground water supply was plentiful, enlisted men, both skilled and unskilled, constructed a new water well at Fort Bayard in December 1893. They installed temporary plank curbing to hold up the walls of this well, and in the following spring they installed a stone circle about eighteen feet in diameter, confident that the large well would furnish water for all the needs of the post.[50]

The ample water supply at Bayard was a factor in the soldiers' success in extinguishing a potentially disastrous fire. At 7:40 P.M. on November 1, 1893, a fire broke out in the hay stored in the third stable from the guardhouse. The sentinel reported that he smelled smoke and soon saw a light about as big as his hat near the south end of the stable. He went towards it, and before he could go half the length of the stable the fire burst forth. He gave the alarm and the men of the garrison were immediately on the scene. By the time the post commander arrived, the hay stable was fully ablaze and the side of a second stable near the burning one was on the verge of igniting. Neither stable could be saved. Other adjoining stables were soon smoking, and a granary in front of the hay stable as well as buildings of the corral were in imminent danger. The men applied water with hoses and fire buckets, their vigorous work saving the buildings.

The fire caused not only the loss of two cavalry stables — one of which had been used to store hay — but also the loss of about forty-two tons of hay (the post's total supply), some quartermaster property, and camp and garrison equipage. Miraculously, the only horse in First Cavalry Troop B's stable was rescued. The wind, which was light, was from the west, and had blown the flames from the hay directly against the side of Troop B's stable. Had the wind been from the southeast, the magazine and other buildings undoubtedly would have been destroyed. But conditions were good for fighting a fire: little wind, plenty of water, and quick response from the men of the garrison. Bliss praised the men for their work, under the guidance of two officers, in saving the other buildings.[51]

Much less exciting than firefighting were the routine duties of the soldiers at Bayard. Some of them spent time performing escort service for both military personnel and civilians. In January 1892 Lt. Isaac C. Jenks and five men of the Twenty-fourth traveled to Fort Selden to pick up doors, windows, and new transportation for Fort Bayard.[52] Even duller duty was "guarding the post," which was often the only entry in the monthly returns reporting the enlisted men's activities.

But there were times when duty on the frontier was neither dull nor easy. In January 1892 Bliss contended that service on the frontier was "about as hard for regiments stationed there as it has been at any time in the last 40 years," detailing a number of soldiers' activities in the previous year to support his contention. Troop D, Tenth Cavalry, did a total of sixty-nine days of detached service, marching 968 miles, and Troop C did about the same amount of detached service. Four companies of infantry marched 185 miles each. Various members of the troops and companies did a total of 6,720 days of detached service.

More specifically, Bliss tallied the number of logs that the soldiers had cut, hauled from the mountains, and helped saw and split into lumber. These soldiers sawed and split enough firewood to supply the needs of a large garrison of soldiers and about one hundred noncombatants. Other soldiers cultivated a large garden, while still others manufactured all the ice needed by the post. In addition, the soldiers built a target range and kept it in good repair, and they built and operated a military telegraph line. They spent hours policing the post, their duties including caring for the sewers and water supply. Finally, they spent a great deal of time heliographing over long lines. All of this was done in addition to participating in ordinary drills, target practice, signal drills, parades, and reviews. These activities plus others caused Bliss to remark that "it is a mistake to conclude that with the cessation of Indian Wars . . . there is a period of 'inactivity' now existing on the frontier."[53]

One of the activities the men of Bayard performed was the permanent closing down of Fort Selden. Because the extension of railroads into the Southwest resulted in the army's being able to move soldiers rapidly over long distances, political and military officials decided to close many of the small forts in the region and to concentrate the military presence there in a few large posts. In fact, in the early 1880s these officials seriously considered transforming Selden from a neglected, minor, one-company fort into a permanent, major, twelve-company post. But after several years of consideration that also involved Fort Bliss, the authorities finally decided to expand the latter. This decision doomed Fort Selden.[54]

In 1887 the army began Selden's final abandonment. In May 1888 the last full company of soldiers (who were white) to be stationed at the fort left, and Selden became a subpost of Fort Bayard.[55] In August ten black soldiers from Companies A, D, and F of the Twenty-fourth Infantry on temporary duty from Fort Bayard arrived at Selden to close the neglected and decaying fort permanently.[56]

Company F's leader, Lt. James E. Brett, was post commander for all but five months of the last two and one half years of Selden's existence. During this final period, the commanding officer and his men faced a number of problems. Living conditions were admittedly wretched because the adobe buildings were in a state of disrepair and were rapidly disintegrating under the influence of rain and wind. Furthermore, in October and November 1888 nearly twenty-four inches of rain, three times the annual average, fell on the Mesilla Valley, causing the fort's dirt roofs to leak and endangering supplies.[57]

In addition to these hardships, Fort Selden experienced a disaster when at 12:45 A.M. on the morning of June 7, 1889, a fire broke out in the quartermaster's corral. Brett reported: "The rapidity with which the fire spread was, to say the least, astonishing." After hearing the sentinel's first shot, Brett was at the corral within one minute, finding the place already enveloped in flames and the animals "succumb[ing] with lightning rapidity." "The heat was so intense," he reported, "that it was also impossible to save much of the transportation." Brett acknowledged that "such a holocaust, such agony, which was equal to Dante's description of Hell, was previously beyond my description."

Despite the promptness, energy, and courage that all the troopers displayed, the fire gutted the corral, an adobe structure with a dry brush roof. Five horses and seven mules were lost, as well as one Doherty wagon, one Red Cross ambulance, one army wagon, two escort wagons, three carts, eleven sets of harnesses, assorted wagon fixtures, and a quantity of lumber. Several of the men were nearly burned to death in their desperate efforts to extinguish the fire and to save government animals and property. After the fire the post had only two horses, one mule, one escort wagon, two water wagons, one buckboard, and some harnesses, and Brett was obliged to borrow three animals from the post trader for temporary use.

Brett theorized that the fire had been caused by a match that accidentally dropped from a teamster's pocket and was ignited by the foot of an animal. The weather, he acknowledged, had been excessively warm, but because the men had kept the stalls scrupulously clean, he discounted the possibility of spontaneous combustion. He also dismissed the possibility of arson, as he had seen no strangers around the corral and the troopers had no motive for incendiarism. Some suspicion of arson did arise when troopers found two half-pound powder cans near the fire's origin, but the cans were quite old and showed signs of rust and exposure. Brett therefore concluded that the containers had been under rubbish on the roof for a long time, only to be discovered when the rubbish burned.[58]

An area newspaper argued subsequently that the force then at Selden was too small to take care of government property adequately.[59] The army agreed; shortly after the fire seven men of Company H, Twenty-fourth Infantry, out of Fort Bayard temporarily joined the troopers already at Selden. But this numerical strength did not last long; soon thereafter, Selden's enlisted force was again reduced to ten men.[60]

As Fort Selden's closure drew near, the enlisted men helped crate and ship to Fort Bayard all serviceable property, including a field

Howitzer, several other guns and cannons, cartridges, clothing, a box of medical books, and miscellaneous equipment. They tore lumber from the old buildings in order to pack these items for shipment. They also shipped all usable doors, windows, and window frames. By auction the soldiers helped dispose of tents, firewood, hay, coal, and similar items. As Fort Bayard did not need Selden's pack-covers, aparejos, riding saddles, packsaddles, or water wagons, they were either sold or taken to other posts. Some worthless items were destroyed.[61]

When the hospital corps detachment at Selden was reassigned for duty at Fort Bayard in October 1890, thereby closing the medical department, the end for the entire post was clearly at hand.[62] It came three months later.[63] Brett left one noncommissioned officer and three privates to guard the post's buildings, and in June 1891 these members of the military guard at Selden finally were removed to Fort Bayard. On March 30, 1892, the Fort Selden military reservation was transferred to the Department of the Interior.[64]

The end of Fort Stanton came a few years later. In June, July, and August 1896 one commissioned officer and seven enlisted men taken from four of Bayard's infantry companies were temporarily assigned to Stanton, their duty being to close it permanently.[65] With the closing of Selden and Stanton, the only military fort remaining in southern New Mexico was Fort Bayard.

VIII. Off-Duty Soldiers: Fort Bayard, 1887–1896

B ecause the Indians essentially had been subdued in New Mexico by the early 1880s, time for leisure and other off-duty activities existed for the soldiers stationed in the territory thereafter. Sometimes these other activities were closely related to the routine work of the soldiers. For instance, in 1879 the army ordered each soldier to fire twenty rounds each month on a target range. At the same time, it adopted an official policy of awarding prizes and furloughs to the best marksmen in each unit, injecting a strong competitive element into the target shooting. Beginning in 1888 competitions were held at the post, department, and divisional levels, with the best marksmen pitted against opponents in army-wide matches.[1] Many soldiers became enthusiastic target shooters in the 1880s and 1890s, taking pride in their skills and in the marksmen's and sharpshooters' badges and certificates the army awarded them. Compared man for man with the standing armies of other nations, U.S. soldiers were probably the world's best military marksmen when the Spanish–American War began in 1898.[2]

The men at Fort Bayard did not resist required target practice, and many of them eagerly worked to win awards and competitions. The Twenty-fourth Infantry hardly had arrived at Bayard in June 1888 when post commander Col. Zenas R. Bliss pointed out that because of the recent move and lack of target frames, the men had lost many days of target practice. Furthermore, because another week would be lost before the men could resume practice, he requested permission that the thirty-eight days lost in May and June be made up beginning September 15 and continuing until the following July.[3] One of the first jobs assigned to the men after their arrival at Bayard, in fact, was to erect

Black Cavalrymen, 1894. (Photo by A. B. Coe, Courtesy Montana Historical Society, Helena.)

new butts for target practice.[4] Even without proper facilities these troopers engaged in skirmish target practice within two weeks after their arrival, and their superiors forwarded to the inspector of rifle practice, Department of Arizona, reports of scores for both sharpshooters and marksmen.[5] At the same time, the men of the Tenth Cavalry stationed at Bayard engaged in pistol practice.[6]

In July 1888 three of Bayard's infantrymen (Pvt. Henry Daniels and Sgts. Lewis W. McNabb and William Wilkes) and three cavalrymen (Pvts. George Bonds and Adrian Jones and Cpl. Richard Harrison) were selected to compete in the annual regional rifle competition, held that year at Fort Wingate.[7]

In 1889 Bayard's Calvin Chapman, an enlisted man in Troop L of the Tenth Cavalry, won a first place gold medal in the cavalry small arms competition.[8] In 1890 Bayard sent three men (trumpeter Edward Parnell and Pvts. Jones and Bonds) as its contestants in the small arms competition. These men had taken their target practice seriously in the weeks before the competition, often being on the target practice range as early as 7 A.M. Their diligence paid off: Jones won a second-place silver medal.[9]

A hint of the importance of these contests occurred in 1891, when Fort Bayard made plans to host the annual regional shooting competitions. In preparation for the event, Bliss asked for $300 for the improvement of the post's target range, buildings, and platforms.[10] The event returned to Wingate the following year and alternated between the two posts for the next few years. The men of the Twenty-fourth Infantry out of Bayard continued to win their share of distinguished marksman medals.[11]

Another off-duty activity closely related to work was hunting. In the mid-1890s Bayard's commander encouraged hunting among both enlisted men and officers. Although the men tracked game for the pleasure of the hunt, their commanding officer viewed the expeditions from another point of view. He wrote: "Of all the experiences short of those gained in actual warfare I consider none more important than those gained in the hunting field." He went on to say such activity led men to gain knowledge of the country, to sharpen observation powers and shooting skills, to develop habits of self-reliance and confidence, and in many instances to manifest bravery. In regard to the latter trait, he recalled that a wounded bear had turned on a group of soldier-hunters and grappled with one of the men, "who but for coolness and bravery on his own part and one of his companions would have lost his life." The officer concluded that an accident resulting from hunting should be considered as if it had been incurred in the line of duty.[12] Since wild game was plentiful in the mountains north of Fort Bayard, another result of hunting was a supplementation of the meat the army purchased from private contractors.

Vegetables were not included in the rations issued to soldiers during most of the years of the late nineteenth century, but because the army recognized their nutritional value, it encouraged post gardens. All over the frontier enlisted men on fatigue details laid out garden plots, dug irrigation ditches, and assisted in planting, weeding, cultivating, and harvesting vegetable crops.[13] The men of Bayard were among them. Shortly after the Twenty-fourth Infantry arrived at Bayard, the men of the regimental band and Company D were authorized to put in two separate gardens. Company D's garden covered about three-quarters of an acre and contained seventy-five rows of onions, fifty rows of cabbages, fifteen rows of cauliflowers, and six rows of lettuce, each row being eighty feet long. It also contained a patch of beans twelve feet by eighty feet and a patch of turnips eleven paces by twenty-six paces. By the middle of August the onions, cabbages, and cauliflowers were in good condition, though the beans and turnips proved less satisfactory. In the late summer of 1888 Colonel Bliss wrote that the band's garden was being "reappraised," a euphemism indicating that it was unsuccessful. The bandsmen had the leisure time to plant a garden, but apparently they did not have the skills to make it thrive.[14]

By contrast, the success of the garden of Company D was such that in future years, the companies at the post planted a single, large garden. In 1890 the post garden, cared for by one gardener and six assistants, covered between thirteen and fifteen acres. Although lack of water for irrigation slowed down the growth process early on and later floods destroyed one-fourth of the garden (about twenty thousand pounds of bearing plants), it nevertheless produced sixty-five thousand pounds of vegetables, including spinach, cabbage, lettuce, okra, celery, cauliflower, squash, corn, salsify, radishes, onions, peas, turnips, beets, beans, melons, cucumbers, tomatoes, pumpkins, peppers, carrots, and parsnips. All the vegetables, valued at nearly $2,000, were sold to officers and organizations on the post.

Colonel Bliss concluded that "on the whole the garden is considered to have been very satisfactory, and as having added greatly to the health and diet of the men."[15] But he pointed out that for the garden to continue to be successful, men must be carefully selected for plowing and planting and even for hoeing and weeding the vegetables. He wrote: "Very few enlisted men are competent gardeners or sufficiently skilled to do satisfactorily or profitably all the work necessary in a large vegetable garden even under a man detailed as chief gardener."[16]

If bandsmen did not spend a lot of time gardening, what kind of life did they generally lead? Army regulations permitted any qualified enlisted man to apply for a position in the band, which was financed through contributions and the post fund. Sometimes provision was even made for additional musical training after a soldier joined the band.[17] Generally he was allowed to stay in the band indefinitely, although if he wanted to return to his company or troop, that was his prerogative. While a band member, he normally forewent the usual regimen of his unit or other common activities.[18]

Fort Bayard had a barrack specifically set aside for the regimental band. It had facilities for nineteen men, the usual number of musicians in the Twenty-fourth Infantry band, which was stationed there for over eight years.[19] The army provided the Twenty-fourth's band with instruments and kept them in good repair. The band members generally had an adequate ration of clothing, including uniforms with chevrons on them.[20] Excused from many other duties, band members spent considerable time in marching drills and practicing music.

The Twenty-fourth's band at Bayard performed at a number of official ceremonies. For example, in April 1891 it marched ninety-six miles to and from Deming, where its members spent nearly a week waiting for and then playing for President Benjamin Harrison, who was moving through the territory.[21] In October 1895 its members and the men of four of Bayard's six infantry companies marched over two miles to Halls Station accompanying the body of Col. Thomas G. Pitcher.[22] In addition to these solemn ceremonies, the band sometimes filled private requests. Within a few days after it arrived at Bayard in 1888, for instance, Silver City leaders engaged it to play at their Fourth of July celebration. Perhaps to encourage local residents' attendance, the city's newspaper editor wrote of the band: "[It] is one of the largest and best in the service. The musicians are all colored. The drum major stands six feet four inches, and is a show by himself."[23] Two years later it entertained delegates to the territory's Democratic convention in Silver City,[24] and in 1893 it filled a request to play at the Deming Irrigation Convention.[25]

One citizen of Silver City objected to the military band's being used for such occasions, pointing out that it competed with local bands. But other residents ignored this complaint and continued to invite the band on whatever occasion they deemed appropriate.[26] Even so, military leaders were careful not to offend local citizens. Perhaps fearing disapproval, they denied a request of Private Potter, Company A, Twenty-fourth Infantry, that the band accompany his minstrel troupe to Silver City for a performance.[27]

This reference to an enterprising soldier's minstrel troupe is a reminder that the men entertained themselves and others when work was slow at the post. Among other buildings at Bayard was an amusement hall with a stage for theatrical performances and lectures. The fact that an officers' lyceum was held in the amusement hall may have indicated that such programs were available to the enlisted personnel as well. The amusement hall was used for dancing, parties, and social gatherings of all sorts. In addition, the post exchange had an amusement room with several billiard tables for the use of the enlisted men.[28]

Special events brought out large crowds, as when on December 25, 1889, Troop D, Tenth Cavalry, held a midnight ball in its barrack. On that occasion Bayard's commander brought charges against the sergeant of the post guard for allowing several members of the guard to leave the guardhouse to attend this Christmas event.[29] On another occasion, much excitement was generated when the army granted Willis Stanley of Silver City permission to perform a balloon ascension on the military reservation on a September Sunday afternoon. Perhaps the military leaders felt that the ascension provided enough excitement for one day, for they rejected Stanley's request to give a theatrical performance in the amusement hall that evening.[30]

When Pvt. James Dickerson, Company F, Twenty-fourth Infantry, requested on behalf of the enlisted men of the post, a half-day holiday in each week to encourage athletic sports, his superiors demurred, citing the large amount of work to be done.[31] Despite the rejection of this request for more free time for athletic sports, however, the men found time for games and exercise.

For most of the enlisted men the preference for physical exercise was stronger than that for religious worship or intellectual stimulation, but the latter were not totally nonexistent. In the 1890s at Fort Bayard a ward of the old hospital building was used as a chapel, and if the commanding officer is to be believed, worship services were held regularly and were well attended. Throughout the army, many enlisted men benefited from libraries and reading rooms established at almost every post or garrison. Shortly after the Civil War, post libraries were merely the sum of company and regimental libraries, these units usually taking their books along when they were reassigned. The War Department attempted to remedy this inefficient system by authorizing only permanent post libraries, financed mainly by expenditures from the post fund. In 1879 the quartermaster general was authorized to supply books, newspapers, and periodicals to post libraries, but the available funds were sharply limited, even though Q.M. Gen. Montgomery Meigs was an enthusiastic supporter of post libraries.[32]

Bayard had two good libraries, one belonging to the post and one belonging to the Twenty-fourth Infantry, the latter existing despite the army's attempts at consolidation. The post library subscribed to many newspapers and magazines, as did several of the cavalry troops and infantry companies.[33] Among fifteen newspaper subscriptions ordered for the post library were the *Albuquerque Democrat and Morning Journal, Kansas City Times, New York Herald, Puck, Nation, Harper's Weekly,* and *Forest and Stream.*[34] The garrison was well supplied with books, newspapers, and magazines; how many of them the enlisted men read is a moot question.

The Army Reorganization Act of 1866 authorized the army to establish schools at its various posts, the post or garrison commanders being responsible for providing the requisite suitable rooms or buildings.[35] This statute also provided for the creation of cavalry and infantry regiments composed only of black enlisted men and stipulated that chaplains be assigned to these newly created black regiments. Because army chaplains were usually assigned to an entire post rather than to an individual regiment, this provision was unique. Besides performing regular religious duties, these chaplains were responsible for secular educational programs for black recruits, who were assumed to be relatively illiterate.[36] This use of chaplains as educators in black regiments quickly became an accepted practice.

The first chaplain of the Twenty-fourth Infantry was John N. Schultz, who began to serve in that capacity in 1869. Schultz had previously served as the first, and only, chaplain for the Thirty-eighth Infantry in Kansas and New Mexico, which was consolidated with the Forty-first Infantry to form the Twenty-fourth. During those early years on the frontier, Schultz set up and ran a school for enlisted men, continuing his educational work with black infantrymen until 1875, when he resigned from the army.[37] D. Ellington Barr was the first regimental chaplain of the Twenty-fifth Infantry, inaugurating a school for enlisted men in Louisiana soon after the regiment was formed. He continued to develop an educational program as the regiment moved westward.[38] These and other early chaplains began a program of education in the black infantry units that was to expand throughout the regiments' service on the American frontier.

Another important early educational leader was Chaplain George Gatewood Mullins, who more than any other person pioneered the army's modern-day education program. When black soldiers responded to Mullins's enthusiastic innovations, he sensed in the men a fierce determination to be free citizens in a free society. His educational program was designed not only to lessen black illiteracy but also to articulate the social and military value of education in the army.[39]

Chaplain Allen Allensworth. (Courtesy Spirit Productions, San Francisco, California.)

When many commanders did not follow the letter of the 1866 act concerning the establishment of schools, in 1878 the War Department began to require all posts, garrisons, and permanent camps to operate schools for all enlisted men, an important step forward for education in the army. Previously, schooling had been an optional service on each post, except on those where black regiments were stationed. The War Department directed the quartermaster department to construct schoolrooms, libraries, reading rooms, and chapels at these posts, supplying them with chairs, tables, desks, lamps, bookshelves, and fuel. Although these new orders served to highlight the existing required programs for the black soldiers, they were deficient in two respects: they did not provide for compulsory schooling for the undereducated enlisted men, and they did not provide for the hiring of trained schoolteachers.[40] Yet even with these deficiencies, progress was made on the army's educational front.

While serving on detached duty as assistant to Gen. Alexander McDowell McCook, the army's chief of education, Chaplain Mullins devised a system to organize all post schools on a similar basis — a move to standardize education in the army. After Mullins himself was elevated to chief of education, in April 1881 he began to implement a program of standardization of textbooks and subject matter in post schools. Before his retirement in 1891, Mullins realized his major goal when in 1889 the Congress passed legislation making attendance at post schools a military obligation for all men without an elementary education.[41]

An important educational leader who built upon the reforms begun by Mullins was Chaplain Allen Allensworth, a well-educated black clergyman affiliated with the Baptist denomination. Allensworth's success was partly the result of his complete acceptance of the racial status quo in the army. When applying for a chaplain's appointment in 1886, for instance, this former slave wrote the adjutant general that he would give no offense because of his race: "I know where the official ends and where the social line begins and have therefore guarded against social intrusion."[42] He reported for duty with the Twenty-fourth Infantry at Fort Supply in Indian Territory, where he operated the post school for over a year and a half, until the regiment was transferred to the Department of Arizona.

When the headquarters of the Twenty-fourth Infantry was established at Fort Bayard in 1888, Allensworth settled there, establishing a broad educational program for the entire regiment. As a trained educator, Allensworth introduced a graded curriculum at Fort Bayard's school, and he devised a study outline for the enrollees. In March 1889 he wrote a booklet entitled *Outline of Course of Study, and the Rules Governing Post Schools of Ft. Bayard, N.M.*, which detailed the graded levels of his program and reviewed the content of each subject taught at every level. His program was divided into two parts, one for the soldiers and one for the children who lived on the post. He designated the subject matter to be taught each day of the week. For example, in the soldiers' program, on Mondays he taught grammar, on Tuesdays arithmetic, on Wednesdays bookkeeping and writing (with emphasis on military records and writing), and so on for the remainder of the week until all the basic subjects had received attention.[43]

Allensworth arranged for Bayard's post chapel to double as a schoolroom. Because it was inconvenient to move standard desks in and out of a room used for two purposes, he recommended that more-easily movable desks be built by men of the Bayard command.[44] When more space to teach noncommissioned officers was needed, he arranged for a gun storage shed to be converted into a classroom. He was diligent in obtaining textbooks, stationery, slates, crayons, pencils, visual aids, and other supplies. He even made contact with the civilian population in his search for support and supplies.[45] So dedicated was he that when funds were short, he sometimes spent his own money for such items.

Allensworth made classroom instruction available both during the day and in the evening. He recruited enlisted men to take instruction in the post school, and when they did not attend voluntarily, the officers of the companies and troops ordered them to attend.[46]

Like other chaplains of black regiments, Allensworth was hard pressed to find competent teachers. If qualified teachers were not among the men at Bayard, he did not hesitate to have men from other posts temporarily assigned to him. In this manner he obtained Twenty-fourth Infantry Pvts. James W. Abbott, John R. Green, and David Holden, all from Arizona (San Carlos, Fort Apache, and Fort Huachuca, respectively), to teach in his school.[47] He also used Pvt. Willis Bailey of Company F of Bayard, retaining Bailey's services even after he was appointed corporal.[48] (Most teachers were privates. Problems sometimes arose because noncommissioned officers often resisted schooling under their tutelage after having commanded them during working hours.)

Because of his achievements and reputation, in 1891 Allensworth was invited to Toronto, Canada, to deliver a paper entitled "Education in the United States Army" at the annual meeting of the National Education Association. Although the War Department turned down his request for official permission to attend this meeting, Allensworth attended by receiving a leave of absence and paying his own expenses. In his paper Allensworth pointed out that the army's educational program was a means to provide soldiers' lives with new and greater dimensions and to make soldiers more responsible and useful citizens.[49]

Allensworth desired to display a model army schoolroom at the 1892 Chicago World's Fair, but his superiors rejected his proposal because they did not feel post schools at that time were as good as the model might indicate.[50] Even though Allensworth was disappointed that his proposal was denied, he was not unaware that his model was more ideal than real, an issue that did not concern him. The larger purpose of his request was to use the occasion further to publicize and improve the status of the army's schools.

Committed to the moral worth of education and able to demonstrate to the army the practical value of education, chaplains in the black infantry regiments, including Allensworth at Fort Bayard, made vital and significant contributions to the army's educational program. They demonstrated that a post educational program, when properly conducted under competent teachers, had a beneficial effect upon the morale, discipline, and esprit de corps of a garrison. The army's records revealed that emphasis upon learning paid dividends because the military service contained a better-educated group of enlisted men. Furthermore, chaplains and commanders claimed that school attendance made the men more obedient soldiers and kept them from undesirable activities.

That may have been true in some cases, but despite the presence of a school at Bayard, some of the men there continued to indulge in gambling, fighting, and drinking, mainstays in the life of many ordinary enlisted men stationed at frontier military posts. Gambling seemed to increase in the days immediately following a payday, the men finding both time and secret places to gamble, even though the army frowned upon this activity. A blatant incident of gambling occurred in October

1888, when John D. Sparling, Company F, Twenty-fourth Infantry, while serving as sergeant of the post guard, permitted prisoners in his charge to play cards and gamble in the general prison room of the post guardhouse. To make matters worse he gambled with them. For this action, Sparling was court-martialed.[51]

Sometimes gambling and fighting coincided. Of the two, fighting was the more serious offense. Tension among the enlisted men often resulted in altercations during holidays. In one case, on December 25, 1888, Pvt. Richard Cox attacked Pvt. H. Lambert (both of Company D, Twenty-fourth Infantry) with a hatchet. When Sgt. E. Ramber and others took the weapon from Cox, Cox then attacked the unarmed Lambert with a knife.[52] In another incident exactly one year later, two infantrymen, Pvts. Dick Richardson and Lee Chisholm, got into a fight during which Richardson slashed Chisholm's face with a knife, whereupon Chisholm drew a razor on Richardson. Later Chisholm threatened to shoot Richardson with a loaded shotgun.[53]

But trouble was not limited to Christmastime. In the following summer, infantry Pvts. George Tilman and Charles L. Anderson engaged in a fistfight, after which Tilman acquired a shotgun and threatened to kill Anderson. Other men of Company D had to disarm him by force to prevent further trouble.[54] In March 1891 Tenth cavalrymen Pvts. Stanley Chester and James Smith got into an argument in Carey and Givens's saloon in Central City, and Smith struck Chester with a chain, fracturing his skull. While Smith languished in the post guardhouse, Chester lay in the post hospital in a dangerous condition with a temperature of 105.5°.[55]

Sometimes fighting or other antisocial behavior was the result of drunkenness, whether liquor was consumed while the men were on work detail or during leisure hours. On one occasion the sergeant of the guard sent Cpl. Lawrence J. Julius, Company F, Twenty-fourth Infantry, to quell a disturbance in the quarters of the post laundress. Upon arriving there Julius placed his gun in a corner of the room, accepted a drink of whiskey, and then added to the disorder and confusion by his own "uproarious conduct." Another corporal of the guard had to quiet the disturbance, of which Julius was then a part.[56]

A few weeks later infantryman Pvt. Edward Williams got drunk and used violent and abusive language concerning an absent member of his company, refusing to stop after being ordered to do so. In addition, he refused to go to the guardhouse, and he had to be taken there forcibly. At the guardhouse he assaulted Sgt. James Watkins, striking him several times in the face, this action bringing additional charges against him. In another incident, when Pvt. Charlie Stargall of Troop L, Tenth Cavalry, drank too much, he began to use loud and profane language. Sgt. Shelborn Shropshire ordered him to cease, to which Stargall responded: "I would like to see some God Damn nigger make me stop. . . . I am ready to go to the guard house now." He was placed in the guardhouse, but he continued to curse.[57] On a different occasion, when Charles Ridley, trumpeter for Troop L, Tenth Cavalry, got intoxicated, he was thrown into the guardhouse and for his insolence there, he was court-martialed.[58]

Charges were also brought against Cpl. Ernest Rowland, Company A, Twenty-fourth Infantry, when, after drinking too much, he went to a performance at Fort Bayard's theatrical hall. While there, he became loud and boisterous in the presence of an audience including ladies, and he used obscene language, refusing to stop when the sergeant of the guard tried to keep him quiet.[59] More serious was the action of Pvt. Robert Jones, Company D, Twenty-fourth Infantry, who with a bottle of whiskey in his hand, broke into the bedroom of Lizzy McCarthy, a domestic servant employed by assistant surgeon Capt. W. H. Arthur.[60] A few days later Cpl. Henry James of the same company entered the backyard of an officer's quarters, after which he was found in the room of a woman servant in a drunken condition.[61]

By 1893 drunkenness was a serious problem among the black enlisted men at Bayard. The post surgeon reported an increase in the cases of alcoholism, which concerned the army, although its leaders did not take responsibility for this development. Colonel Bliss wrote: "Thirty years ago, or twenty five, say[,] the Colored race was perhaps the most temperate people in the world in regards to drink. During that time they have steadily increased in intemperance, from causes unknown, but which are outside of the army."[62] On the contrary, in view of the isolation, lack of social opportunities, hard work, and boredom, sometimes all mixed together, it is small wonder that soldiers, both black and white, turned to drink.

Attempts to obtain alcohol created another set of problems. While cavalryman Clay Pointer served as corporal of the stable guards and was in charge of the herd guards of his troop, he quit his post and rode his horse to Central City to visit a saloon.[63] Filled with saloons, Central City was about a mile from the Bayard military reservation, and its proximity created temptation not only for Pointer but also for other enlisted men. Because of this undesirable situation and the lack of a post canteen, in 1889 the commanding officer at Bayard wanted to authorize the post trader to sell beer and light wines, which in his opinion would prevent many minor offenses.[64] The army, however, disallowed the commander's recommendation.

Another of Central City's major attractions for the soldiers at Bayard was the fifty or so prostitutes there. According to Bayard's commander, most of the prostitutes were supported by the enlisted men, and "in order that this may be done a great deal of going out of the Post must take place, either with or without permission."[65] When the army discouraged the men from going to Central City to visit prostitutes, some of the soldiers attempted to satisfy their sexual urges by bringing women onto the post. While on detached service at Fort Cummings, Sgt. Mailton Ross, Troop D, Tenth Cavalry, permitted Daisy Shropshire and Luella Brooke, women of admitted bad repute, to enter the post and remain overnight, ordering other soldiers to vacate a room and to sleep in a kitchen so that he could occupy the room with the two women. To make matters worse, he fed the women from government stores, depriving his men of their designated rations.[66]

Other men dealt with their sexual urges by approaching women already on the post. For example, Pvt. Peter McCann, Troop D, Tenth Cavalry, on two occasions was found at reveille in his sleeping habit in the servants' quarters of an officer.[67] On another occasion, Pvt. Henderson Hucksty, Troop L, Tenth Cavalry, entered the servants' room of the post trader, where he assaulted a female servant whose cries attracted the attention of members of the post guard.[68] In yet another instance, Pvt. James W. Snyder of Company D, Twenty-fourth Infantry, made advances toward Nora Brasshe, a cook at the teamster's mess at Bayard. When she resisted him, he knocked her down and beat her with a heavy stick, then threatened and struck her with a pistol.[69] Finally, Pvt. William Parker, Troop L, Tenth Cavalry, beat and kicked Fannie Potter, a servant, when she did not yield to his advances.[70]

Sometimes trouble concerning women involved the wives of the enlisted men. Pvt. Charles Waters, Troop L, Tenth Cavalry, wrote a letter containing improper proposals to Ella Johnson, wife of Pvt. James

Black Soldiers at Fort Stanton Army Hospital, ca. 1900. (Photo by John J. Hensley, Courtesy Rio Grande Historical Collections, New Mexico State University Library, Las Cruces, Neg. #RG80–102–10.)

M. Johnson, Company A, Twenty-fourth Infantry. Not offended by Waters's overtures, Mrs. Johnson in turn complained to the commanding officer that her husband had threatened her, perhaps because of her receptiveness to Waters. In another incident, the wife of Corporal Jones, Company D, Twenty-fourth Infantry, carried a concealed weapon into the post and shot and killed her husband, after which the sheriff at Central City arrested her for murder.[71]

In the fall of 1890 a Bayard soldier killed his mistress and the town constable at Central City. He was arrested and placed in the Grant County jail in Silver City. After languishing in jail for nine months, during which time the army refused to pay him, the soldier reportedly sued the government for back pay.[72] The outcome of his trial for murder and his suit for money is not known. These stories are not intended to suggest that black soldiers were less moral or more violent than white soldiers; rather, these antisocial demonstrations are reminders that like the whites, the blacks were not immune to crimes of passion.

Also like white soldiers, black soldiers contracted social diseases. Those stationed at Fort Bayard were infected during their visits with the prostitutes of Central City. Some were given disability discharges for constitutional syphilis, and at least one was discharged because he had syphilitic rheumatism. In all cases the army made it clear that these diseases were not contracted in the line of duty, the degree of disability thus being listed as either one-half or one-fourth.[73] Despite these cases, on the basis of admittedly incomplete records, the numbers of black enlisted men contracting social diseases appears to have been extremely small.

Other communicable diseases were also of concern to military leaders. In the spring of 1891 when both the grippe and measles appeared within the civilian population near Fort Bayard, the army attempted to prevent their spread to the men of the garrison. But in the case of a measles epidemic, they were unsuccessful. Shortly thereafter, cases of diphtheria appeared at the post, keeping the surgeon and his helpers busy.[74] A lone reference to dysentery in the 1880s records indicates that this disease was not common at Bayard at that time,[75] and the scourge of scurvy had long since passed.

Another antisocial behavior was thievery. The men stole various personal items from each other: Pvt. Charles Waters, for instance, took a pair of leather gauntlets valued at $1 from Sgt. James H. Alexander, both men of Troop L, Tenth Cavalry.[76] More serious, however, were the actions of farrier James Livingston, Troop D, Tenth Cavalry, who without permission rode to Central City on a pony owned by Capt. A.S.B. Keyes.[77] A form of stealing occurred when enlisted cavalrymen failed to pay a total of $90 owed to a Chinese laundryman named Yee Wah for washing their clothes over a period of time. Because the Chinese businessman was known as industrious and honest, the commanding officer was convinced that the request for payment was valid, and he encouraged the men's officers to pressure the soldiers to pay their debts.[78] On another occasion, during a night in January 1891 a discharged soldier named James Williams broke into the post corral and stole two sets of double harnesses. A burro disappeared the same night, and Williams was accused of taking it; certainly the circumstantial evidence was against him.[79]

Sometimes the actions of convicted thieves revealed their characters. Enlisted man Albert S. Crouch was a case in point. Confined to Bayard's guardhouse, Crouch, who had a reputation as a bad and dangerous man, was insubordinate, going out of his way to annoy others. In violation of army regulations he wrote letters directly to military superiors, including the secretary of war, asking that he be confined at Leavenworth Military Prison, where he apparently believed he would be more comfortable. His bad conduct was contagious.

He executed a successful escape plan along with Pvt. Peter McCann, who was in the guardhouse because he, in turn, had allowed a prisoner to escape while he himself was a guard. Although the sheriff of Deming captured and returned Crouch and McCann, their escape had been initially successful because of the cooperation of guard Cpl. Lawrence J. Julius, whom Crouch had bribed. As a result, McCann was placed in irons and tried for desertion, while Crouch continued to languish in the Bayard guardhouse. For allowing prisoners to escape, Julius was dishonorably discharged and sentenced to four years at Alcatraz Island. Bayard's commanding officer recommended that Crouch also be sent to Alcatraz.[80]

Related to thievery was a case of forgery involving a soldier. Pvt. Thomas Pearce, Troop L, Tenth Cavalry, wrote a check to the post trader for $3, claiming that he was Pvt. William Wilson of the same troop and signing Wilson's name to the check. Pearce was charged with forgery and perjury and placed in the guardhouse. When he escaped, Bayard's commanding officer offered a $30 reward for his capture.[81] Apparently he was never found, for he was added to the list of army deserters.

The causes of thievery and forgery were numerous and surely varied in each instance. Perhaps the men wanted more money for entertainment and services. Even though the army supplied the men with food and shelter, their small paychecks often did not cover the cost of items such as laundry service, whiskey, and sex. Another contributing factor may have been a desire for more material possessions. Certainly the enlisted men of that era were not wealthy in that regard. When Pvt. Job Reed of the Twenty-fourth Infantry deserted from his temporary post at Fort Selden in November 1889, he left behind the following property:[82]

    a number of cartridges
    1 Springfield rifle
    1 field belt
    4 shirts
    1 pillow
    1 mattress
    1 mattress cover
    1 canteen

1 tin cup
1 knife
1 fork
1 spoon
1 meat can
1 haversack
1 sack cover
1 locker
1 shelter tent, half
3 blankets
5 undershirts
1 undershirt, civilian
1 pair stockings
2 pairs Berlin gloves

This list not only reveals the specific material possessions of one deserter but also gives an indication of the kinds and amount of property most soldiers owned at that time. If soldiers joined the post–Civil War army in order to increase their material wealth, they surely were disappointed.

Of all the problems associated with soldiers in the West, the most serious was desertion. Such action on the part of a trooper struck at the very heart of the army. In 1889 Brig. Gen. Nelson A. Miles, commander of the Division of the Pacific, asserted: "The principal evil besetting the army is desertion." Two years later Secretary of War Redfield Proctor published statistics that illustrated the breadth of the problem. From January 1, 1867, to June 30, 1891, 88,475 men had deserted from an army that numbered only twenty-five thousand soldiers annually throughout most of that period. He estimated that the annual average desertion rate for those twenty-four and one half years was 14.8 percent. The peak years were 1871 and 1872, when nearly one-third of the men in the army deserted in each of those years.[83]

Black soldiers as a group had a considerably lower rate of desertion than whites. From 1880 through 1889, deserters from the Ninth and Tenth Cavalry Regiments totalled 393 and 180, respectively. By comparison, the lowest white cavalry regiment was the First with 703, while the Fourth had the highest number at 1,116. More remarkable was the record of the black infantry regiments. Throughout the 1880s only 59

Mansfield Robinson, Twenty-fourth Infantry. (Courtesy Edward M. Coffman.)

men deserted from the Twenty-fourth, while 104 left the Twenty-fifth. The lowest number among white regiments, by contrast, was the Second with 281, while the Fifteenth, with 676 deserters, had the highest number.[84]

Soldiers deserted for many reasons directly related to army life: the inordinate demands of hard labor, poor quarters, poor or inadequate food, lack of recreation, harsh officers, low pay, lengthy intervals between paydays, restlessness, drunkenness, poor quality of recruits, and the indifference, if not outright hostility, of civilian society. Sometimes the men deserted for personal reasons, such as homesickness, missing their families, or the desire to return to civilian life. Then, too, the rise and fall of the nation's economy affected desertions, the numbers being lower during economic depressions when jobs outside the army were less readily available. A relationship also existed between desertion and seasonal economic activity: those men who enlisted in the fall, served through the winter, and then deserted in the spring when jobs were more plentiful were known as snowbirds. One officer estimated that almost two-thirds of all desertions occurred in the spring months.[85]

Adj. Gen. Richard C. Drum believed that restlessness and lack of understanding of the difference between the enlistment oath and an ordinary job contract were the culprits behind desertions. This assertion placed the problem in the perspective of American society. In the last quarter of the nineteenth century, industrial corporations had difficulties with absenteeism, and turnover among factory workers was large. If a person did not like a job, he simply left it, especially if another appeared to be available.[86] Seemingly, many men approached enlistment in the same vein.

Deserters usually were not caught, and if they were, punishment was not terribly severe, despite the fact that the army considered desertion a serious crime. As time passed, punishment for deserters was made even lighter. The army's deliberate efforts to better the conditions of military life, however, cut the general desertion rate in the 1890s to about 5 percent.[87]

The end of the Indian Wars was the stimulus for these improved conditions. Dangers were reduced and more time for athletics and other off-duty activities was available. Although these more desirable conditions in the 1890s were a factor in reducing desertions among white troopers, but black desertions did not decrease; indeed, their numbers rose. Fewer blacks had deserted in the late 1870s and early 1880s when Indian resistance was high than in the 1890s when danger was less and leisure time was greater. How can this be explained? Although many other factors were involved in black desertion in the 1890s, boredom surely played a role.[90]

Despite increased desertion among black soldiers during the 1890s, they still deserted in lower percentages than did white soldiers, a fact that had been true throughout the post–Civil War period. More than likely, the lower incidence of desertion among black soldiers resulted from their realizing that life in the military — hard though it was — was more desirable than life in the civilian population, where racial prejudice and discrimination were harsher and often interfered with their work, as well as other aspects of their lives.

IX. The Final Years, 1898–1900

When 273 soldiers of the Twenty-fourth Infantry vacated Fort Bayard in October 1896, for exactly two years New Mexico Territory had no black soldiers stationed within its borders, a condition that ended on October 4, 1898, when 152 enlisted men of Companies E and F of the Twenty-fifth Infantry arrived at Forts Wingate and Bayard, respectively. These men had traveled by rail from Montauk Point, the easternmost tip of Long Island, New York, a distance of over 2,600 miles. In June 1899 these infantry companies left Forts Bayard and Wingate, concluding the presence of black infantrymen in New Mexico Territory. During this final nine-month stay, the number of black infantrymen totalled nearly 250.[1]

Serving along with these infantrymen in New Mexico were troops of the Ninth Cavalry. On January 8, 1899, Troop H arrived at Wingate, and on June 22, 1899, Troop K arrived at Bayard, just two days before the black infantrymen there moved out. Troop K had been stationed at Fort Huachuca, Arizona, and had moved to Bayard by rail and by horseback. In November 1899 all but twenty-one men of Troop K moved out of Bayard, and a month later the remaining detachment left. In February 1900 Troop L from San Antonio, Texas, joined Troop H at Wingate, the two troops residing there until July 1900. Each of these troops averaged just over one hundred enlisted men.

Counting new enlistments, about 325 individual cavalrymen were in New Mexico during this time.[2] Counting both cavalrymen and infantrymen, from October 1898 to July 1900 the monthly average of black enlisted men in New Mexico was just over two hundred. In all, about 575 black troopers served in New Mexico during this final

Enlisted Men and Officers, Troop H, Ninth Cavalry, Fort Wingate, New Mexico, ca. 1899. (Photo by Phelps, Courtesy Museum of New Mexico, Santa Fe, Neg. #98372.)

period.[3] As had been true in the past, the movements and stations of black soldiers in New Mexico at this time were not unrelated to those of white troopers, specifically the Fifteenth Infantry and the Seventh Cavalry.[4]

During the waning years of the existence of Forts Bayard and Wingate, the few cavalrymen present continued to do some of the jobs their predecessors had done. In May 1899, for example, a lieutenant and a detachment of thirty enlisted men of Troop F, Ninth Cavalry, traveled to Arizona Territory to help authorities disinfect and quarantine an Indian village.[5] In August a lieutenant and twenty-five dismounted enlisted cavalrymen proceeded by rail from Fort Wingate to Navajo Springs, Arizona Territory, to assist with suppressing a possible Indian uprising. But the trouble was not serious and they returned to New Mexico almost immediately.[6] Less than a month later, a captain and sixty-eight men of Troop H left Wingate on a practice march. After five days of marching they arrived at Albuquerque and went into camp. For a week they participated in exercises at the Territorial Fair, after which they returned to their post.[7]

While the cavalrymen were engaging in these routine activities, the infantrymen who were tied down at the posts led even more humdrum lives. With little real work to do, they worked at keeping busy. The routine of army life was lax, and boredom was a way of life. Post returns for this period were virtually devoid of reports of activities. The most common entry was: "The men of the command performed usual garrison duties."

Under such conditions, leisure activities, especially baseball, provided diversion and contact with the outside world. Soldiers in the postwar West had taken up the popular sport of baseball early on, many finding time to play the game during the many years that troops were called upon to suppress Indians. Companies and troops often had their own ball teams, some of which were composed of both officers and enlisted men. When conditions and time permitted, the teams competed with others whose members were stationed at the same post. Sometimes all-post teams played those at other posts or teams composed of civilians from nearby communities. Company and troop funds provided money for baseball equipment, as the army did not provide athletic gear.[8] When the Indian Wars ended in the early 1890s, activity was stepped up to fill the available time with what would soon become a national pastime. The Ninth Cavalry's Troop L at Fort Wingate had a baseball team, complete with matching uniforms for its dozen members. They had bats, balls, gloves, and full equipment for the team's catcher. In view of the dwindling numbers of military forts in New Mexico, they played whatever opposition was available, usually nearby civilian teams.

During these years of relative inactivity, even picture-taking became a big event. The noncommissioned officers of Troop L, with dress uniforms and stacked arms, posed in front of a wooden military building draped with a giant American flag. About the same time, all the members of Troop H posed for a picture, soldiers with guns and officers with swords.

The army had feared fires, or the prospects of them, at its western posts throughout the late nineteenth century, and at Fort Wingate the year 1899 revealed that such fears were not without justification. At 3:15 A.M., July 27, a fire broke out in a vacant cavalry stable. The guard sounded the alarm and the men of the garrison promptly rushed to the scene with fire-fighting apparatus. The fire quickly spread to a nearby

Baseball Team, Troop L, Ninth Cavalry, Fort Wingate, New Mexico, ca. 1900. (Photo by Imperial Photo Gallery, Courtesy Museum of New Mexico, Santa Fe, Neg. #98374.)

empty stable, but realizing the two empty stables could not be saved, the men turned their efforts to the occupied stables, which they were able to protect, saving the public animals in them, as well as nearby property. The post commander wrote: "The officers and men of the command worked well and it was only by the greatest exertion on the part of all that the other stables were not destroyed." Including the buildings, quartermaster supplies, and ordnance stores, the losses amounted to $3,194.22. The cause of the fire was unknown.[9]

Before year's end, Wingate had two other fires. When an unknown person attempted to rob the commissary safe and caused a fire, the soldiers extinguished the blaze so rapidly that the damage done to the commissary amounted to only $100 and repairs were relatively easy to make.[10] A few weeks later the post sawmill burned, the loss being $5,500. The post commander believed that someone had deliberately set this fire.[11] Three fires in six months certainly justified suspicion, if not accusation. To say that a soldier or soldiers set the fires to enliven life at Wingate is hardly fair, but in view of the boredom, the possibility

Noncommissioned Officers, Troop L, Ninth Cavalry, Fort Wingate, New Mexico, ca. 1900. (Photo by Imperial Photo Gallery, Courtesy Museum of New Mexico, Santa Fe, Neg. #98373.)

is there. Certainly the fires did break the routine of an otherwise dull existence.

When the 221 enlisted men of the Twenty-fifth Infantry moved out of Forts Wingate and Bayard in June 1899, they traveled by rail to San Francisco, where the Wingate men boarded the *Valencia* and the Bayard men boarded the *Pennsylvania,* both ships bound for the Philippine Islands. The other companies of the Twenty-fifth Infantry stationed in Arizona, Texas, and Colorado were shipped to the Philippines at the same time, forming part of the 4,425 men transferred from San Francisco via Honolulu to Manila.[12] When the Ninth Cavalry left Fort Wingate in July 1900, Troop L moved to Fort Apache, Arizona, and Troop H was transferred to the Philippines via San Francisco.[13] The soldiers were shipped to the Philippine Islands at the turn of the century to help put down Filipino insurgents led by Emilio Aguinaldo. These black infantrymen and cavalrymen were among the last to serve in New Mexico before it became a state in 1912.

Between 1868 and 1891 the army abandoned twelve of New Mexico's sixteen forts. In 1894 and 1896, Forts Marcy and Stanton were evacuated permanently. Only Forts Bayard and Wingate remained, the former closing in 1900 and the latter in 1912. Because black soldiers had served at Bayard until a few months before its final closing and at Wingate until a few years before its end, the removal of these enlisted men closely coincided with the end of the army's military presence in New Mexico Territory. The two nearly simultaneous events marked the end of an era.[14]

X. Prejudice and Discrimination

Following the Civil War, the American people regularly praised the veterans of that great conflict, holding celebrations and awarding numerous accolades and honors to those citizens who had served as temporary soldiers. For these men, the U.S. government was generous with monuments, commemorations, and pensions. All of this, however, was in stark contrast to the treatment afforded the professional soldiers who served the country in the postwar period. After 1866 a pervasive anti-military ethos enveloped men who served in the army. Although these men served during the period of the Indian Wars, they were considered peacetime soldiers, and they did not command the respect directed toward the thousands of volunteer citizen-soldiers who had fought in the Civil War. Another strike against them was that this postwar army had few members who were from the upper or middle classes. Rather, it was composed primarily of lower-class urban workers, European immigrants, and blacks, toward whom Americans often expressed contempt, especially as members of this peacetime army.

Except for a few artillerymen who served in forts along the Atlantic and Gulf coasts, most men in the post–Civil War army served on the frontier, stationed there to protect Americans as they traveled to and settled in the West. They broke the resistance of marauding Indians and patrolled reservation boundaries. In many specific instances they protected individual settlers, and their presence discouraged additional attacks upon others. Farmers, ranchers, miners, and railroad construction workers often called upon the military establishment, assuming without question that help would be forthcoming.

Under these circumstances, one might assume that all westerners were appreciative of the soldiers' efforts. Such was not the case. Members of the nonmilitary population, in fact, often criticized the soldiers for not taking action or not acting quickly enough. And when the soldiers were unsuccessful in a specific mission, the wrath of an unappreciative population poured out. To be sure, some frontiersmen praised the soldiers, but for every person who could say that the army protected him, another — and perhaps more — were critical.

In an era when Americans were committed to a strong work ethic, many civilians in the West could find little to admire in the spectacle of drunken soldiers carousing on payday. And when a few enlisted men ran afoul of local authorities, the population often generalized that all soldiers were non-law-abiding no-accounts. Fighting, gambling, and stealing on the part of the men did not help endear them to the civilians. The presence of houses of prostitution, saloons, and gambling halls near almost every fort — and the soldiers frequenting them — offended the Puritan ideals of local inhabitants, even when these inhabitants did not always live up to those ideals themselves.

Of all the services the multipurpose army provided after the Civil War, in the long run probably the most important was its economic contribution to western development.[1] It significantly strengthened local economies when it purchased meat, vegetables, lumber, fuel, forage, and other supplies in great quantities. Although soldiers' paychecks were individually small, when a hundred or more men were at a post their collective income further stimulated the local economy. But even those westerners who often made money because of the presence of the army and its troopers did not necessarily respect them. Prostitutes, saloon keepers, horse and mule dealers, freighters, beef contractors, producers of agricultural products, and others were glad the army was in the West, but they did not necessarily like its enlisted men and they did not hesitate to prey upon them.

Black soldiers represented nearly one-tenth of the army's effective strength. In many western commands, they made up more than one-half of the available military force. The civilian population's prejudice toward peacetime soldiers was exacerbated when those soldiers were black. Local newspapers did not help the situation when they published derogatory statements. The editor of a New Mexico newspaper, for example, was sharply critical when Chief Victorio was frustrating the

White Mountain Apaches (Sgt. Jim and Bonito) and "Renegade Negro" (a former soldier?), ca. 1883. (Photo by Ben Wittick, Courtesy Museum of New Mexico, Santa Fe, Neg. #102053.)

army: "The experiences through which the people of Southern New Mexico have passed during the past two months are sufficient to convince any sane man that the portion of the United States Army known as the Ninth Cavalry is totally unfit to fight Indians." He continued: "We simply state the concrete fact that negro companies in Southern New Mexico have been whipped every time they have met Indians, except when the instinct of self-preservation has caused them to run away just in time to keep from being whipped." The Las Cruces editor concluded his diatribe by writing: "Let the Ninth be dismounted or disbanded . . . [so that its members] might contribute to the nation's wealth as pickers of cotton and hoers of corn, or to its amusement as a travelling minstrel troupe. As soldiers on the western frontier they are worse than useless — they are a fraud and a nuisance."[2]

When an officer of the Ninth Cavalry visited the newspaper editor and set him straight concerning the performance of black enlisted men, in the next issue the editor admitted that the men had done better than he had been led to believe. But he could not resist concluding: "Our faith in negro troops is not strong. We know that the African race is lacking in that best substitute for bravery — pride."[3] Despite his request that his readers "give the Ninth another chance," within a few months, his prejudiced diatribes again were appearing in his columns.

Further revealing unfounded white prejudice was a lengthy newspaper article in which the writer claimed that black men lacked the ambition necessary to make good soldiers, and that blacks were unable to endure the hardships of mountain warfare. The writer claimed that during military engagements "the colored troops have repeatedly thrown away their cartridges for an excuse to get to the rear." He continued: "They have repeatedly refused to follow their officers, who, placing themselves in front, have ordered a charge, and rushed forward only to find themselves alone." He concluded: "Such troops may do for garrison duty, but in the field, especially against Indian[s], they are of no more account than so many wooden men."[4] Although the blacks' excellent record speaks for itself, these writers unfortunately were expressing or reinforcing the cherished myths of many whites.

Hostile whites often harassed the black soldiers when the latter were outside the forts' gates during their leisure hours or on other occasions. Disputes in bars and gambling houses invariably took on racial overtones if black troopers were involved. An unwritten rule appeared to be that white civilians could murder black soldiers with impunity, for these individuals were seldom punished for such crimes. A black soldier suspected of a law violation, however, often became the target of unrestrained abuse and violence at the hands of the local authorities.

Sometimes soldiers experienced the prejudice of a civilian population even while performing soldierly duties. The previously mentioned refusal of a New Mexico rancher to lend a saddle to a black private sent to secure help for a group of his buddies pinned down by Indian fire surely was such an example.[5] At other times black soldiers ran up against unofficial but strict customs that called for the separation of the races. In 1890 while returning to Fort Bayard from the Army General Hospital at Hot Springs, Arkansas, a recuperating black soldier reportedly had to go forty-eight hours without food because neither on the train nor at a station could he buy even a cup of coffee.[6]

Plenty of references reveal that many people doing business with the army did not hesitate to provide inferior animals, food, and supplies for the soldiers, and the evidence that black soldiers were the objects of a considerable share of this cheating is great. In 1867 supposedly fresh vegetables furnished to the men at Fort Cummings quickly spoiled, and thirty-seven thousand pounds of bacon and eighteen hundred pounds of ham were of such poor quality when purchased that almost immediately it was unfit for human consumption.[7] When poor beef was supplied to the men of the One Hundred Twenty-fifth Infantry at Fort Bascom in 1867, a white officer threatened to annul the contract.[8] A quarter of a century later, the post commander at Fort Bayard was forced to make a similar threat.[9] In 1879 a veterinary surgeon of the Ninth Cavalry charged that recently purchased horses to be used by black cavalrymen had been "bishoped" — that is, the sellers had filed and fixed the animals' teeth to deceive the purchasers in regard to their ages.[10]

When a few black troopers were closing down Fort Selden, railroad expressmen, whose conduct was of "contemptuous indifference," had thrown a delivery of fresh beef off a fast-moving train. When the beef struck the ground it rolled about fifty feet, whereupon the sack burst and the meat became unfit to eat because of dirt and bruises. Selden's commander wrote that "this inflicts a grave injury upon the inhabitants of this command," and he pressured the agents of Wells Fargo and

Company to halt this practice, which might have resulted from racial prejudice.[11] These examples alone are not sufficient to prove civilian workers' and businessmen's contempt for black soldiers, but they are representative of many similar references in the military records and they raise legitimate questions concerning discrimination.

When the army decided to move the Twenty-fourth Infantry from Fort Bayard to Fort Douglas, Utah, in 1896, not everyone in Salt Lake City liked the idea. The Salt Lake *Tribune* published an editorial entitled "An Unfortunate Change," claiming that the people of the city had serious reservations: they did not like the possibility of "direct contact with drunken colored soldiers on the way from the city to Fort Douglas."[12] When word of this opposition to black troopers reached the members of the Twenty-fourth Infantry at Fort Bayard, Pvt. Thomas A. Ernest of Company E wrote the following letter to the editor of the *Tribune:*

> The enlisted men of the Twenty-fourth infantry, as probably the people of Salt Lake City know, are negroes, but there are some things about the twenty-fourth that the people of Salt Lake City probably do not know. There are as many gentlemen in the Twenty-fourth infantry as there are in any other regiment of like arm of service. The Twenty-fourth ranks as one of the cleanest, best-drilled and best-disciplined regiments in the United States Army. . . . They are soldiers now, it is true, but they believe that they are engaged in an honorable calling. They have enlisted to uphold the honor and dignity of their country. . . .
>
> The negro is known for his obedience to and respect for law and order, and we object to being classed as lawless barbarians. We were men before we were soldiers, we are men now, and will continue to be men after we are through soldiering. We ask the people of Salt Lake City to treat us as such. . . . It is true that we have been stationed on the frontier for the past twenty-two years, but none of us have become savages. We are proud of our regiment's reputation, and confident of our ability to maintain it, and the people of Salt Lake City have nothing to fear from the men of the Twenty-fourth infantry even though they are negroes.[13]

To the credit of the newspaper, it printed this letter a few days before the infantrymen from New Mexico arrived in Utah. A year later the *Tribune* published an extensive apology, concluding with the complimentary statement that "the regiment has lived down the apprehensions awakened when the announcement of their coming was made and they are now appreciated at their worth, as citizens and soldiers above reproach."[14] Despite this turnaround, many of the citizens of the West, including New Mexicans, continued to hold prejudices toward black troopers.

Throughout the late nineteenth century, white and black soldiers often served at the same posts concurrently. What did white soldiers think and do when they were stationed with black soldiers? When both groups were in the field together, they often depended on each other for survival: danger tended to obliterate the color line. While fighting Indians, neither group had the time nor inclination to be concerned about color. But occasionally prejudice showed itself on the posts. From time to time fights between whites and blacks occurred, sometimes, but not always, manifesting racial overtones. A white officer perhaps best summarized conditions at the mixed garrisons when he wrote: "There appears to be no trouble or bad feelings between white and colored troops . . . they do not mix, neither do they quarrel." White soldiers usually shunned their black comrades, and members of both races participated in their own social and recreational activities.

Normally the posts had segregated company athletic teams, but garrisons sponsored integrated teams when they competed with those from other posts or from the civilian population. Blacks occasionally attended on-post dances, but always with the tacit understanding that they would bring their own companions and would not attempt to dance with white women. The records suggest that the attention of black soldiers to white women precipitated most of the quarrels between enlisted men of the two races. Despite such occasional conflict, the daily military contact and social relations between the races and the fact that black soldiers shared equally in the dangers and boredom of frontier service probably tended to dissipate some of the prejudices of both groups.[15]

Was the army itself prejudiced toward the black soldiers? When Civil War–era politicians debated whether blacks were to be a part of the peacetime army, some military officers spoke against it, even though many blacks had distinguished themselves during the wartime emergency. When the decision was made to allow blacks in the peacetime army, many military leaders were quick to support a segregated army. Black enlisted men could join the army, but they had to serve in all-black cavalry and infantry regiments.

In terms of structure, the postwar black regiments were exactly the same as the white regiments, except that the former were assigned chaplains with specific instructions to provide schooling. Was this a sign of prejudice or was it simply a sign of the army's concern for its enlisted men? Educated northern black soldiers did not need rudimentary schooling, but illiterate former southern slaves could profit from it. Whatever the army's motivation or the black reaction to the educational provisions of the law, a more educated group of enlisted men meant a better army, and the educational program proved to be more than a qualified success.

The claim has been made that the army was unfair because it assigned most black soldiers to serve in the West, where conditions were more likely to be harsh. But generally speaking, most post–Civil War soldiers were in the West — where they were needed — and both whites and blacks struggled with hardship.

Officially the same rules and regulations governed the entire army, and, therefore, duties and routine experiences of the blacks were to a great extent similar to those of white soldiers. Because the army was small and faced a demanding mission on the frontier, white leaders — like it or not — depended on black soldiers to carry a share of the load of field and garrison duty. Shortages of manpower prevented prejudice from remanding blacks to noncombatant status.

Were blacks the victims of discrimination within the army's system? Evidence to affirm that question existed in New Mexico, where in 1867 Fort Cummings's post commander reported that the flour that Fort Bliss had sent his black troopers was old and in sacks of such poor material that they burst with ordinary handling.[16]

In 1880 when two sergeants and seventeen privates drawn from three companies of the Ninth Cavalry temporarily were stationed at Camp French, New Mexico, a sympathetic white officer visiting the camp reported the following undesirable conditions: the men's clothing was old and worn out; the tents, with seams ripped out to increase air circulation in hot weather, were worn and torn and unfit for service; the men cooked in a small house that they erected themselves; they had no table to eat on, rather they ate from their knees or from the ground; and the corn they ate was of poor quality and stored in rotting sacks. The men had only two government horses at the camp, one being "so low in flesh and generally worn out or broken down as to be considered not worth the cost of feeding for the months before he can be recuperated." The other horse had a very bad open sore on its back, and with no protection it was filled with both flies and dirt. Finally, some of the men had not been paid for several months, one of them claiming he had not received any pay for over a year.[17] The military records are filled with similar reports of the poor food, equipment, supplies, and stations the army made available to black soldiers.

Officers who commanded black enlisted men often complained about the number and quality of horses and mules the army furnished them. In 1868 Fort Cummings's commander reported that the post had only twenty-four horses and mules, that four of these were unserviceable, and that only ten were available for scouting duties,[18] the implication being that he and his Thirty-eighth infantrymen could not do their jobs due to the shortage and quality of the animals at hand. Hardly had the Ninth Cavalry moved to New Mexico in 1876 when field commanders began to report upon the inadequate quantities and quality of their animals. For instance, the captain of the Ninth's Company E reported that the six-mule teams used to transport him and his men and supplies on a fifty-seven-day trip from Fort Clark, Texas, to Fort Wingate were totally inadequate.[19]

A year later a special inspector reported that the mules at Fort Selden were in very poor condition, most of them — even in one case the ambulance team — appearing to have been used as pack animals. Furthermore, most of the mules were twenty years old or older. He recommended that eighteen of the thirty-six mules at Selden be turned over to the Fort Union depot for recuperation or sale and that an equal number of young, sound mules be transferred to the post for draft and packing purposes.[20] Military records do not indicate that this recommendation was effected. In 1879 Col. Edward Hatch of the Ninth Cavalry complained that the horses the army furnished his troopers were too small for the service they had to perform.[21]

Do such complaints prove that blacks got a raw deal regarding animals assigned to them? Could not a military historian find an equal number of references to officers who argued that their white troopers were not being provided with adequate animals? With black and white men often stationed together and sometimes depending upon each

other in the field, it would have been unwise and impractical — as well
as a violation of regulations — to maintain a policy of providing
supplies of inferior quantity and quality to blacks. Although specific
instances of discrimination in supplying animals no doubt occurred,
apparently a pattern of general discrimination did not.

Did black regiments receive the same arms and equipment as white
regiments? Military records indicate they did. When the army converted to the improved Springfield rifle in the 1870s, black units got
their issues at approximately the same time as white units got theirs.
In other instances army authorities gave both races the privilege of
testing new weapons and equipment.[22]

That the army was discriminatory in regard to the presence and
promotion of black officers is easily proved. Although regulations did
not prohibit the commissioning of black officers or the promotion of
qualified black noncommissioned officers to the commissioned ranks,
not a single black enlisted man rose from the ranks to a commission
between 1866 and 1898, the year of the Spanish-American War.
Between 1870 and 1889 only twenty-two black youths received ap-
pointments to the U.S. Military Academy. Of the twelve who passed
the West Point entrance examination, only three were able to over-
come four years of social ostracism, discrimination, and many other
tribulations to graduate from the academy: Henry O. Flipper, John H.
Alexander, and Charles Young graduated in 1877, 1887, and 1889,
respectively.[23] Sheer numerical facts present a prima facie case for
discrimination against blacks in the army's officer corps.

Even though the army insisted that its official policies were non-
discriminatory, it could not guarantee equality or social acceptance.
Most white Americans — both military and civilian — believed blacks
were inferior to whites, and official policy could not change those
beliefs. William T. Sherman, general of the army from 1869 to 1883,
stated before a congressional committee: "If I were compelled to choose
5,000 men to go into a fight with, I would rather take 5,000 white
men."[24] He further declared: "The blacks are a quiet, kindly, peaceful
race of men. Naturally not addicted to war; better suited to the arts of
peace." Despite the considerable military virtues demonstrated by
black soldiers by the time Sherman wrote these remarks, the general's
attitude remained unchanged: he believed that allowing blacks into
the military service was only a partial success and that the army should

not be viewed as a charitable institution.[25] Other high-ranking army officers freely expressed their reservations about blacks in the military services; some of them, in fact, supported political efforts to remove blacks from the army and to abolish the black regiments.[26]

Many army officers acted upon their prejudices. One of the most telling illustrations was the choice of assignments West Point graduates made. Their opportunity of choice was based on class standing, and throughout the 1870s and most of the 1880s the highest-ranking cadets opted to command white companies or troops. Furthermore, some experienced officers preferred to resign from the army, rather than accept a vacancy existing in a black regiment. Others remained in the military service but harmed their careers when they turned down opportunities to command black units. Eugene A. Carr and Frederick Benteen, who became noted in the Indian Wars, were among those officers who sacrificed higher rank because they refused to command black men.[27] George A. Custer, who refused a lieutenant colonelcy with the Ninth Cavalry but wangled the same rank in the Seventh Cavalry, is the best known of those officers who allowed color directly to affect their careers. Some blacks saw a certain poetic justice when Custer fell at the Battle of the Little Big Horn ten years later. Certainly his military career and his niche in history would have been far different had he fought with the Ninth in New Mexico against the Apaches instead of with the Seventh in Montana against the Sioux.

When officers were assigned to command black units, they often allowed their prejudices to show; prejudice was so common that no doubt many of these officers were totally unaware of their expressions of it. Perhaps a white lieutenant was revealing his prejudice when he wrote: "No men of the 38th Infantry at this Post [Bayard] are competent to discharge the duties [as clerk and acting commissary sergeant]." He requested he be allowed to keep a private of the Third Cavalry who earlier had been loaned to him for this dual job.[28] When the commander of Fort Cummings wrote: "As this post is garrisoned by colored troops, I find it impossible to procure from among the enlisted men a person competent to perform the duties of QM clerk,"[29] he may have been revealing the generally low level of education and training of black infantrymen, but more likely he was expressing his prejudice toward blacks in general. As a third example, a white officer requested to keep Pvts. Isaac Carter and Milton Harris of Company A, Thirty-eighth Infantry, as workers in the quartermaster department at Fort Cummings, saying they were trustworthy, reliable, and faithful. But he undermined these comments by prejudicially concluding that "such men can seldom be found among colored soldiers."[30]

When a black soldier charged that a white army surgeon had provided inadequate medical care that resulted in the death of Pvt. Samuel Motley of Company F, One Hundred Twenty-fifth Infantry, at Fort Selden, he implied that the medical doctor was racially prejudiced.[31] He may have been correct. Nevertheless, army surgeons sometimes provided inadequate care for white soldiers as well. We may never know the facts in this specific case.

Countless army officers cursed their enlisted men, depending on the situation and the officer's habits. Whatever their color, soldiers on the western frontier endured such abuse. But the blacks endured more than the whites. The records are filled with black soldiers' charges that officers used abusive language with them, often employing racial epithets. Even if the blacks at times may have been overly sensitive to officers' language, the charges are frequent enough to conclude that many of them were justified.

Sometimes the officers' prejudice and the black men's response to it had dire consequences for the army's frontier mission. When in September 1879 Chief Victorio's band killed five soldiers and three civilian herd guards and captured nearly all the horses of Capt. Ambrose E. Hooker's Company E, Ninth Cavalry — inaugurating the most serious phase of the army's attempt to subdue the New Mexico Apaches — the Indian attack at Camp Ojo Caliente may not have been successful had the captain and his men not been at odds with each other because of Hooker's racial prejudice. Shortly after the tragic event, men of the company wrote an anonymous letter to the captain's superiors blaming Hooker for the deaths of the men of the herd guard, claiming that Hooker had been warned that the Indians might attack and that he had not taken proper precautions to protect his men, insufficiently arming and equipping them. They further charged that after the incident, he had said that he wished all the men of his command had been killed and that he would try to get as many of them killed as possible. Finally, the enlisted men of Company E charged that Hooker's conduct toward his men had been unofficerlike for a long time and that they had made earlier complaints against him, to no avail.

The consequences of the successful Indian raid and the anonymous letter stimulated the army to send Fifteenth Infantry Capt. Charles Steelhammer to Ojo Caliente to investigate. In December Steelhammer personally interviewed all fifty-one enlisted men of Company E. He also interviewed Hooker, two other commissioned officers of the company, and a private citizen, reporting these interviews in a 111-page document.[32]

Almost all the men testified that Hooker regularly cursed his enlisted men, claiming that he called them, collectively or individually, "damned Negro sons of bitches," "a pack of god damned sons of bitches," "damned worthless sons of bitches," "damned monkey son of a bitch," "god damned black son of a bitch," "god damn dirty niggers," "damned idiot," "puppies," "dogs," "apes," "brutes," "a parcel of cowards," "damned nigger," "damned dog," "baboons," "Arabs," "kangaroos," "worthless dog," and "scoundrels." Lt. Frank B. Taylor testified that Hooker had quite frequently used abusive language with his troopers.

Hooker denied that he cursed his men and called them names, saying: "I have ever carefully avoided from my first service with these troops, the use of any expressions, calculating or tending to originate, cultivate, or foster any question as to distinction on account of race or color." However, he undercut his denial as he elaborated upon it. He admitted that after years of experience as commander of Company E, "my limited supply of refined English became exhausted and worn out, and . . . from constant association with men who seemed to have no proper comprehension of refined English I found myself gradually adopting language better comprehended and appreciated and much more effective with men to whom choice English expression were much the same as Greek." He said: "I plead guilty, at times, to the use of strong emphatic language in individual cases. I have been free to express my opinion of thieves, shirks and malingerers as contemptible dogs."

He further admitted that he said some of his men were "as fit to be soldiers as our dogs to be saints," and he told a sergeant that he did not want to listen to "any of his barrack gambling, nigger slang." He said he tried to impress upon his men that there was a great difference between soldiers in the U.S. Army and "cornfield Niggers" and admitted that in private he had referred to the men as apes, baboons, chimpanzees, monkeys, kangaroos, orangutans, and gorillas. The charge that Hooker had been unofficerlike was, indeed, well founded.

Some of the men of Company E believed that Hooker's discipline was overly harsh. He hit his men with his riding whip, he forced them to work in silence, and he compelled one man to walk instead of ride when the man misunderstood an order. Several men reported that Hooker had forced them to carry logs as punishment, even when justification for punishment appeared groundless. When one man resisted, Hooker had him bucked and gagged, with a forty-pound log placed on his shoulder and a heavy chain fastened to his wrist and wound around his neck.

When a corporal and some privates were driving cattle through a canyon, the corporal shot a wild turkey, contrary to orders. Hooker cursed the soldier, instructed a sergeant to cut off his chevrons, and ordered "the damned dog to carry the turkey until it rots on his back." The man was handcuffed and the turkey tied to his back, where he carried it from 2 P.M. until taps one day and from reveille until 9 A.M. the next day. Another man reported that Hooker had "lariated me . . . out on herd with the horses, as if I had been one of them."

When a private took down the captain's tent and was putting it and the tent pins in a wagon, Hooker appeared and said that he had never seen a "nigger" who could put away anything straight. The soldier looked up, and Hooker shouted: "God damn you when I speak I don't want you to look up at me," to which the man replied: "Captain, what do you take me for? I am a soldier and want to be treated as such." Hooker then struck and kicked the man, told him to "shut up your god damn mouth," and ordered the man to be bucked and gagged. When Hooker called the man a dog, the soldier replied that he was no more of a dog than the captain was, at which time Hooker kicked the man three times in the neck, telling him not to utter another word, or he "would kick every god damned tooth in my head down my throat." Then the man was handcuffed to a wagon and dragged for about thirty feet. Later he was made to walk for five days handcuffed to the wagon.

Because many of the punishments of which the men complained were relatively common on the frontier, Hooker ignored most of them in his rebuttal. However, he admitted that he had had a turkey tied to the back of a man but when it began to smell badly, he had had it

Capt. Ambrose E. Hooker. (Courtesy Massachusetts Commandery of the Military Order of the Loyal Legion and the U.S. Army Military History Institute, Carlisle, Pennsylvania.)

removed. Hooker was probably more severe in his punishment than many other frontier officers, but he may not have been too far out of line in comparison. The problem was the racial slurs he meted out with the punishment, as well as the generally condescending attitude he projected toward the black soldiers. A private summed up the situation well when he said that he had been trying to do his duty, "but when I have done my best, I have been reprimanded as freely as if the reverse had been the case."

More serious than the soldiers' complaints about cursing and what they considered unfair punishment were their charges that Hooker had been warned that Indians were in the vicinity, that he had not properly armed and equipped the herd guard, and that he therefore was responsible for the deaths of the men. Lieutenant Taylor and a citizen named John Sullivan testified that the captain had, indeed, been told that Indians had been seen nearby. Hooker did not deny that he had heard of the presence of the Indians, but he considered Sullivan's report an incidental remark because the man had come on other business. Hooker justified reducing the guard to five soldiers instead of the usual eight because a large portion of the company was on detached service. When he was reminded that twenty-five privates were at the post and were available for duty at the time of the fatal attack, he responded: "I could have sent more men but I did not feel they were needed. Besides five men are better because they keep working; send more and they gamble under a shade tree or stay around a fire in cold weather."

The men who guarded the herd were on unsaddled horses and carried Colt .45 pistols rather than carbines. When their fellow soldiers complained that Hooker had placed the herdsmen in an untenable position, Hooker stated that he had told the herd guard that they could saddle their horses and carry their carbines, but they preferred not to. Then he argued that carbines were useless encumbrances to soldiers guarding a moving herd and that saddles were not necessary.

In accusatory and blunt language, Hooker stated that the herders shared a considerable amount of the responsibility for the fiasco. He believed that they should have posted a sentinel and that the guard was negligent and inattentive. He maintained that it was the herders, not he, who were responsible for their own deaths. The investigator disagreed, concluding that a sentinel would have been useless because of the terrain where the herd was grazing.

Hooker then placed the soldiers' charges against him in a larger perspective. He was convinced that the men were engaged in a conspiracy that had existed since the time the company was formed. He reported that in the spring of 1867, shortly after the company was organized and while it was in central Texas on its way to duty on the frontier, the enlisted men of the company broke out in open mutiny, seriously wounding its lieutenant and killing the officer of the day. When Hooker joined the company nearly two years later, a number of the mutinous soldiers were still in it. Hooker claimed he had been with the company only one day when a soldier told his maidservant about the previous mutiny, finishing his story by threatening that the new captain had better be gentle with them or else.

In 1874 when the company was in Indian Territory these men had complained to Col. George Buell about Hooker's leadership, but Buell had pronounced the complaints "the result of a spirit of insubordination bordering on mutiny." In 1876 when three enlisted men at Fort Wingate objected to Hooker's harsh discipline, Colonel Hatch dismissed their objections as frivolous. Hooker stated that "there has always been a spirit of insubordination in my company from its organization, which has required the most rigid discipline with a firm and unwavering hand to suppress and keep it down."

Hooker believed that Private Nance, one of his detractors in 1876 and "an agitator and malcontent of long standing," was responsible for the current unrest among the troopers. He saw Nance as "a champion of his race and extensively engaged in the amelioration of its present condition, more particularly in the service and more especially in my Co[mpany]." From Hooker's viewpoint, his men "esteemed [Nance] to be something of an oracle in the Co[mpany]." Hooker believed that Nance continued to encourage a spirit of insubordination in others, citing as examples an occasion when the men resisted both drills and the drill sergeant, and another occasion when two men drew their guns on Hooker after he tried to give them orders. He justified his strong discipline in light of these past events and this present resistance to orders.

When some of the men engaged in stealing, Hooker was prompted to say: "It is doubtless well known that these men are from force of circumstances and education (for which they are perhaps not entirely to blame) natural born thieves and liars." When earlier he had refused to talk to the men about their complaints, he justified his action by saying that he did not want to have the "annoyance and disgust of listening to their preconcerted and concocted lies."

Hooker believed that sometimes ridicule was more effective than punishment. He reported: "I often tell awkward men that they mounted and dismounted their horse more like an Indian squaw, or a Texas cowboy, or a confused Nigger than like a soldier — or perhaps, that he sat on his horse more like a baboon than a well drilled soldier. The other soldiers make fun of people I talk to this way and this sometimes has a salutary effect."

Hooker ended his defense by stating that he was confident the department commander surely held the class of men composing Company E in the same estimation as Hooker himself did. Thus, a similar anonymous communication from a company of white soldiers would doubtless have received the treatment it merited: silent contempt and indifference.

But Hooker was not allowed off so easily. After hearing all the witnesses, Steelhammer wrote:.

> It will be found I think that Captain Hooker's own statement corroborates the essential portion of the allegations made. Surely we must have patience and forebearance in the management of our colored troops as well as of white soldiers. Anger like any other passion increases when constantly indulged and will hardly ever become the proper agent for increasing the efficiency of an Army, whatever material its soldiery may be composed of. Hooker expects too much of his men. Scolding and arbitrary exercise of power only make matters worse. Hooker probably acted the way he sincerely believed was the best, but he thinks it is the only way; his way. It is therefore more than unfortunate that Captain Hooker has contracted such strong and seemingly ineradicable prejudices against the colored race as soldiers.

In view of the testimony of the enlisted men serving under Hooker and because of Hooker's obviously increased irritability after the loss of the herd, Steelhammer recommended that Company E be stationed at a post where the commanding officer would be superior in rank to Hooker, relieving the captain of some responsibilities and thus making life easier for him and perhaps more satisfactory to his men.

Basic factual information about Hooker's background gives no hints as to how and when the officer's strong racial prejudices developed. Born in New York and living in California as an adult, he joined the California Infantry in the middle of the Civil War, shortly after the end of which he became a lieutenant colonel in the Second California

Cavalry. In July 1866 he became a lieutenant in the U.S. Army's Eighth Cavalry, and in March 1867 he was elevated to captain and transferred to the Ninth Cavalry. Unlike other officers who commanded black troopers, Hooker, who led black cavalrymen for over two years prior to the Ojo Caliente fiasco, never developed a sense of respect for his men. This difference in opinion may have resulted from racial predispositions among the commanders rather than direct experience. No doubt Hooker believed his experiences with black men proved their inferiority. Even though little of his background is known, surely it was the context for his beliefs and actions in 1879.[33]

Hooker's example may have been extreme, but this was an era when prejudice was pervasive, often just beneath, if not actually above, the surface of the civilian and military societies. Far too many officers thought like Hooker, even if they did not act like him. Unknowingly they created conditions for the subtleties of racism to exist.

Although prejudice permeated the prevailing climate and some officers publicly expressed their contempt for the black soldiers, others who worked with the men over time came to admire them, and some praised them. Edward Hatch and Benjamin Grierson, commanders of the Ninth and Tenth Cavalry Regiments, respectively, expressed their appreciation numerous times.

Zenas R. Bliss, longtime commander of the Twenty-fourth Infantry, showed genuine concern when his enlisted men were treated unfairly. This was exemplified in an incident concerning a black recruit who was issued one day's rations and was sent to join the regiment at Fort Supply, Indian Territory. As a result of fouled-up transportation schedules, the new soldier was without rations for four days. Bliss called attention to this improper treatment in a letter to the assistant adjutant general of the Department of the Missouri, requesting that army personnel be more sensitive to black soldiers under his command.[34] On more than one occasion while Bliss was commander at Fort Bayard, he praised the performance of his enlisted men, such compliments reflecting his generally high regard for all black soldiers.

Another officer who became known for being fair and honest in his relationships with his men and who was particularly sensitive to any evidence of prejudice against them was Col. George Lippitt Andrews, a Civil War veteran who remained in the army in the postwar years. He joined the Twenty-fifth Infantry in December 1870, later becoming its commander.[35] While the Twenty-fifth was stationed in Dakota Territory, Col. Andrews had reason to believe that an inspecting officer visiting Fort Randall was strongly prejudiced against black soldiers. He reported the officer to the assistant adjutant general of the Department of Dakota and asked that he be reprimanded.[36]

The military records are filled with statements of praise from lesser officers who worked closely with blacks. Two New Mexico examples will suffice. In 1868 a Thirty-eighth Infantry lieutenant reported that Pvt. Benjamin Meadows of Company A was a reliable and trustworthy person, and he requested permission to retain him for much-needed work in the subsistence department at Fort Cummings.[37] In 1881 a Fifteenth Infantry lieutenant borrowed Pvt. Richard Jones, Company I, Ninth Cavalry, to work in his quartermaster corps. In a letter requesting permission to retain Jones, the lieutenant wrote: "I kept him principally as guard over a large quantity of corn . . . and was obliged at times to leave him solely in charge of the property. He is a reliable man."[38]

Some officers praised the black soldiers as fighting men. In 1878 a new West Point graduate who was with a white cavalry regiment at a post that had black infantry companies wrote home: "It does not take very long for one to change entirely his ideas in respect to these troops. They make excellent soldiers."[39] When the men of Company D, Ninth Cavalry, made a forced march of seventy miles out of New Mexico to reinforce a white column under fire at Milk Creek, Colorado, and assisted in breaking the back of an Indian siege, a white captain awarded them what he considered the highest possible accolade when he called them "the whitest men" he had ever seen.[40] A significant indication of the growing reputation of the black soldiers was that with each passing year between 1877 and 1891 West Point graduates of increasingly higher class rank chose to serve in the Ninth or Tenth Cavalry Regiments.[41]

Although blacks constituted about 9 percent of the enlisted men in the army between 1866 and 1891, during that same period black enlisted men constituted only 4 percent of those who won the coveted Medal of Honor. That lower percentage was more likely a function of white prejudice in awarding the medal than a measure of black bravery. Colonel Bliss pointed out that during the Indian Wars, blacks had many gallant deeds to their credit, and he believed that they ranked among the best soldiers on the frontier.[42] When Gen. John Pope wrote of one black unit that "everything that men could do they did," he unknowingly made a statement that could have been used as the collective epitaph of the black soldiers who served during the Indian Wars.[43] An objective assessment of the record is that blacks as a group were, by any standard, competent as fighting men. Over forty black soldiers died while serving in the military forces in New Mexico. Five of these men died after fights resulting from racial prejudice and at least thirty of them were killed in the line of duty.

Despite the hardships that all soldiers experienced on the frontier and despite general and specific prejudices directed toward black soldiers, the more than three thousand black troopers who served in New Mexico Territory from 1866 to 1900 made individual and collective contributions. First, during the Indian Wars, they helped subdue the hostile Indians. Second, they protected a growing, law-abiding white population from both Indians and unruly whites. Third, they had an impact upon the economy of New Mexico. Finally, they participated in a temporary military society that interacted with the territory's civilian population, resulting in a cultural exchange between them and the general population of New Mexico. The buffalo soldiers' significant contributions deserve more acknowledgment than they have previously received.

Appendix

The New Mexico posts where black soldiers served had varied histories. Five of them had been established before the Civil War, four were established during the war itself, and two were founded after the war.

Fort Union was the oldest of the forts serving as stations for black soldiers in post–Civil War New Mexico Territory. The fort was established in July 1851 about twenty-four miles northeast of Las Vegas on the Mountain Branch of the Santa Fe Trail on the west side of the valley of Wolf Creek, a tributary of the Mora River. Its purpose was threefold: to deter the Jicarilla Apache and Ute Indians, to protect the Santa Fe Trail, and to serve as a supply depot. At the beginning of the Civil War, in anticipation of a Confederate attack, the federal commander of the post ordered it moved approximately one mile, the new site located on the valley floor east of Wolf Creek. In 1863 the fort was moved to its third and final location, almost immediately north of its second site. For many years Fort Union served as the general supply depot for the military garrisons of New Mexico. The construction of railroads into the area lessened its importance, and in 1882 the arsenal was discontinued. In 1891 the fort was vacated, except for a caretaker detail.

Fort Craig came into existence in 1854. It was located on land that gently sloped eastward to the Rio Grande a mile away, about four miles south of the present site of San Marcial. Beyond rose the dark profile of Contadera Mesa. Craig's major task was to guard the north-south route along the Rio Grande, providing travelers with protection against roving bands of Apaches. Its closure came in 1885.

Originally built on the Bonito River in May 1855, Fort Stanton was established to control the Mescalero and White Mountain Apache Indians. Federal soldiers evacuated and partially burned the fort in August 1861 when Confederates from Texas entered New Mexico and temporarily held Stanton until late 1862, when Col. Kit Carson of the First New Mexico Infantry reoccupied it. Rebuilt in 1868 on its original site, the post was later moved two miles north to its present location. In 1896 it was abandoned as a military post.

Although Camp Ojo Caliente was established in 1859 and troops were stationed there as late as 1882, it was never officially designated a fort. It was located on the right bank of the Alamosa River, near the foothills of the San Mateo Mountains, about eighteen miles north of the present town of Winston. In its early years the camp served as an advanced picket post for Fort Craig, its purpose being to control the Navajo Indians. The camp was abandoned before the end of the Civil War, and in the early 1870s it began serving as agency headquarters for the Ojo Caliente Reservation. Military troops were stationed there from 1877 to 1882, during the height of the Apache resistance.

Fort Wingate II (originally named Fort Fauntleroy and, for a time, renamed Fort Lyon) was established in 1860 at Ojo del Oso at the northern end of the Zuni Range near the headwaters of the Rio Puerco of the West. The federal garrison was withdrawn in late 1861 because of the Confederate invasion of New Mexico. In 1868 federal soldiers reoccupied the post after returning about seven thousand Navajos and a few hundred Apaches to the area following the Indians confinement at Fort Sumner, New Mexico. At this time, the post was designated Fort Wingate. In 1912 it was evacuated, except for a caretaker detail.

Fort McRea came into existence in April 1863, located near Ojo del Muerto, about five miles west of the *Jornada del Muerto* (literally, journey of the dead one), a ninety-mile, waterless strip of land in south-central New Mexico along the east side of the Rio Grande. It was situated on the historic caravan routes from Chihuahua, Mexico, to Santa Fe, and was intended to protect travelers following the trade routes and to prevent Indian depredations in the general area. In 1867 it was abandoned but later reopened, closing permanently in 1876.

Fort Bascom was established in August 1863 on the north bank of the Canadian River, about eight miles north of the present town of Tucumcari. Its job was to protect travel routes across central New Mexico — including the Fort Smith–Santa Fe Trail — and to encourage settlement in the Canadian Valley by controlling the Kiowa and Comanche Indians in the region. In 1870 it was abandoned.

Fort Cummings was founded in October 1863, located at Cooke's Springs in Cooke's Range, fifty-three miles west of the Rio Grande on the Mesilla-Tucson Road. Its purpose was to restrain the Apache Indians and guard the most dangerous point on the southern route to California, with the exception of Apache Pass, Arizona. It was evacuated in 1873, reoccupied in 1880, evacuated again in 1884, and reoccupied again in 1886. Later that same year it was abandoned for the final time.

Fort Selden, established in May 1865, was situated near the southern end of the Jornada del Muerto, about one and one half miles east of the Rio Grande, approximately twelve miles north of the town of Doña Ana. Like Craig it was to protect the route along the Rio Grande as well as provide safety for the settlers of the Mesilla Valley. It was not garrisoned from mid-1879 through 1880 but was regarrisoned from 1881 until 1888, after which a caretaker detail remained until early 1891, when the post was officially closed.

Fort Bayard, established in August 1866, was located ten miles east of Silver City, near the base of the Santa Rita Mountains. Before its closure in 1900, Bayard's mission was to protect the Pinos Altos mining district against the Warm Springs Apache Indians.

The last New Mexico fort at which black soldiers were garrisoned was Fort Tularosa, established in 1872. It was located in present-day Catron County, the original site being on the west bank of Tularosa Creek, about fifteen miles north of the town of Reserve. A reservation for Apache Indians had recently been opened in that vicinity and Tularosa was to protect the government agency there. Before the post was completely built, however, the Bureau of Indian Affairs moved the agency headquarters to Horse Creek, approximately eighteen miles east of the original site. Tularosa was abandoned in 1874 when the Indians on the nearby reservation were returned to their former home at Ojo Caliente, located east and south of the Tularosa site but still west of the Rio Grande. Although officially abandoned, Tularosa was occasionally manned by soldiers temporarily residing there at the height of the Indian Wars.

The five New Mexico posts at which black troopers were not garrisoned in the postwar era were Forts Webster, Wingate I, Sumner, Lowell, and Marcy. Fort Webster was established in 1851, and during its lifetime it occupied three separate locations, all of them in the general vicinity of the Santa Rita copper mines in the Mimbres Valley. The fort was abandoned between 1853 and 1866, after which it apparently was used as a temporary post during the post–Civil War Indian hostilities.

Located at El Gallo, the great spring near present-day San Rafael, Fort Wingate I came into existence in 1862 and was evacuated in 1868 when its garrison was transferred to Fort Wingate II.

Fort Sumner existed between 1862 and 1868 in the Bosque Redondo on the east bank of the Pecos River south of the present town of Fort Sumner. Fearful of Indian uprisings when the army's western commands were moved east during the Civil War, the U.S. government established Fort Sumner as a place to confine a large number of both Navajos and Apaches. After the war ended, the Indians were returned to their homelands in western New Mexico, and the post was shut down.

Located on the Chama River southwest of Tierra Amarilla, Fort Lowell was founded in November 1866 to protect the area against Ute Indians. It was abandoned in 1869, when the army concluded that the Utes were pacified.

Erected in 1846, Fort Marcy was adjacent to the Palace of the Governors off the central plaza in Santa Fe. The fort was deactivated in 1867, and from then until 1875 the military establishment in Santa Fe was designated the Post at Sante Fe, New Mexico, this post being the headquarters for the Military District of New Mexico for a part of this time. In 1875 Marcy was reactivated, functioning until its permanent closing in 1894.

Of the five New Mexico forts where black soldiers were not stationed, only Fort Marcy played a major role during the era of the Indian Wars. The other four were relatively short-lived or insignificant. Lowell, Sumner, and Wingate I ceased to exist within three or four years of the end of the Civil War, and Webster was nothing more than a minor, temporary post.[1]

Notes

Introduction

1. Frederick H. Dyer, *A Compendium of the War of the Rebellion* (New York: 1959), vol. 3: 1718–1740; Dudley Taylor Cornish, *The Sable Arm: Negro Troops in the Union Army, 1861–1865* (New York: 1966), 126–131, 232–235, 254–255, 288; *The Army Lineage Book, Volume II: Infantry* (Washington, D.C.: 1953), 22. To avoid excessive documentation, on occasion, as in this footnote, the sources for a story or incident are combined into a single reference.

2. Cornish, *The Sable Arm*, 266–267, 286–287; James M. McPherson, *The Negro's Civil War: How American Negroes Felt and Acted During the War for the Union* (New York: 1965), 237.

3. Robert M. Utley, *Frontier Regulars: The United States Army and the Indian, 1866–1891* (New York, 1973), 11–12, 15; Mary Lee Stubbs and Stanley Russell Connor, *Armor-Cavalry, Part I: Regular Army and Army Reserve* (Washington, D.C.: 1969), 19–20; *The Army Lineage Book. Volume II: Infantry*, 25–26.

4. Brief histories of these post–Civil War forts are included in the Appendix.

5. Post Returns, Fort Bascom, August 1866–October 1867; Fort Bayard, August 1866–October 1869, December 1875–December 1881, October 1887–April 1892, October 1898–December 1899; Fort Craig, September 1866–October 1869, October 1876–May 1877, December 1880–December 1881; Fort Cummings, August 1866–September 1869, July 1880–November 1881; Fort McRae, August 1866–October 1869, May–October 1876; Fort Selden, August 1866–October 1869, March 1876–March 1877, December 1880–November 1881, August 1888–January 1891; Fort Stanton, November 1866–October 1867, December 1875–November 1881, June-August, 1896; Fort Union, August–November 1866, December 1875–March 1881; Fort Wingate, January 1876–October 1881, October 1898–July 1900; Returns from U.S. Military Posts, 1800–1916, Microcopy No. 617, Records of the Adjutant General's Office, Record Group 94; and Records of United States Army Continental Commands, 1821–1920, Record Group 393, National Archives, Washington, D.C. (Hereafter cited as Post Returns.) See also S. C. Agnew, *Garrisons of the Regular U.S. Army: New Mexico, 1846–1899* (Santa Fe: 1971).

6. Lee Myers, "Military Establishments in Southwestern New Mexico: Stepping Stones to Settlement," *New Mexico Historical Review* 43 (January 1968): 5–48.

7. A modern-day sign of the presence of these black troopers expresses itself in two of New Mexico's place names: Dead Negro Hill and Nigger Hill. For details on the naming of these sites, see Monroe Billington, "Black History and New Mexico's Place Names," *Password* 29 (Fall 1984): 112.

Chapter I

1. Dyer, *Compendium of the War*, vol. 3: 1718–1740; Cornish, *The Sable Arm*, 288.

2. Dyer, *Compendium of the War*, vol. 3: 1733; Post Returns, Forts Union and Bascom, August–November 1866.

3. Dyer, *Compendium of the War*, vol. 3: 1740.

4. Companies A, E, F, and I went to Selden; Company B stopped at Bayard; Company D was stationed at Cummings; and Companies C and K went to McRae. Soon Company A was transferred from Selden to Craig and then to Bayard. Company B moved from Bayard to Craig, while Company C moved from McRae to Craig. Meanwhile, Company E left Selden and went to Stanton. After three months at Selden, Company I was temporarily assigned to both Cummings and Bayard. When the Fifty-seventh's three companies left Bascom in October 1866, Company K of the One Hundred Twenty-fifth moved from McRae to replace them. Post Returns, Forts Bascom, Selden, Bayard, Cummings, McRae, Craig, and Stanton, August–December 1866.

5. Anticipating removal from New Mexico, in September 1867 Company A had marched out of Bayard, and in October Companies B and C had vacated Craig. At the same time, Companies D, E, F, I, and K had vacated Cummings, Stanton, Selden, Bayard, and Bascom, respectively. Post Returns, Forts Bascom, Bayard, Craig, Cummings, Stanton, and Selden, September–October 1867; Fort Union, October–December 1867; Bvt. Maj. Gen. [George W.] Getty, Special Orders No. 43, August 27, 1867, Headquarters Records, Fort Cummings, 1863–1873 and 1880–1884, M1081, Records of United States Army Continental Commands, 1821–1920, Record Group 393, National Archives Washington, D.C. (Hereafter cited as Headquarters Records, Fort Cummings.)

6. For details of this war, see Utley, *Frontier Regulars*, 111–115.

7. Arlen L. Fowler, *The Black Infantry in the West, 1869–1891* (Westport, Conn: 1971), 17; Elizabeth Bacon Custer, *Tenting on the Plains: General Custer in Kansas and Texas* (Norman, Okla.: 1971), 677–678.

8. Company A was first stationed at Cummings and then at Bayard, and the reverse was true of Company F. Company C was first stationed at Craig and then at Bayard, and the reverse was true of Company D. Company H remained at McRae during its entire stay in New Mexico, and Company K was at Selden for the whole time. Post Returns, Forts Cummings, Bayard, Craig, McRae, and Selden, September–December 1867. The first members of the Thirty-eighth Infantry entered New Mexico in August, when Companies A and K arrived at Fort Union before proceeding to Cummings and Bayard. At the same time, the regimental staff stopped at Union before it moved on in September to establish headquarters at Craig. In July 1869 the headquarters were moved from Craig to Bayard. Thirty-eighth Infantry Returns, August and September 1867, July 1869, Returns from Regular Army Infantry Regiments, June 1821–December 1916, Microcopy No. 665, Records of the Adjutant General's Office, Record Group 94; and Records of United States Regular Army Mobile Units, 1821–1942, Record Group 391, National Archives, Washington, D.C. (Hereafter cited as Thirty-eighth Infantry Returns.); C. E. Clarke to adjutant general of the army, Washington, D.C., October 3, 1867, Headquarters Records, Fort Cummings.

9. William G. Muller, *The Twenty Fourth Infantry Past and Present* (Ft. Collins, Colo.: 1972), 25.

10. Post Returns, Forts Bayard, Craig, McRae, and Selden, September–October 1869; Fowler, *Black Infantry*, 17.

11. Agnew, *Garrisons of New Mexico*, 119, 121, 125.

12. Post Returns, Forts Bascom, Bayard, Craig, Cummings, McRae, Selden, Stanton, and Union, August 1866–October 1869.

13. Post Returns, Fort Bascom, August 1866–October 1867; Fort Bayard, August 1866–October 1869; Fort Craig, September 1866–October 1869; Fort Cummings, August 1866–September 1869; Fort Selden, August 1866–October 1869; Fort Stanton, November 1866–October 1867; Fort Union, August–November 1866. See also Agnew, *Garrisons of New Mexico*, 43–45, 57–59.

14. R. B. Foutts to C. H. DeForrest, August 29, 1866, Post Records, Fort Cummings, Records of the United States Army Continental Commands, 1821–1920, Record Group 393, National Archives, Washington, D.C. (Hereafter cited as Post Records, Fort Cummings.)

15. R. B. Foutts, Special Orders No. 81, October [?] 1866, Post Records, Fort Cummings.

16. B. B. Javitts to C. H. DeForrest, September 11, 1866, Letters Received by Headquarters, District of New Mexico, September 1865–August 1890, M1088, Records of United States Army Continental Commands, 1821–1920, Record Group 393, National Archives, Washington, D.C. (Hereafter cited as Letters Received by Dist. N.M., 1865–1890.); Post Returns, Fort Cummings, September 1866; R. B. Foutts to C. H. DeForrest, September 11, 1866, Post Records, Fort Cummings.

17. E. P. Horne to C. H. DeForrest, September 28, 1866, Letters Received by Dist. N.M., 1865–1890.

18. E. P. Gressey to C. H. DeForrest, May 24, 1867, Letters Received by Dist. N.M., 1865–1890.

19. J. G. Tilford to E. Hunter, November 22, 1867, Letters Received by Dist. N.M., 1865–1890.

20. *Santa Fe Weekly New Mexican,* November 26, 1867; October 6, 1868; March 16, 1869; Post Returns, Fort Selden, February 1869.

21. James Monroe Foster, Jr., "History of Fort Bascom, New Mexico, 1863–1870" (Master's thesis, Eastern New Mexico University, 1955), 55–56.

22. H. C. Merriam to assistant adjutant general, District of New Mexico, January 19, 1868, Letters Received by Dist. N.M., 1865–1890.

23. Post Returns, Fort Bayard, June 1868.

24. R. B. Foutts to C. H. DeForrest, May 20, 1867, Post Records, Fort Cummings.

25. R. B. Foutts to C. McKeever, September 23, 1867, Post Records, Fort Cummings; H. F. Leggett to J. N. Morgan, February 14, 1868, Headquarters Records, Fort Cummings.

26. A. Moore to acting assistant adjutant general, District of New Mexico, September 2, 1869, Post Records, Fort Cummings. Military commanders often hired guides to lead soldiers in their chase after Indians. The daily rate was between $2.50 and $3 plus rations, and the monthly rate was not to exceed $45 plus daily rations. W. R. Gerhart to C. H. DeForrest, November 10, 1866, Letters Received by Dist. N.M., 1865–1890; A. Moore to H. J. Cuniffe, March 22, 1869, Post Records, Fort Cummings; Bvt. Brig. Gen. J. H. Carleton, Special Orders No. 43, Headquarters, District of New Mexico, Santa Fe, N.M., November 14, 1868, Headquarters Records, Fort Cummings.

27. Francis B. Heitman, *Historical Register and Dictionary of the United States Army, From Its Organization, September 29, 1789, to March 2, 1903* (Urbana, Ill.: 1965), vol. 1: 721.

28. James Monroe Foster, Jr., "Fort Bascom, New Mexico," *New Mexico Historical Review* 35 (January 1960): 48–49.

29. Foster, "History of Fort Bascom," 96–97.

30. R. B. Foutts to C. H. DeForrest, June 10, 1862, Headquarters Records, Fort Cummings.

31. J. C. McBride, Special Orders No. 60, July 3, 1868, Post Records, Fort Cummings.

32. C. E. Clarke to E. Hunter, February 18, 1868, Headquarters Records, Fort Cummings.

33. Foster, "History of Fort Bascom," 56.

34. A. Duncan to C. H. DeForrest, March 6, 1867; A. Duncan to C. H. DeForrest, March 28, 1867, Letters Received by Dist. N.M., 1865–1890; Post Returns, Fort Bayard, March 1867.

35. J. N. Morgan, Special Orders No. 1, January 1, 1868; J. N. Morgan to E. Hunter, January 6, 1868, Post Records, Fort Cummings.

36. A. Moore to the post adjutant, Fort Bayard, January 20, 1868; H. C. Merriam note, January 28, 1868, Letters Received by Dist. N.M., 1865–1890.

37. B. M. Custer to D. M. Page, January 19, 1868, Letters Received by Dist. N.M., 1865–1890.

38. E. Bloodgood to E. Hunter, September 18, 1868, Letters Received by Dist. N.M., 1865–1890.

39. Post Returns, Fort Bayard, August–November 1868; B. M. Custer to D. M. Page, August 27, 1868; C. E. Clarke to D. M. Page, September 15, 1868, Letters Received by Dist. N.M., 1865–1890.

40. A. Moore to acting assistant adjutant general, District of New Mexico, August 21, 1868, and September 4, 1868, Post Records, Fort Cummings; Thirty-eighth Infantry Returns, September 1868; Post Returns, Fort Cummings, September 1868; A. Moore to assistant adjutant general, Dist. N.M., September 23, 1868, Post Records, Fort Cummings.

41. Post Returns, Fort Selden, September–December 1868.

42. Post Returns, Fort Selden, January 1869.

43. W. B. Lane to acting assistant adjutant general, District of New Mexico, April 19, 1869, Letters Sent from Fort Selden, New Mexico, vol. 7A–7, Records of the Office of the Quartermaster General, Record Group 92, National Archives, Washington, D. C. (Hereafter cited as Letters Sent from Fort Selden.)

44. Post Returns, Fort Selden, May 1869; W. B. Lane to acting assistant adjutant general, District of New Mexico, May 9, 1869, Letters Sent from Fort Selden.

45. Post Returns, Fort Selden, June 1869; W. B. Lane to acting assistant adjutant general, District of New Mexico, May 11, 1869; W. B. Lane to W. A. Kobbe, May 31, 1869; E. A. Rigg to Messrs. Shedd and Blake, July 26, 1869, Letters Sent from Fort Selden.

46. Post Returns, Fort Selden, August 1869.

47. F. Stanwood to acting assistant adjutant general, District of New Mexico, October 28, 1869, Letters Sent from Fort Selden.

48. D. R. Clendenin to W. A. Kobbe, June 5, 1870, Letters Sent from Fort Selden.

49. Foster, "History of Fort Bascom," 85.

50. *Santa Fe New Mexican,* February 23, 1869.

51. Rupert Noval Richardson, *The Comanche Barrier to South Plains Settlement* (Glendale, Calif.: 1933), 319.

52. *Santa Fe New Mexican,* February 23, 1869.

53. A. Moore to E. Hunter, March 1, 1869, Headquarters Records, Fort Cummings; Post Returns, Fort Cummings, June 1869; W. B. Lane to acting assistant adjutant general, District of New Mexico, April 12, 1869, Letters Sent from Fort Selden; Post Returns, Fort Bayard, June 1869; A. Moore to acting assistant adjutant general, District of New Mexico, June 22, 1869, Post Records, Fort Cummings.

54. H. C. Merriam to C.N.W. Cunningham, August 13, 1868, Letters Received by Dist. N.M., 1865–1890.

55. Post Returns, Fort Bayard, August 1868; C.N.W. Cunningham to D. M. Page, September 1, 1868, Letters Received by Dist. N.M., 1865–1890.

56. Post Returns, Fort Cummings, November and December 1866, May 1867; C. E. Clarke, Special Orders No. 31, March 18, 1868, Post Records, Fort Cummings.

57. E. P. Horne to C. H. DeForrest, April 27, 1867, Letters Received by Dist. N.M., 1865–1890; Post Returns, January 1869.

58. H. F. Leggett, Special Orders No. 46, June 1, 1868, Post Records, Fort Cummings.

59. R. B. Foutts, Special Orders No. 70, September 24, 1866, Post Records, Fort Cummings.

60. R. B. Foutts, Special Orders No. 31, June 18, 1867, Post Records, Fort Cummings.

61. J. C. McBride, Special Orders No. 72, August 4, 1868, Post Records, Fort Cummings.

62. R. B. Foutts, Special Orders No. 40, August 3, 1867; O. Elting, Special Orders No. 9, January 23, 1868, Post Records, Fort Cummings.

63. Special Report of the Inspection of Fort Selden by Maj. A. J. Alexander, April 3, 1867, Letters Received by Dist. N.M., 1865–1890.

64. J. H. Carleton to commanding officers of Forts Selden, Cummings, and Bayard, December 16, 1866, Letters Sent by the 9th Military Department, the Department of New Mexico, and the District of New Mexico, 1849–1890, M1072, Records of United States Army Continental Commands, 1821–1920, Record Group 393, National Archives, Washington, D.C. (Hereafter cited as Letters Sent by 9th Military Department.)

65. E. Hunter to commanding officer, Fort Selden, October 25, 1868, Letters Sent by 9th Military Department.

66. J. G. Tilford to C. H. DeForrest, February 27, 1867, Letters Received by Dist. N.M., 1865–1890.

67. O. Elting to L. Merrill, October 9, 1869, Letters Sent from Fort Selden.

68. J. G. Tilford to C. H. DeForrest, August 21, 1867, Letters Received by Dist. N.M., 1865–1890.

Chapter II

1. A. Duncan to W. R. Shoemaker, August 17, 1866, Letters Sent from Fort Selden.

2. A. Moore, General Orders No. 5, July 3, 1868, Post Records, Fort Cummings.

3. J. C. McBride, General Orders No. 6, July 28, 1868, Post Records, Fort Cummings.

4. E. Hunter to H. C. Merriam, July 15, 1868, Letters Sent by 9th Military Department; C. E. Clarke to W. M. Beebe, Jr., October 27, 1867, Headquarters Records, Fort Cummings; J. W. Steele, Special Orders No. 108, December 17, 1868; J. C. McBride, Special Orders No. 72, August 4, 1868; J. W. Steele, Special Orders No. 97, November 11, 1868, Post Records, Fort Cummings.

5. Darlis A. Miller, *Soldiers and Settlers: Military Supply in the Southwest, 1861–1885* (Albuquerque: 1989), 225.

6. E. P. Horne to C. H. DeForrest, April 27, 1867, Letters Received by Dist. N.M., 1865–1890.

7. Miller, *Soldiers and Settlers*, 229.

8. A. J. Alexander to C. H. DeForrest, January 4, 1867, Letters Received by Dist. N.M., 1865–1890.

9. J. G. Tilford to W. J. Mitchell, January 24, 1867; J. G. Tilford to E. A. Rigg, February 22, 1868; W. B. Lane to M. I. Ludington, May 14, 1869, Letters Sent from Fort Selden.

10. Timothy Cohrs, "Fort Selden, New Mexico," *El Palacio* 79:4 (March 1974): 16.

11. R. B. Foutts to C. McKeever, January 25, 1867, Headquarters Records, Fort Cummings.

12. R. B. Foutts, Endorsement on Letter of Quartermaster, District of New Mexico, to acting assistant quartermaster, Fort Cummings, June 3, 1867; J. A. Corbett to chief quartermaster, District of New Mexico, October 3, 1867, Post Records, Fort Cummings.

13. W. E. Sweet to chief quartermaster, District of New Mexico, November 9, 1867, Post Records, Fort Cummings.

14. J. W. Steele to chief quartermaster, Department of the Missouri, May 26, 1869, Post Records, Fort Cummings.

15. John Gregory Bourke, *On the Border with Crook* (New York: 1891), 7.

16. For a study of the considerable impact of the army upon the Southwest's economy before the Civil War, see Robert W. Frazer, *Forts and Supplies: The Role of the Army in the Economy of the Southwest, 1846–1861* (Albuquerque: 1983).

17. J. DuBois to C. H. DeForrest, June 7, 1867, Letters Received by Dist. N.M., 1865–1890.

18. J. A. Corbett to W. E. Sweet, October 14, 1867; J. A. Corbett to chief, Commissary of Subsistence, October 18, 1867, Post Records, Fort Cummings.

19. C. E. Clarke, Special Orders No. 25 ½, March 3, 1868; W. E. Sweet to the post adjutant, Fort Cummings, March 4, 1868, Post Records, Fort Cummings.

20. Quoted in Miller, *Soldiers and Settlers*, 122.

21. A. J. Alexander, Endorsement to Accompany Special Inspection Report of Fort Selden, New Mexico, April 3, 1867, Letters Received by Dist. N.M., 1865–1890; W. B. Lane to M. I. Ludington, May 14, 1869, Letters Sent from Fort Selden.

22. R. B. Foutts, General Orders No. 1, January 1, 1867, Post Records, Fort Cummings.

23. J. A. Corbett to chief, Commissary of Subsistence, District of New Mexico, October 18, 1867; J. A. Corbett to chief quartermaster, Department of the Missouri, October 12, 1867, Post Records, Fort Cummings.

24. H. F. Leggett, Special Orders No. 17, February 14, 1868, Post Records, Fort Cummings.

25. Miller, *Soldiers and Settlers*, 122.

26. Special Orders No. 2, January 15, 1867, Post Records, Fort Cummings.

27. J. W. Steele to Marrick and Bascom Saw Mill, March 15, 1869, Post Records, Fort Cummings.

28. G. Sykes to commanding officer, Fort Bayard, April 22, 1867, Letters Sent by 9th Military Department; E. P. Gressey to C. H. DeForrest, May 1, 1867, Letters Received by Dist. N.M., 1865–1890.

29. A. J. Alexander, Special Report of the Inspection of Fort Bayard, March 6, 1867, Letters Received by Dist. N.M., 1865–1890.

30. R. B. Foutts, Special Orders No. 47, August 14, 1866, Headquarters Records, Fort Cummings; W. E. Sweet, Special Orders No. 70, November 4, 1867; R. B. Foutts, Special Orders No. 80, [1867]; J. C. McBride, Special Orders No. 61, July 4, 1868; J. W. Steele, Special Orders No. 108, December 17, 1868, Post Records, Fort Cummings.

31. W. E. Sweet, Special Orders No. 78, November 27, 1867; J. W. Steele, Special Orders No. 97, November 11, 1868; J. C. McBride, Special Orders No. 71, July 31, 1868; R. B. Foutts, Special Orders No. 41, August 5, 1867, Post Records, Fort Cummings.

32. Jack D. Foner, *The United States Soldier Between Two Wars: Army Life and Reforms, 1865–1898* (New York: 1970), 16.

33. Francis Paul Prucha, *Broadax and Bayonet: The Role of the United States Army in the Development of the Northwest, 1815–1860* (Lincoln, Nebr.: 1953), 152.

34. R. B. Foutts, Endorsement on Letter of Post ACS, June 29, 1867, Post Records, Fort Cummings.

35. R. B. Foutts, Endorsement on Letter from Captain Corbett to CLS, District of New Mexico, September 6, 1867, Post Records, Fort Cummings.

36. C. E. Clarke, General Orders No. 8, November 13, 1867, Post Records, Fort Cummings.

37. J. A. Corbett to chief, Commissary of Subsistence, District of New Mexico, February 22, 1867, Post Records, Fort Cummings.

38. Miller, *Soldiers and Settlers*, 143.

39. E. Hunter, Circular, Headquarters, District of New Mexico, October 16, 1867, Headquarters Records, Fort Cummings.

40. A. B. Eaton to H. F. Clarke, March 26, 1868, Headquarters Records, Fort Cummings.

41. Prucha, *Broadax and Bayonet*, 156.

42. J. W. Steele, General Orders No. 6, July 4, 1869; A. Moore to adjutant general of the army, August 26, 1869, Post Records, Fort Cummings.

43. R. B. Foutts, Special Orders No. 76, October 10, 1866, Post Records, Fort Cummings.

44. Miller, *Soldiers and Settlers*, 140–141.

45. S. Hunter to C. H. DeForrest, October 3, 1866, Letters Received by Dist. N.M., 1865–1890.

46. W. F. DuBois to E. G. Marshall, August 29, 1866, Letters Received by Dist. N.M., 1865–1890; Miller, *Soldiers and Settlers*, 42–43.

47. Thirty-eighth Infantry Returns, September and December 1867.

48. A. Moore to E. Hunter, March 6, 1869, Post Records, Fort Cummings.

49. J. C. McBride to Acting Assistant Surgeon Warwoth, January 16, 1869, Headquarters Records, Fort Cummings.

50. R. B. Foutts, Endorsement on Letter of Acting Assistant Surgeon John E. Beers, May 28, 1867, Post Records, Fort Cummings.

51. A. Moore, Special Orders No. 58, July 19, 1869, Post Records, Fort Cummings.

52. E. A. Rigg to C. Styer, July 8, 1869, Letters Sent from Fort Selden.

53. A. Moore to J. B. Ketchum, August 25, 1869, Post Records, Fort Cummings.

54. C. E. Clarke, Special Orders No. 76, November 20, 1867; J. W. Steele, General Orders No. 2, March 30, 1869, Post Records, Fort Cummings; Thirty-eighth Infantry Returns, November 1867.

55. A. Duncan to C. DeForrest, November 12, 1866; J. G. Tilford to E. Hunter, February 26 and March 26 and 30, 1868, Letters Sent from Fort Selden; Cohrs, "Fort Selden," 18, 19, 20–21.

56. E. Hunter to commanding officer, Fort Selden, August 16, 1868, Letters Sent by 9th Military Department.

57. A. Duncan to C. H. DeForrest, November 12, 1866; O. Elting to acting assistant adjutant general, District of New Mexico, October 20, 1869, Letters Sent from Fort Selden.

58. A. Moore, Charges and Specifications Against Private Allen Townsend, 1868; J. C. McBride, Charges and Specifications Against Private William H. Russell, 1868, Headquarters Records, Fort Cummings.

59. A. Moore, Charges and Specifications Against Private Henry Perkins, 1868, Headquarters Records, Fort Cummings.

60. A. Moore to E. Bloodgood, July 26, 1869, Post Records, Fort Cummings.

61. R. B. Foutts to D. Alexander, June 16, 1867, Headquarters Records, Fort Cummings.

62. Miller, *Soldiers and Settlers*, 335–33.

63. Miller, *Soldiers and Settlers*, 336.

64. A. Moore to acting assistant adjutant general, District of New Mexico, March 1, 1869, Headquarters Records, Fort Cummings.

65. A. Moore to acting assistant adjutant general, District of New Mexico, July 24, 1869, Post Records, Fort Cummings.

66. R. Booker to assistant adjutant general, Department of the Missouri, July 15, 1869, Headquarters Records, Fort Cummings.

67. W. A. Kobbe to commanding officer, Fort Cummings, December 15, 1868; E. Hunter to commanding officer, Fort Cummings, February 25, 1869, Headquarters Records, Fort Cummings; Post Returns, Fort Bayard, March 1869.

68. Special Orders No. 62, August 22, 1866, Post Records, Fort Cummings.

69. W. E. Sweet to post adjutant, Fort Cummings, November 26, 1867, Headquarters Records, Fort Cummings.

70. Foster, "History of Fort Bascom," 77.

71. Thirty-eighth Infantry Returns, 1867 Annual Returns.

72. Post Returns, Fort Cummings, October 1867.

73. Courts Martial, 00–3148, trial of Cpl. Robert Davis, Sgt. William Yeatman's testimony, Records of the Office of the Judge Advocate General, General Courts Martial, 1812–1938, Record Group 153, National Archives, Washington, D.C. (Hereafter cited as Courts Martial.)

74. Courts Martial, 00–3460, trial of Sgt. Thornton Reeves.

75. Courts Martial, 00–3148, judge advocate's summation.

76. Courts Martial, 00–3148, judge advocate's summation.

77. Courts Martial, 00–3148, Sgt. William Yeatman's testimony.

78. Courts Martial, 00–3148, Sgt. William Yeatman's testimony.

79. Courts Martial, 00–3460, Mrs. Henry Tally's testimony. Mrs. Tally was the wife of a Company A private; apparently Mattie Merritt lived with her.

80. Courts Martial, 00–3148, Sgt. William Yeatman's testimony.

81. Courts Martial, 00–3148, Sgt. William Yeatman's testimony.

82. Courts Martial, 00–3148, Sgt. William Yeatman's testimony.

83. C. E. Clarke to W. M. Beebe, Jr., December 3, 1867, Headquarters Records, Fort Cummings.

84. Courts Martial, 00–3148.

85. Courts Martial, 00–3549, trials of Privates Henry Watkins and George Stratton, Lt. James N. Morgan's testimony; Charges and Specifications Against Private Henry Watkins and Private George Newton, undated, Headquarters Records, Fort Cummings; Post Returns, Fort Cummings, December 1867; J. N. Morgan to E. Hunter, December 7, 1867, Headquarters Records, Fort Cummings.

86. Post Returns, Fort Cummings, December 1867; E. Hunter to commanding officer, Fort Cummings, December 19, 1867, Headquarters Records, Fort Cummings.

87. Courts Martial, 00–3148.

88. Courts Martial, 00–3148, summation, Sgt. William Yeatman's testimony; Courts Martial, 00–3527, trial of Sgt. Samuel Allen, summation.

89. Courts Martial, 00–3527, summation.

90. Courts Martial, 00–3527.

91. Courts Martial, 00–3460.

92. Courts Martial, 00–3549, trials of Pvt. Henry Watkins and Pvt. George Stratton; Charges and Specifications Against Private George Stratton, undated, Headquarters Records, Fort Cummings.

93. Courts Martial, 00–3527.

94. Based upon similar sources, this account and interpretation of the mutiny is in general agreement with Lee Myers, "Mutiny at Fort Cummings," New Mexico Historical Review 46 (October 1971): 337–350. For an entertaining account filled with fiction and almost devoid of fact, see William Thornton Parker, Annals of Old Fort Cummings, New Mexico, 1867–8 (Northampton, Mass.: 1916), 11–14.

Chapter III

1. Agnew, *Garrisons of New Mexico*, 43–45, 69–71, 99–103, 119.

2. C. E. Drew to commanding officer, Fort Cummings, October 11, 1869, Headquarters Records, Fort Cummings.

3. Utley, *Frontier Regulars*, 189–196; William H. Leckie, *The Buffalo Soldiers: A Narrative of the Negro Cavalry in the West* (Norman, Okla.: 1967), 172–173.

4. Utley, *Frontier Regulars*, 357; Leckie, *Buffalo Soldiers*, 174–175.

5. Agnew, *Garrisons of New Mexico*, 71, 101.

6. Heitman, *Historical Register*, 1: 510.

7. Ninth Cavalry Returns, December 1875–October 1881, Returns from Regular Army Cavalry Regiments, 1833–1916, M744, Records of the Adjutant General's Office, 1780s to 1917, Record Group 94, and Records of United States Regular Army Mobile Units, 1821–1942, Record Group 391, National Archives, Washington, D.C. (Hereafter cited as Ninth Cavalry Returns.)

First to arrive at its New Mexico post was Company C, which marched into Fort Bayard on December 9, 1875. Company A joined Company C there the following April. Companies H and L reached Fort Stanton in the middle of December, and before the month ended, the regimental headquarters and band arrived at Fort Union. The headquarters group and band had left Fort Clark, Texas, on October 19, marching 1,100 miles to Union. In January 1876 Company D arrived at Union and Company L moved there from Stanton. In February the command's headquarters were transferred to Santa Fe, Companies D and L and the band remaining at Union. The following August, Company K joined these two companies and the band at Union. Post Returns, Fort Bayard, December 1875, April 1876; Fort Union, December 1875–February 1876, August 1876.

In January 1876 Company E, led by Capt. Ambrose E. Hooker, took station at Fort Wingate, moving to Union in September. In March 1876 Company F arrived at Fort Selden, in April Company M arrived at Stanton, and in May Company I, led by Capt. Frank T. Bennett, settled at Wingate. Company B was stationed at Fort McRae from May through October and at Fort Craig from November to the following May, when it went to Bayard. In April 1877 Company F moved from Selden to Stanton, and four months later Company G, which had been at Fort Garland, Colorado, first arrived in New Mexico, settling at Bayard. Post Returns, Fort Wingate, January and May 1876; Fort Union, September 1876; Fort Selden, March 1876; Fort Stanton, April 1876, April 1877; Fort McRae, March 1876; Fort Craig, November 1876; Fort Bayard, May 1876, August 1877.

In May and November 1877 Companies K and L, respectively, left Union and New Mexico, and in November 1878 Company D left Union and the territory. In the meantime, in 1877 and 1878 Company E at Union and Company H at Stanton each spent two months on temporary duty at Camp Ojo Caliente. Post Returns, Fort Union, May and September–November 1877, November 1878.

In 1879 Companies F, H, and M each spent two or three months stationed temporarily at Fort Tularosa. In the same year, Company G was away from Bayard at Ojo Caliente for four months, and Company E was temporarily at Ojo Caliente from May 1879 until July 1880. After its duty at Tularosa, Company H did not return to Stanton but moved on to Bayard in September 1879. Post Returns, Fort Stanton, August–October 1879; Fort Bayard, May–September 1879; Fort Union, May 1879–July 1880.

The year 1880 opened with Company A still at Stanton. Companies B and C remained at Bayard, although in 1880 and 1881 Company B spent twelve months at Fort Cummings and Company C spent a year at Cummings and three months at Ojo Caliente. In July and August 1880 Company D returned to New Mexico for temporary duty at Cummings. In December it was assigned permanently to Craig but spent ten of its remaining thirteen months temporarily at Ojo Caliente. Rather than returning to Union when it finished its duty at Ojo Caliente, Company E moved on to Wingate in August 1880. Although Company F's home station was Bayard, it spent the last half of 1880 and the first two months of 1881 at Cummings. Post Returns, Fort Stanton, January 1880; Fort Bayard, January 1880–November 1881; Fort Craig, December 1880–October 1881; Fort Wingate, August 1880.

The year 1880 began with Companies G and M transferring to Stanton and Bayard, respectively. Company M remained at Bayard for all of 1880, going on to Selden in January 1881. For three months during its year at Selden, the company was temporarily stationed at Cummings. Other movements in 1880 and 1881 included Company K's returning to New Mexico, where it served at Ojo Caliente from March until August. For the next eight months, Company K was officially assigned to Union, but it spent most of its time at Cummings; in March 1881 it was permanently assigned to Wingate. In 1880 and 1881 Companies H and I kept their home bases at Bayard and Wingate, respectively, but Company I spent most of 1880 at either Ojo Caliente or Cummings, and for two separate months in 1880 and 1881 Company H was temporarily at Cummings. Post Returns, Fort Stanton, January 1880; Fort Selden, January–December 1881; Fort Union, September 1880–March 1881; Fort Bayard, January 1880–December 1881; Fort Wingate, January 1880–December 1881. See also Agnew, *Garrisons of New Mexico*, 76–79.

8. Post Returns, Forts Bayard, Cummings, Craig, Selden, Stanton, Union, and Wingate, December 1875–December 1881. Temporary troopers at Tularosa and Ojo Caliente were counted as being at their home posts. McRae's incomplete returns do not reveal troop numbers from May through October 1876, but because only one company was there during that time, the estimates are sound. See also Russell F. Weigley, *History of the United States Army* (New York: 1967), 567.

9. S. R. Stafford to commanding officer, Fort Stanton, December 21, 1875; G. Granger to assistant adjutant general, Department of the Missouri, December 28, 1875, Letters Sent by 9th Military Department.

10. *Historical and Pictorial Review, 2nd Cavalry Division, U.S. Army* (N.p.: 1941), 46.

11. Dan L. Thrapp, *Victorio and the Mimbres Apaches* (Norman, Okla.: 1974), 175–176.

12. Post Returns, Fort Selden, September 1876; C. Steelhammer to acting assistant adjutant general, District of New Mexico, September 18, 1876, Letters Sent from Fort Selden.

13. Post Returns, Fort Selden, October 1876.

14. Ninth Cavalry Returns, November 1876. For an excellent study of the army's use of Indians for scouting purposes, see Thomas W. Dunlay, *Wolves for the Blue Soldiers: Indian Scouts and Auxiliaries with the United States Army, 1860–90* (Lincoln, Nebr.: 1982).

15. J. M. Shaw to E. Hatch, September 8, 1876; A. P. Morrow to acting assistant adjutant general, District of New Mexico, October 6, 1876; Sworn Statements of 9th Cavalry Enlisted Men to 2nd Lt. C. W. Merritt, Sept. 25, 1876; Sworn Statements of Navajo Indian Scouts, Camp Vincent, N.M., Sept. 25, 1876; H. H. Wright to commanding officer, Camp Vincent, N.M., September 25, 1876; A. P. Morrow to acting assistant adjutant general, District of New Mexico, October 6, 1876, Letters Received by Dist. N.M., 1865–1890.

16. Thrapp, *Victorio*, 182.

17. Ninth Cavalry Returns, January 1877; *Army and Navy Journal* 14 (May 12, 1877): 18; Leckie, *Buffalo Soldiers*, 178–179; Preston E. Amos, *Above and Beyond in the West: Black Medal of Honor Winners, 1870–1890* (Washington, D.C.: 1974), 8.

18. Ninth Cavalry Returns, January 1877; *Army and Navy Journal* 14 (May 12, 1877): 18.

19. *Annual Report of the Commissioner of Indian Affairs to the Secretary of the Interior for the Year 1877* (Washington, D.C.: 1877), 34–35; Ninth Cavalry Returns, April and May 1877; C. L. Sonnichsen, *The Mescalero Apaches*, 2nd ed. (Norman, Okla.: 1972), 178. See also John P. Clum, "The Apaches," *New Mexico Historical Review* 4 (1929): 107–127.

20. Post Returns, Fort Bayard, May 1877; J. Con line to acting assistant adjutant general, District of New Mexico, July 30, 1877, Letters Received by Dist. N.M., 1865–1890.

21. *Annual Report of the Commissioner of Indian Affairs 1877*, 157; Ninth Cavalry Returns, July and August 1877.

22. Ninth Cavalry Returns, April and May 1877.

23. Post Returns, Fort Bayard, August and September 1877; *Mesilla Independent*, August 25, 1877.

24. Ninth Cavalry Returns, September 1877; Post Returns, Fort Bayard, September 1877; *Grant County Herald*, September 8, 1877; *Mesilla Independent*, September 15, 1877; *Annual Report of the Commissioner of Indian Affairs 1877*, 20–21.

25. C. D. Beyer to acting assistant adjutant general, District of New Mexico, October 3, 1877, Letters Received by the District of New Mexico, 1876–1881, Records of United States Army Continental Commands, 1821–1920, Record Group 98, National Archives, Washington, D.C. (Hereafter cited as Letters Received by Dist. N.M., 1876–1881.)

26. Leckie, *Buffalo Soldiers*, 186.

27. *Mesilla Independent*, September 15, 1877; H. Jewett to assistant adjutant general, District of New Mexico, October 8, 1877, Letters Received by Dist. N.M., 1876–1881.

28. P. T. Swain to assistant adjutant general, District of New Mexico, November 1, 1877; J. Pope to R. C. Drum, October 18, 1877, Letters Received by Dist. N.M., 1876–1881; Post Returns, Fort Wingate, October 1877; Ninth Cavalry Returns, October 1877.

29. Thrapp, *Victorio*, 213–255; Leckie, *Buffalo Soldiers*, 185.

30. Donald E. Worcester, *The Apaches: Eagles of the Southwest* (Norman, Okla.: 1979), 216–217.

31. F. C. Godfroy to N.A.M. Dudley, April 22, 1878; N.A.M. Dudley to acting assistant adjutant general, District of New Mexico, May 24, 1878, Selected Letters Received, 1875–1880, Records of the Adjutant General's Office, Record Group 94, National Archives, Washington, D.C. (Hereafter cited as Selected Letters Received, 1875–1880.); Post Returns, Fort Stanton, May and July 1878.

32. Acting assistant adjutant general, District of New Mexico, to commanding officer, Fort Stanton, June 13, 1878, Letters Sent by 9th Military Department.

33. Acting assistant adjutant general, District of New Mexico, to commanding officer, Fort Stanton, June 13, 1878, Letters Sent by 9th Military Department.

34. Post Returns, Fort Stanton, August 1878; N.A.M. Dudley to assistant adjutant general, District of New Mexico, July 12, 1878, Letters Received by Dist. N.M., 1876–1881; Leckie, *Buffalo Soldiers*, 191.

35. Post Returns, Fort Stanton, August 1878; H. Carroll to post adjutant, Fort Stanton, August 12, 1878, Letters Received by Dist. N.M., 1876–1881.

36. Leckie, *Buffalo Soldiers*, 192.

37. Post Returns, Fort Stanton, August 1878.

38. Post Returns, Fort Wingate, August 1878.

39. *Grant County Herald*, September 14, 1878.

40. H.H.R. Carter to post adjutant, Fort Bayard, January 15, 1879, Letters Received by Dist. N.M., 1865–1890.

41. W. H. Hugo to post adjutant, Fort Bayard, January 13, 1879, Letters Received by Dist. N.M., 1865–1890.

Chapter IV

1. Norman Cleaveland and George Fitzpatrick, *The Morleys — Young Upstarts on the Southwest Frontier* (Albuquerque: 1971), 61.

2. Larry Murphy, *Out In God's Country: A History of Colfax County, New Mexico* (Springer, N.M.: 1967), 80.

3. Victor Westphall, *Thomas Benton Catron and His Era* (Tucson: 1973), 100–101.

4. Lawrence R. Murphy, *Philmont: A History of New Mexico's Cimarron Country* (Albuquerque: 1972), 117.

5. Murphy, *God's Country,* 74; Murphy, *Philmont,* 118.

6. Westphall, *Catron,* 98–101.

7. Murphy, *Philmont,* 119.

8. Morris F. Taylor, *O. P. McMains and the Maxwell Land Grant Conflict* (Tucson: 1979), 1ff.

9. Murphy, *Philmont,* 119–120.

10. The most detailed and balanced account of the events surrounding these deaths is Taylor, *O. P. McMains,* 33–56.

11. E. Hatch to assistant adjutant general, March 9, 1876, Letters Received by Dist. N.M., 1876–1881; Chris Emmett, *Fort Union and the Winning of the Southwest* (Norman, Okla.: 1965), 372.

12. Murphy, *Philmont,* 121.

13. Cleaveland and Fitzpatrick, *The Morleys,* 73, 83–87, 114.

14. Murphy, *Philmont,* 122.

15. Cleaveland and Fitzpatrick, *The Morleys,* 118–119.

16. Cleaveland and Fitzpatrick, *The Morleys,* 119.

17. Post Returns, Fort Union, March 1876; Emmett, *Fort Union,* 372.

18. Cleaveland and Fitzpatrick, *The Morleys,* 120; Norman Cleaveland, *Colfax County's Chronic Murder Mystery* (Santa Fe: 1977), 7–8.

19. See Norman Cleaveland comp. and ann., *An Introduction to the Colfax County War, 1875–78* ([Santa Fe]: 1975); Norman Cleaveland, "The Great New Mexico Cover-Up: Frank Warner Angel's Reports," *Rio Grande History* 5 (Summer 1975): 4–9; Lee Scott Theisen, "Frank Warner Angel's Notes on New Mexico Territory, 1878," *Arizona and the West* 18 (Winter 1976): 333–336.

20. Cleaveland and Fitzpatrick, *The Morleys,* 120–121.

21. Cleaveland and Fitzpatrick, *The Morleys,* 121.

22. *Cimarron News and Press,* quoted in *Mesilla News,* April 8, 1876.

23. F. Moore to J. F. Wade, March 25, 1876, Letters Received by Dist. N.M., 1865–1890.

24. J. S. Loud to commanding officer, Fort Union, New Mexico, March 29, 1876, Letters Received by Dist. N.M., 1865–1890.

25. Emmett, *Fort Union,* 372.

26. Post Returns, Fort Union, April 1876; J. F. Wade to F. Moore, April 12, 1876, Letters Received by Dist. N.M., 1865–1890; Emmett, *Fort Union,* 372.

27. *Las Vegas Gazette,* October 7, 1876; William A. Keleher, *Maxwell Land Grant: A New Mexico Item* (Santa Fe: 1942), 69–70.

28. *Santa Fe Daily New Mexican*, May 9, 1877; Emmett, *Fort Union*, 373, 376.

29. Murphy, *Philmont*, 126–129.

30. Maurice G. Fulton, *History of the Lincoln County War* (Tucson: 1968), 75–76; *Mesilla Independent*, September 8, 1877; J. Sherman, Jr., to E. Hatch, December 3, 1877; J. S. Loud to commanding officer, Fort Stanton, December 10, 1877, Letters Received by Dist. N.M., 1865–1890.

31. Westphall, *Catron*, 78–86.

32. Fulton, *Lincoln County War*, 45–47. For a detailed account of the economic power and influence of the house of Murphy, see John P. Wilson, *Merchants, Guns, and Money: The Story of Lincoln County and Its Wars* (Santa Fe: 1987), 27–48.

33. Harwood P. Hinton, Jr., "John Simpson Chisum, 1877–1884," *New Mexico Historical Review* 31 (July 1956): 188–196.

34. Fulton, *Lincoln County War*, 57–64; Wilson, *Merchants, Guns, and Money*, 63–67.

35. Ninth Cavalry Returns, February 1878; Post Returns, Fort Stanton, February 1878.

36. G. A. Purington to E. Hatch, March 14, 1878, Letters Received by Dist. N.M., 1865–1890.

37. S. B. Axtell to E. Hatch, February 25, 1878; W. L. Rynerson to S. B. Axtell, February 25, 1878, Letters Received by Dist. N.M., 1865–1890.

38. Post Returns, Fort Stanton, February 1878; Ninth Cavalry Returns, February 1878.

39. G. A. Purington to acting assistant adjutant general, District of New Mexico, February 27, 1878, Letters Received by Dist. N.M., 1865–1890.

40. G. A. Purington to E. Hatch, March 14, 1878, Letters Received by Dist. N.M., 1865–1890.

41. J. S. Loud to commanding officer, Fort Stanton, March 24, 1878, Letters Sent by 9th Military Department.

42. Ninth Cavalry Returns, March 1878; Donald R. Lavash, *Sheriff William Brady: Tragic Hero of the Lincoln County War* (Santa Fe: 1986), 102.

43. Lavash, *William Brady*, 103; Fulton, *Lincoln County War*, 170–171.

44. Ninth Cavalry Returns, April 1878; Frederick W. Nolan, *The Life & Death of John Henry Tunstall* (Albuquerque: 1965), 310–311; William A. Keleher, *Violence in Lincoln County, 1869–1881: A New Mexico Item* (Albuquerque: 1957), 113.

45. Dee Dwight Greenly, "The Military Career of Nathan Augustus Monroe Dudley, 1843–1889" (Master's thesis, New Mexico State University, 1986); Heitman, *Historical Register*, vol. 1: 386; Leckie, *Buffalo Soldiers*, 181–183, 197–198.

46. N.A.M. Dudley to J. S. Loud, May 4, 1878, Letters Received by Dist. N.M., 1865–1890.

47. J. N. Copeland to N.A.M. Dudley, April 8, 1878, Letters Received by Dist. N.M., 1865–1890.

48. W. Bristol to N.A.M. Dudley, April 20, 1878, Letters Received by Dist. N.M., 1865–1890.

49. N.A.M. Dudley to J. S. Loud, May 4, 1878, Letters Received by Dist. N.M., 1865–1890.

50. T. Dale to commanding officer [E. Hatch], May 1, 1878, Letters Received by Dist. N.M., 1865–1890.

51. J. S. Loud to commanding officer, Fort Stanton, April 14, 1878, Letters Sent by 9th Military Department.

52. J. Sherman, Jr., to N.A.M. Dudley, April 15, 1878; W. Bristol to N.A.M. Dudley, April 18, 1878; J. N. Copeland to N.A.M. Dudley, April 24, 1878, Letters Received by Dist. N.M., 1865–1890; Post Returns, Fort Stanton, April 1878.

53. Fulton, *Lincoln County War*, 210–215.

54. J. N. Copeland to N.A.M. Dudley, April 30, 1878, Letters Received by Dist. N.M., 1865–1890.

55. G. W. Smith to post adjutant, Fort Stanton, May 1, 1878, Letters Received by Dist. N.M., 1865–1890.

56. N.A.M. Dudley to J. S. Loud, May 4, 1878, Letters Received by Dist. N.M., 1865–1890.

57. J. N. Copeland to N.A.M. Dudley, May 2 (two letters), 4, and 7, 1878; deputy sheriff of Lincoln County to N.A.M. Dudley, May 2, 1878; M. F. Goodwin to N.A.M. Dudley, May 2, 1878, Letters Received by Dist. N.M., 1865–1890.

58. S. B. Axtell to [E. Hatch], May 30, 1878, Letters Received by Dist. N.M., 1865–1890; Leckie, *Buffalo Soldiers*, 198; J. S. Loud to commanding officer, Fort Stanton, June 1, 1878, Letters Sent by 9th Military Department; Post Returns, Fort Stanton, June 1878.

59. M. F. Goodwin to post adjutant, Fort Stanton, June 19, 1878; N.A.M. Dudley to acting assistant adjutant general, District of New Mexico, June 22, 1878, Letters Received by Dist. N.M, 1865–1890.

60. H. Carroll to post adjutant, Fort Stanton, July 1, 1878, N.A.M. Dudley to acting assistant adjutant general, District of New Mexico, June 29, 1878, Letters Received by Dist. N.M., 1865–1890.

61. For a clear explanation of the legal bases for the use of soldiers in civil disorders as a posse comitatus, see Robert W. Coakley, *The Role of Federal Military Forces in Domestic Disorders, 1789–1878* (Washington, D.C.: 1988), 344–345. Coakley details two examples of the use of the army as a posse comitatus prior to the passage of the Posse Comitatus Act in 1878. See pp. 128–144.

62. Acting assistant adjutant general, District of New Mexico, to commanding officer, Fort Stanton, June 25, 1878, Letters Sent by 9th Military Department; N.A.M. Dudley to acting assistant adjutant general, District of New Mexico, July 11, 1878, Letters Received by Dist. N.M., 1865–1890.

63. D. M. Appel to post adjutant, Fort Stanton, July 15, 1878; Statement of Deputy Sheriff John Long, July 21 or 22, 1878, Letters Received by Dist. N.M., 1865–1890; Robert M. Utley, *Four Fighters of Lincoln County* (Albuquerque: 1986), 44; Keleher, *Violence in Lincoln County*, 141–142; Nolan, *Tunstall*, 374–375.

64. G. W. Peppin to N.A.M. Dudley, July 16, 1878; N.A.M. Dudley to G. W. Peppin, July 16, 1878, Letters Received by Dist. N.M., 1865–1890.

65. Proceedings of a Board of Officers Convened at Fort Stanton, New Mexico, July 7, 1878, Letters Received by Dist. N.M., 1865–1890.

66. N.A.M. Dudley to acting assistant adjutant general, District of New Mexico, July 6 and 18, 1878; G. A. Purington and others to N.A.M. Dudley, July 18[?], 1878, Letters Received by Dist. N.M., 1865–1890.

67. N.A.M. Dudley to acting assistant adjutant general, District of New Mexico, July 20, 1878, Letters Received by Dist. N.M., 1865–1890; Post Returns, Fort Stanton, July 1878; Greenly, "Military Career of Dudley," 87; Utley, *Four Fighters*, 46.

68. N.A.M. Dudley to acting assistant adjutant general, District of New Mexico, July 20, 1878, Letters Received by Dist. N.M., 1865–1890.

69. Utley, *Four Fighters*, 46; N.A.M. Dudley to acting assistant adjutant general, District of New Mexico, July 20, 1878, Letters Received by Dist. N.M., 1865–1890.

70. Keleher, *Violence in Lincoln County*, 145.

71. Keleher, *Violence in Lincoln County*, 146; N.A.M. Dudley to acting assistant adjutant general, District of New Mexico, July 23, 1878; Fillipi Marendo and others, Report of the Proceedings of the Coroner's Jury, July 20, 1878, Letters Received by Dist. N.M., 1865–1890.

72. Nolan, *Tunstall*, 378–379; N.A.M. Dudley to acting assistant adjutant general, July 23, 1878, Letters Received by Dist. N.M., 1865–1890.

73. Leckie, *Buffalo Soldiers*, 202.

74. N.A.M. Dudley to S. B. Axtell, August 15, 1878; G. W. Peppin, sworn statement, August 15, 1878; N.A.M. Dudley to acting assistant adjutant general, District of New Mexico, September 7 (two letters), 14, 28, and 29, 1878, Letters Received by Dist. N.M., 1865–1890.

75. N.A.M. Dudley to acting assistant adjutant general, District of New Mexico, August 3, 1878, Letters Received by Dist. N.M., 1865–1890.

76. Acting assistant adjutant general, District of New Mexico, to commanding officer, Fort Stanton, August 15, 1878, Letters Sent by 9th Military Department.

77. Acting assistant adjutant general, District of New Mexico, to commanding officer, Fort Stanton, October 27, 1878, Letters Sent by 9th Military Department; Post Returns, Fort Stanton, November and December 1878, January 1879; L. Wallace to E. Hatch, February 14, 1879, Letters Received by Dist. N.M., 1865–1890.

78. Philip J. Rasch, "Exit Axtell: Enter Wallace," *New Mexico Historical Review* 32 (July 1957): 231–233.

79. Leckie, *Buffalo Soldiers*, 203; *Santa Fe New Mexican*, December 14, 1878.

80. Keleher, *Violence in Lincoln County*, 200–202.

81. G. Kimbrell to commanding officer, Fort Stanton, New Mexico, February 15, 1879; N.A.M. Dudley to acting assistant adjutant general, District of New Mexico, February 19, 1879; B. Dawson to post adjutant, Fort Stanton, February 19, 1879, Letters Received by Dist. N.M., 1865–1890; Wilson, *Merchants, Guns, and Money*, 117.

82. J. B. Wilson and others to N.A.M. Dudley, February 19, 1879; G. Kimbrell to N.A.M. Dudley, February 19, 1879; N.A.M. Dudley, Special Orders No. 26, February 19, 1879; G. Kimbrell to M. F. Goodwin, February 20, 1879; N.A.M. Dudley to acting assistant adjutant general, District of New Mexico, February 21, 24, and March 1, 1879; M. F. Goodwin to post adjutant, Fort Stanton, February 23, 1879, Letters Received by Dist. N.M., 1865–1890; Ninth Cavalry Returns, February 1879.

83. L. Wallace to E. Hatch, March 5, 1879; M. F. Goodwin to post adjutant, Fort Stanton, March 7, 1879, Letters Received by Dist. N.M., 1865–1890.

84. E. Hatch to commanding officer, Fort Stanton, March 5, 1879, Letters Sent by 9th Military Department.

85. L. Wallace to E. Hatch, March 6, 1879, Letters Received by Dist. N.M., 1865–1890.

86. L. Wallace to E. Hatch, March 7, 1879; E. Hatch to assistant adjutant general, Department of the Missouri, March 8, 1879, Letters Received by Dist. N.M., 1865–1890.

87. Indictment, Territory of New Mexico vs. N.A.M. Dudley, Territory of New Mexico, County of Lincoln, in the District Court at the County of Lincoln in the April A.D. 1879 Term, no date, Letters Received by Dist. N.M., 1865–1890.

88. Charges and Specifications Against Lieutenant Colonel N.A.M. Dudley, no date, Letters Received by Dist. N.M., 1865–1890; Leckie, *Buffalo Soldiers*, 204–205.

89. Lee Scott Theisen, ed., "The Fight in Lincoln, N.M., 1878: The Testimony of Two Negro Participants," *Arizona and the West* 12 (Summer 1970): 182–198. Tragedy struck Washington a few weeks after he testified, when he shot at a dog and accidentally killed his wife and child. *Thirty-Four*, June 18, 1879.

90. H. Carroll to acting assistant adjutant general, District of New Mexico, March 10 and 15, 1879; B. Dawson to post adjutant, Fort Stanton, March 28, 1879; G. A. Purington to acting assistant adjutant general, Fort Stanton, March 29 and August 17 and 23, 1879; L. Wallace to E. A. Hatch, April 28, 1879, Letters Received by Dist. N.M., 1865–1890; acting assistant

adjutant general to commanding officer, Fort Stanton, April 28, 1879, Letters Sent by 9th Military Department; Post Returns, Fort Stanton, March–October 1879.

91. Quoted in Leckie, *Buffalo Soldiers*, 205.

Chapter V

1. Worcester, *The Apaches*, 217–218.

2. C. D. Beyer to post adjutant, Fort Bayard, February 22, 1879, Letters Received by Dist. N.M., 1865–1890; *Grant County Herald*, February 15, 1879.

3. C. D. Beyer, Special Orders No. 44, Fort Bayard, May 6, 1879; W. H. Hugo to post adjutant, Fort Bayard, June 9, 1879, Letters Received by Dist. N.M., 1865–1890; *Grant County Herald*, May 10, 1879.

4. A. P. Morrow, Special Orders No. 48, Fort Bayard, May 25, 1879; P. Cusack to post adjutant, Fort Bayard, June 16, 1879, Letters Received by Dist. N.M., 1865–1890.

5. C. D. Beyer to post adjutant, Fort Bayard, June 16, 1879, Letters Received by Dist. N.M., 1865–1890.

6. Amos, *Above and Beyond*, 9–11.

7. Post Returns, Fort Union, October 1879; *Annual Report of the Secretary of War, 1880* (Washington, D.C.: 1881), vol. 1: 86; *Historical and Pictorial Review, 2nd Cavalry Division*, 46; C. Steelhammer to acting assistant adjutant general, District of New Mexico, December 11, 1879, Letters Received by Dist. N.M., 1865–1890.

8. *Annual Report of the Secretary of War, 1880*, vol. 1: 88.

9. Post Returns, Forts Bayard, Cummings, Union, Stanton, and Wingate, September 1879–October 1880; Leckie, *Buffalo Soldiers*, 211, 215–216.

10. J. Pope to assistant adjutant general, Military Division of the Missouri, September 24, 1879, Letters Received, File No. 6058–1879, Records of the Adjutant General's Office, Record Group 94, National Archives, Washington, D.C. (Hereafter cited as Letters Received, File No. 6058–1879.)

11. Amos, *Above and Beyond*, 11–13.

12. Post Returns, Fort Union, October 1879.

13. A. P. Morrow to acting assistant adjutant general, District of New Mexico, November 5, 1879, Letters Received by Dist. N.M., 1865–1890.

14. Post Returns, Fort Bayard, November 1879; Leckie, *Buffalo Soldiers*, 214.

15. Post Returns, Forts Bayard, Stanton, Union, Cummings, and Wingate, January–August 1880; A. P. Morrow to E. Hatch, January 18, 1880; E. Hatch to J. Pope, February 3, 1880, Letters Received, File No. 6058–1879.

16. Thrapp, *Victorio*, 265, 268.

17. Robert M. Utley, "The Buffalo Soldiers and Victorio," *New Mexico Magazine* 62: 3 (March 1984): 50, 53; Thrapp, *Victorio*, 270–271; Dan L. Thrapp, *The Conquest of Apacheria* (Norman, Okla.: 1967), 195–197; *Annual Report of the Secretary of War, 1880*, vol. 2: 94–95.

18. W[alter] F. Beyer and O[scar] F. Keydel, eds., *Deeds of Valor: How America's Heroes Won the Medal of Honor* (Detroit: 1901), vol. 2: 273; Leckie, *Buffalo Soldiers*, 217–219.

19. Leckie, *Buffalo Soldiers*, 220.

20. E. Hatch to assistant adjutant general, Department of the Missouri, May 17, 1880, Letters Received, File No. 6058–1879; Beyer and Keydel, *Deeds of Valor*, vol. 2: 273–276.

21. *Annual Report of the Secretary of War, 1880*, vol. 1: 109; E. Hatch to assistant adjutant general, Department of the Missouri, May 27, 1880, Military Division of the Missouri, Special File, Victorio Papers, 1880, Records of United States Army Continental Commands, 1821–1920, Record Group 98, National Archives, Washington, D.C. (Hereafter cited as Special File, Victorio.); Utley, *Frontier Regulars*, 362; Thrapp, *Conquest of Apacheria*, 201; Sonnichsen, *Mescalero Apaches*, 208.

22. E. Hatch to J. Pope, June 1, 1880, Letters Received, File No. 6058–1879; Thrapp, *Conquest of Apacheria*, 202–203; Thrapp, *Victorio*, 281–282.

23. For a study of the diplomatic negotiations between the United States and Mexico regarding Victorio and the advantage he took of the international border, see Bruce J. Dinges, "The Victorio Campaign of 1880: Cooperation and Conflict on the United States–Mexico Border," *New Mexico Historical Review* 62 (January 1987): 81–94.

24. Victorio's last battle is described in Thrapp, *Victorio*, 293–314.

25. For more information on the Tenth Cavalry's role in the Victorio War, see William H. Leckie and Shirley A. Leckie, *Unlikely Warriors: General Benjamin H. Grierson and His Family* (Norman, Okla.: 1984), 258–267, and Leckie, *Buffalo Soldiers*, 217–220, 222–229.

26. *New Southwest and Grant County Herald*, October 30, 1880.

27. P. Cusack to adjutant, Ninth Cavalry, September 15, 1880, Letters Received by Dist. N.M., 1865–1890.

28. N.A.M. Dudley to acting assistant adjutant general, District of New Mexico, November 2, 10, and 24, 1880, Post Records, Fort Cummings; N.A.M. Dudley to acting assistant adjutant general, District of New Mexico, November 4, 1880, Headquarters Records, Fort Cummings.

29. T. Bills to N.A.M. Dudley, October 26, 1880, Headquarters Records, Fort Cummings.

30. N.A.M. Dudley to [Simeon H.] Newman, editor of *Thirty-Four*, Las Cruces, New Mexico, November 4, 1880; N.A.M. Dudley to acting assistant adjutant general, District of New Mexico, November 15, 1880; N.A.M. Dudley to commanding officer, Fort Craig, November 13, 1880, Post Records, Fort Cummings.

31. C. W. Taylor to acting assistant adjutant general, District of New Mexico, November 16, 1880, Letters Received by Dist. N.M., 1865–1890.

32. N.A.M. Dudley to acting assistant adjutant general, District of New Mexico, November 17, 1880 (telegram); N.A.M. Dudley to O. R. Smith, November 17, 1880, Post Records, Fort Cummings.

33. T. C. Davenport to acting assistant adjutant general, District of New Mexico, November 20, 1880, Post Records, Fort Cummings.

34. N.A.M. Dudley to acting assistant adjutant general, District of New Mexico, November 21, 1880 (telegram), Post Records, Fort Cummings.

35. N.A.M. Dudley to commanding officer, Fort Bliss, Texas, November 22, 1880 (telegram); N.A.M. Dudley to acting assistant adjutant general, District of New Mexico, November 22, 1880 (telegram), Post Records, Fort Cummings.

36. N.A.M. Dudley to acting assistant adjutant general, District of New Mexico, November 22, 1880 (telegram), Post Records, Fort Cummings. See also B. S. Humphrey to N.A.M. Dudley, November 30, 1880, Headquarters Records, Fort Cummings.

37. J. S. Loud to commanding officer, Fort Cummings, November 10, 1880, Headquarters Records, Fort Cummings; C. A. Howard, Special Field Orders No. 17, November 12, 1880; N.A.M. Dudley to acting assistant adjutant general, District of New Mexico, November 12, 1880 (telegram); W. F. Blauvelt, Special Field Orders No. 45, February 25, 1881, Post Records, Fort Cummings.

38. E. W. Clift to F. B. Taylor, December 2, 1880, Letters Received by Dist. N.M., 1865–1890.

39. N.A.M. Dudley to E. Hatch, January 25, 1881, Letters Received by Dist. N.M., 1865–1890; Ninth Cavalry Returns, August 1881.

40. N.A.M. Dudley to acting assistant adjutant general, District of New Mexico, January 15, 1881 (two letters); N.A.M. Dudley to commanding officer, Fort Bliss, Texas, January 15, 1881 (telegram); N.A.M. Dudley to [telegraph] operator, Mesilla, New Mexico, January 6, 1881 (telegram), Post Records, Fort Cummings.

41. N.A.M. Dudley to commanding officer, Fort Prescott, Arizona, January 15, 1881; N.A.M. Dudley to acting assistant adjutant general, District of New Mexico, January 14, 1881, Post Records, Fort Cummings.

42. N.A.M. Dudley to H. C. McComas, Silver City, New Mexico, January 15, 1881; N.A.M. Dudley to W. R. Price, District of Arizona, January 16, 1881, Post Records, Fort Cummings.

43. N.A.M. Dudley to E. Hatch, January 23, 1881 (first letter), Post Records, Fort Cummings. By that time not only were Companies C and F chasing these Indians, but also Companies B and H out of Bayard had joined the hunt in the San Francisco Valley. Furthermore, Companies D (out of Craig but temporarily under Dudley at Cummings), M (out of Selden), and E and I (out of Wingate) were in the field north of Cummings. At first Company K remained at Cummings, but later Dudley sent a detachment of it to protect Silver Camp, because Indians had been seen there and apparently had stolen some stock. N.A.M. Dudley to E. Hatch, January 23, 1881 (second letter); N.A.M. Dudley to acting assistant adjutant general, District of New Mexico, January 25, 1881, Post Records, Fort Cummings.

44. N.A.M. Dudley to acting assistant adjutant general, District of New Mexico, January 15, 1881, Post Records, Fort Cummings.

45. N.A.M. Dudley to E. Hatch, January 23, 1881; B. S. Humphrey to acting assistant adjutant general, District of New Mexico, February 5, 1881; N.A.M. Dudley to Colonel W. R. Price, January 24, 1881, Post Records, Fort Cummings; L. H. Rucker to E. Hatch, January 24, 1881, Letters Received by Dist. N.M., 1865–1890.

46. Post Returns, Fort Craig, January 1881; N.A.M. Dudley to W. R. Price, January 18, 1881, Post Records, Fort Cummings.

47. N.A.M. Dudley to E. Hatch, January 28, 1881 (three letters), Post Records, Fort Cummings; L. H. Rucker to N.A.M. Dudley, January 28, 1881, Headquarters Records, Fort Cummings.

48. N.A.M. Dudley to acting assistant adjutant general, District of New Mexico, January 15, 16, and 20, 1881, Post Records, Fort Cummings.

49. N.A.M. Dudley to E. Hatch, January 24, 1881; N.A.M. Dudley to acting assistant adjutant general, District of New Mexico, January 25, 1881, Post Records, Fort Cummings.

50. S. Albert to commanding officer, District of New Mexico, February 2, 1881, Letters Received by Dist. N.M., 1865–1890.

51. N.A.M. Dudley to acting assistant adjutant general, District of New Mexico, February 20, 1881 (telegram), Post Records, Fort Cummings.

52. Harold Miller, "Nana's Raid of 1881," *Password* 19 (Summer 1974): 56; Stephen H. Lekson, *Nana's Raid: Apache Warfare in Southern New Mexico, 1881* (El Paso: 1987), 10.

53. *Annual Report of the Secretary of War, 1881* (Washington, D.C.: 1881), vol. 1: 126; Ninth Cavalry Returns, July 1881; Miller, "Nana's Raid," 59; Thrapp, *Conquest of Apacheria,* 212–213.

54. Miller, "Nana's Raid," 59–60; Lekson, *Nana's Raid,* 17.

55. Miller, "Nana's Raid," 60, 61–62; Thrapp, *Conquest of Apacheria,* 213; Lekson, *Nana's Raid,* 19–20.

56. Post Returns, Fort Cummings, August 1881.

57. Post Returns, Fort Wingate, September 1881; *Annual Report of the Secretary of War, 1881*, vol. 1: 127; Ninth Cavalry Returns, August 1881; Miller, "Nana's Raid," 62; Beyer and Keydel, *Deeds of Valor*, vol. 2: 276; Amos, *Above and Beyond*, 17–22.

58. Ninth Cavalry Returns, August 1881; Miller, "Nana's Raid," 64; Beyer and Keydel, *Deeds of Valor*, vol. 2: 277–281; Amos, *Above and Beyond*, 22–27.

59. N. W. Osborne to E. Hatch, August 19, 1881, Post Records, Fort Cummings; *Annual Report of the Secretary of War, 1881*, vol. 1: 127; Beyer and Keydel, *Deeds of Valor*, vol. 2: 281; Ninth Cavalry Returns, August 1881; Miller, "Nana's Raid," 65–67; Sonnichsen, *Mescalero Apaches*, 214–215; Ralph Emerson Twitchell, *The Leading Facts of New Mexican History* (Cedar Rapids, Iowa: 1911–1917), vol. 2: 439; Amos, *Above and Beyond*, 27–30.

60. Quoted in Don Rickey, Jr., *Forty Miles a Day on Beans and Hay: The Enlisted Soldier Fighting the Indian Wars* (Norman, Okla.: 1963), 305–306.

61. Ninth Cavalry Returns, October 1881.

62. Agnew, *Garrisons of New Mexico*, 95.

63. Miller, "Nana's Raid," 62.

64. On November 1 Fort Wingate's Companies E, I, and K left the territory. Companies I and K, which had recently been on temporary duty at Fort Apache, Arizona Territory, arrived at Wingate in late October, whereupon along with Company E they were dispatched to Fort Hays, Kansas. A few days later Stanton's Companies A and G were transferred to Fort Dodge, Kansas. Craig's Company D left its New Mexico post on December 4, having been assigned to Fort Riley, and on that same day Fort Bayard's Companies B and C left their temporary post at Cummings on regular emigrant trains en route to Hays. On December 19 Fort Selden's Company M left its temporary post at Cummings en route to Riley. Finally, in December Companies F and H left Bayard for assignments at Riley. Post Returns, Fort Wingate, October and November 1881; Fort Stanton, November 1881; Fort Craig, December 1881; Fort Bayard, December 1881; Fort Cummings, December 1881; G. A. Forsyth to J. S. Loud, December 5, 1881, Post Records, Fort Cummings; *Annual Report of the Secretary of War, 1881*, vol. 1: 118; Ninth Cavalry Returns, November and December 1881.

65. *Rio Grande Republican*, October 19, 1881.

66. For biographical sketches of all eighteen of these men, see Amos, *Above and Beyond*.

Chapter VI

1. Post Returns, Fort Stanton, September-November 1876, May 1877.

2. A. S. Kimball to chief quartermaster, District of New Mexico, February 13, 1876; A. S. Kimball to acting assistant adjutant general, District of New Mexico, March 2, 1876, Letters Received by Dist. N.M., 1865–1890.

3. C. W. Merritt, Statement of the amount of clothing lost by Enlisted Men Company I 9th Cavalry while working at a fire at this Post [Fort Wingate] on the 15th of December 1876, Letters Received by Dist. N.M., 1865–1890.

4. Post Returns, Fort Stanton, April 1878; Ninth Cavalry Returns, May 1878.

5. C. W. Merritt to acting assistant adjutant general, District of New Mexico, April 15 and 29, 1879, Letters Received by Dist. N.M., 1865–1890.

6. F. T. Bennett to acting assistant adjutant general, District of New Mexico, November 26, 1879, Letters Received by Dist. N.M., 1865–1890.

7. C. A. Stedman, Estimated Costs of Completing "The North Star Road," May 11, 1877; C. A. Stedman to acting assistant adjutant general, District of New Mexico, October 26, 1877, Letters Received by Dist. N.M., 1865–1890.

8. F. T. Bennett to M. G. Cockey, November 26, 1881; C. A. Howard, Special Field Orders Nos. 24 and 31, November 20 and 29, 1880, Post Records, Fort Cummings; A. E. Hooker to J. S. Loud, October 17, 1877; C. Parker to acting assistant adjutant general, District of New Mexico, August 8, 1876; J. G. Keefe to commanding officer, District of New Mexico, April 26, 1876, Letters Received by Dist. N.M., 1865–1890.

9. P. Cusack to post adjutant, Fort Stanton, September 28, 1881, Letters Received by Dist. N.M., 1865–1890.

10. B. Johnson to P. Cusack, October 2, 1881, Letters Received by Dist. N.M., 1865–1890.

11. P. Cusack to post commander, Fort Stanton, October 6, 1881, Letters Received by Dist. N.M., 1865–1890.

12. M. O'Brien to J. S. Loud, October 13, 1881, Letters Received by Dist. N.M., 1865–1890.

13. Post Commander, Fort Stanton to S. R. Stafford, October 21, 1881, Letters Received by Dist. N.M., 1865–1890.

14. C. A. Howard, General Field Orders No. 2, October 27, 1880, Post Records, Fort Cummings.

15. C. A. Howard, Circular, November 15, 1880, Post Records, Fort Cummings.

16. N.A.M. Dudley to J. A. Wilcox, October 28, 1880 (telegram); N.A.M. Dudley to G. Buell, October 28, 1880; J. F. McBlain, Field Orders Nos. 135 and 140, September 20 and 25, 1881, Post Records, Fort Cummings.

17. Dale Frederick Giese, "Soldiers at Play: A History of Social Life at Fort Union, New Mexico, 1851–1891" (Ph.D. diss., University of New Mexico, 1969), 37–38; Thomas J. McLaughlin, "History of Fort Union, New Mexico" (Master's thesis, University of New Mexico, 1952), 109. See also Thomas C. Railsback and John P. Langellier, The Drums Would Roll: A Pictorial History of U.S. Army Bands on the American Frontier, 1866–1900 (London: Arms and Armour Press, 1987).

18. J. N. Gough and others to E. Hatch, June 10, 1876, Letters Received by Dist. N.M., 1865–1890; Post Returns, Fort Union, June and July 1876; Giese, "Soldiers at Play," 38.

19. Santa Fe Citizens Petition to J. Pope, November 9, 1876, Letters Received by Dist. N.M., 1865–1890.

20. E. R. Platt by command of Brig. Gen. J. Pope on army regulations, November 18, 1876, Letters Received by Dist. N.M., 1865–1890.

21. E. Hatch to assistant adjutant general, Department of the Missouri, March 20, 1877, Letters Received by Dist. N.M., 1865–1890.

22. Post Returns, Fort Stanton, May 1877 and March 1878; Fort Union, April 1878.

23. Acting assistant adjutant general's office, District of New Mexico, to C. Bradley, March 26, 1879, Letters Sent by 9th Military Department.

24. Post Returns, Fort Stanton, May 1879–October 1880; G. A. Purington to acting assistant adjutant general, District of New Mexico, June 2, 1879, Letters Received by Dist. N.M., 1865–1890.

25. Santa Fe Weekly New Mexican, November 1, 1880. See also Santa Fe Daily New Mexican, October 29, 1880. The members of the band and the instruments on which each performed were: Sgt. Stephen Taylor (E flat cornet), Pvt. William Cee (E flat cornet), Pvt. Edward Lyons (E flat cornet), Pvt. John Smith (1st B flat cornet), Pvt. William N. Coleman (2nd B flat cornet), Pvt. Alexander Robinson (3rd B flat cornet), Cpl. Edward Lee (solo alto), Pvt. Patrick Straw (1st alto), Pvt. Fielding Jones (2nd alto), Pvt. Benjamin Seals (3rd alto), Pvt. Richard Reed (1st tenor), Pvt. James H. White (2nd tenor), Sgt. Joseph Marshall (baritone), Pvt. Nicholas Dunlap (B flat tuba), Pvt. John Butler (E flat tuba), Pvt. Samuel H. Asburry (E flat tuba), Pvt. George Camphor (small drum), Cpl. Elijah Mason (bass drum), and Pvt. William T. Lee (bells). Santa Fe Daily New Mexican, March 28, 1880.

26. Post Returns, Fort Bayard, September and November 1877.

27. J. S. Loud to commanding officer, Fort Stanton, January 4, 1879, Letters Sent by 9th Military Department; Ninth Cavalry Returns, January 1881.

28. Charges and Specifications Preferred Against First Lieutenant John Conline, 9th U.S. Cavalry, undated, Letters Received by Dist. N.M., 1865–1890.

29. *Rocky Mountain News*, June 17, 1877.

30. Charges and Specifications Preferred Against First Lieutenant John Conline, 9th U.S. Cavalry, undated, Letters Received by Dist. N.M., 1865–1890.

31. J. Conline to assistant adjutant general, Department of the Missouri, August 19, 1877, Letters Received by Dist. N.M., 1865–1890.

32. Additional Charges and Specifications Preferred Against First Lieutenant John Conline, U.S. Cavalry, Fort Bayard, N.M., undated, Letters Received by Dist. N.M., 1865–1890.

33. Additional Charges and Specifications Preferred Against First Lieutenant John Conline, 9th Cavalry, undated, Letters Received by Dist. N.M., 1865–1890.

34. Heitman, *Historical Register*, vol. 1: 321.

35. Giese, "Soldiers at Play," 140.

36. A. S. Kimball to acting assistant adjutant general, District of New Mexico, May 15, 1877, Letters Received by Dist. N.M., 1865–1890.

37. N.A.M. Dudley to post adjutant, Fort Cummings, October 28, 1880, Headquarters Records, Fort Cummings.

38. N.A.M. Dudley to acting assistant adjutant general, District of New Mexico, November 5, 1880; C. A. Howard, Circular, Fort Cummings, November 9, 1880; C. A. Howard, Special Field Orders No. 15, November 10, 1880, Post Records, Fort Cummings; J. J. Kane to acting assistant adjutant general, District of New Mexico, December 7, 1880, Headquarters Records, Fort Cummings.

39. P. P. Powell to F. B. Taylor, May 12, 1881, Post Records, Fort Cummings.

40. L. Kennon to H. Carroll, January 15, 1877, Letters Received by Dist. N.M., 1865–1890.

41. A. E. Hooker to acting assistant adjutant general, District of New Mexico, September 10, 1879, Letters Received by Dist. N.M., 1865–1890.

42. N.A.M. Dudley to commanding officer, Fort Bayard, October 27 and 29, 1880 (telegrams); D. D. Mitchell to T. B. Hunt, November 4, 1880 (telegram), Post Records, Fort Cummings.

43. N.A.M. Dudley to acting assistant adjutant general, District of New Mexico, November 2, 1880, Post Records, Fort Cummings.

44. N.A.M. Dudley to acting assistant adjutant general, District of New Mexico, November 12 and 17, 1880, Post Records, Fort Cummings.

45. S. C. Benedict to post adjutant, Fort Cummings, November 18, 1880, Headquarters Records, Fort Cummings.

46. N.A.M. Dudley to acting assistant adjutant general, District of New Mexico, October 28, 1880, Headquarters Records, Fort Cummings; N.A.M. Dudley to acting assistant adjutant general, District of New Mexico, December 24, 1880, Post Records, Fort Cummings.

47. N.A.M. Dudley to acting assistant adjutant general, District of New Mexico, October 28 (telegram) and 31, November 5 and 16, 1880, Post Records, Fort Cummings.

48. N.A.M. Dudley to acting assistant adjutant general, District of New Mexico, November 23, 1880 (telegram), Post Records, Fort Cummings.

49. F. T. Bennett to acting assistant adjutant general, District of New Mexico, November 20, 1881 (two letters), Post Records, Fort Cummings.

50. *Grant County Herald*, December 28, 1878; Post Returns, Fort Craig, March 1881.

51. C. W. Taylor to acting assistant adjutant general, November 2, 1880, Headquarters Records, Fort Cummings; Post Returns, Fort Cummings, November 1880.

52. Post Returns, Fort Bayard, October 1877.

53. S. C. Plummer to J. S. Loud, May 23, 1880; Statement of Corporal Charles N. Klein, May 13, 1880, Letters Received by Dist. N.M., 1865–1890.

54. Rickey, *Forty Miles a Day*, 126–127.

55. Rickey, *Forty Miles a Day*, 126, 204, 208.

56. C. Steelhammer to acting assistant adjutant general, District of New Mexico, December 11, 1879, Letters Received by Dist. N.M., 1865–1890.

57. H. Carroll to acting assistant adjutant general, District of New Mexico, June 14, 1876 (telegram), Letters Sent from Fort Selden.

58. M. F. Goodwin to E. F. Kellner, October 19, 1876; T. Smith to E. F. Kellner, October 22, 1876, Letters Sent from Fort Selden.

59. C. A. Howard, General Field Orders No. 13, December 4, 1880; P. P. Powell, General Field Orders No. 3, January 3, 1881, Post Records, Fort Cummings.

60. N.A.M. Dudley to A. M. Barnes, April 20, 1881, Post Records, Fort Cummings.

61. E. R. Platt to commanding officer, District of New Mexico, June 5, 1880, Letters Received by Dist. N.M., 1865–1890.

62. F. T. Bennett to acting assistant adjutant general, District of New Mexico, November 20 and 21, 1881; J. Sherman, Jr. to Sir, Santa Fe, New Mexico, November 25, 1881, Letters Received by Dist. N.M., 1865–1890.

63. J. T. Haskell to acting assistant adjutant general, District of New Mexico, November 17, 1881, Letters Received by Dist. N.M., 1865–1890; Post Returns, Fort Craig, November 1881; *Las Cruces Rio Grande Republican*, November 19, 1881.

64. C. McKibbin to acting assistant adjutant general, District of New Mexico, February 21, 1881; J. S. Loud to Commanding Officer, Company E, 9th Cav., March 19, 1881, Letters Received by Dist. N.M., 1865–1890.

65. N.A.M. Dudley to acting assistant adjutant general, District of New Mexico, May 1, 1881, Post Records, Fort Cummings; Post Returns, Fort Stanton, May 1881; H. H. Wright to adjutant, Fort Bayard, August 9, 1877, Letters Received by Dist. N.M., 1865–1890.

66. M. W. Day to acting assistant adjutant general, District of New Mexico, October 19, 1880, Letters Received by Dist. N.M., 1865–1890; Bureau of the Census, *Statistics of the Population of the United States at the Tenth Census: 1880* (Washington, D.C.: 1883), vol. 1: 402.

Chapter VII

1. By a War Department directive, in 1883 companies of cavalry had been redesignated as troops.

2. Tenth Cavalry Returns, March 1885–September 1886; S. C. Agnew, *Garrisons of the Regular U.S. Army: Arizona, 1851–1899* (Arlington, Va.: 1974), 88–91; Leckie, *Buffalo Soldiers*, 239–245.

3. While the Tenth's headquarters and band were in Santa Fe, the band played numerous concerts for the people of the capital city, its weekly Sunday afternoon plaza entertainment being especially popular and enjoyable. After commenting upon the band's excellent music and its marked progress under the able leadership of a Prof. Goldsbury, a newspaper editor wrote this compliment: "It is not saying too much to assert that this is the most gentlemanly

and best managed military band Santa Fe has had for years." See *Santa Fe Daily New Mexican,* February 11, 1888.

4. In October 1887 the fifty-two men of Troop M moved from Fort McDowell, Arizona, to Fort Bayard. In June 1888 the Tenth's Troops D and L joined Troop M at Fort Bayard. In October 1890 Troops L and M were transferred to Fort Grant, Arizona. In January 1891 Troop C joined Troop D at Bayard. In April 1892 these two troops moved by rail from Silver City to Fort Assinniboine, Montana. Tenth Cavalry Returns, September and October 1887; Z. R. Bliss to assistant adjutant general, Department of Arizona, June 13, 1888, Letters Sent by the Post Commander at Fort Bayard, New Mexico, 1888–1897, Microcopy No. T–320, Records of United States Army Continental Commands, 1821–1920, Record Group 98, National Archives, Washington, D.C. (Hereafter cited as Letters Sent by Fort Bayard.); Tenth Cavalry Returns, June 1888, September 1890, February 1891, April 1892; Agnew, *Garrisons of Arizona,* 90–91.

5. In June 1888 Companies A, D, and F arrived at Bayard and in August 1890 Companies H, K, and L joined them. When Company H moved to Arizona in June 1891, Company E replaced it. When Company A moved to Arizona in December 1891, Company G replaced it. Residing at Fort Bayard from January 1892 until October 1896 were six companies (D, E, F, G, K, and L). Post Returns, Fort Bayard, June and July 1888, August 1890, June and December 1891, January 1892–October 1896; Twenty-fourth Infantry Returns, June 1888; Z. R. Bliss to assistant adjutant general, Department of Arizona, June 8, 1888, and J. F. Kent to R. Crofton, October 18, 1896, Letters Sent by Fort Bayard; Fowler, *Black Infantry,* 81.

6. Heitman, *Historical Register,* vol. 1: 225.

7. Three troops of the white Sixth Cavalry had moved to Bayard in 1884, but though one troop remained there until August 1890, the arrival of three Tenth Cavalry troops in June 1888 provided replacements for the other Sixth Cavalry troops. When the Twenty-fourth Infantry arrived in June 1888, the white Thirteenth Infantry pulled out. When the Tenth Cavalry left Bayard in April 1892, two troops of the First Cavalry arrived and remained there until October 1896. Two troops of the Seventh Cavalry served concurrently with the men of the First. In May 1897 the last of the men of the Seventh exited Bayard. When the Twenty-fourth Infantry left Bayard in October 1896, six companies of the white Fifteenth Infantry arrived, remaining there until May (in the case of one company, October) 1898. Agnew, *Garrisons of New Mexico,* 24–25, 60–65, 96–97, 104–105.

8. Post Returns, Fort Bayard, October 1887–October 1896.

9. Post Returns, Fort Bayard, June 1888–October 1896.

10. Post Returns, Fort Bayard, December 1887, September and October 1888, March, July, and November 1890, June and September 1891; Tenth Cavalry Returns, March, September, and October 1890, September and October 1891; Z. R. Bliss to assistant adjutant general, Department of Arizona, February 18, 1892, Letters Sent by Fort Bayard.

11. Tenth Cavalry Returns, November 1887, October 1888.

12. H. H. Whitehill to Z. R. Bliss, April 30, 1889; Z. R. Bliss to acting assistant adjutant general, District of New Mexico, May 2, 1889, Letters Received by Dist. N.M., 1865–1890.

13. Tenth Cavalry Returns, May–July 1890.

14. Tenth Cavalry Returns, May and June 1891.

15. Post Returns, Fort Bayard, June, July, and November 1888; January, March, and July 1889, April and August 1890, March 1892.

16. Post Returns, Fort Bayard, August 1889.

17. J. J. Brereton to A.S.B. Keyes, July 29, 1890; Z. R. Bliss to assistant adjutant general, Division of the Pacific, August 20 and 22, 1890; Z. R. Bliss to A.S.B. Keyes, August 22 and 24, 1890; A.S.B. Keyes to Z. R. Bliss, August 16 and 21 (telegram), 1890; Z. R. Bliss to H. S. Whipple, September 3, 1890, Letters Sent by Fort Bayard.

18. Z. R. Bliss to assistant adjutant general, Department of Arizona, September 22, 28, and 29, 1890; Z. R. Bliss to commanding officer, San Carlos, Arizona, September 28, 1890; C. J. Crane to A.S.B. Keyes, October 1, 1890; Z. R. Bliss to S. F. Maillefert, October 2, 1890, Letters Sent by Fort Bayard.

19. J. A. Lockhart to Z. R. Bliss, October 3, 1890; Z. R. Bliss to A.S.B. Keyes, October 3, 1890; Z. R. Bliss to J. A. Lockhart, October 3, 1890; Z. R. Bliss to commanding officer, Fort Grant, Arizona Territory, October 3, 1890; Z. R. Bliss to assistant adjutant general, Department of Arizona, October 3, 1890; Z. R. Bliss to L. Bradford Prince, October 5, 1890; Z. R. Bliss, First Endorsement on Letter from Governor Prince Enclosing Letter from Mr. Winston, County Commissioner, Sierra Co., N.M., Asking Protection from Hostile Indians, October 5, 1890, Letters Sent by Fort Bayard.

20. Z. R. Bliss to assistant adjutant general, Department of Arizona, October 15, 1890, Letters Sent by Fort Bayard.

21. Z. R. Bliss to postmaster, Alma, New Mexico, October 20, 1890, Letters Sent by Fort Bayard.

22. Z. R. Bliss to assistant adjutant general, Department of Arizona, October 22, 1890; C. J. Crane to A.S.B. Keyes, October 29, 1890, Letters Sent by Fort Bayard.

23. Z. R. Bliss to assistant adjutant general, Department of Arizona, November 2, 1890, Letters Sent by Fort Bayard.

24. Z. R. Bliss to assistant adjutant general, Department of Arizona, January 16, 1892, Letters Sent by Fort Bayard; Tenth Cavalry Returns, January 1892; Post Returns, Fort Bayard, January 1892.

25. Z. R. Bliss to assistant adjutant general, Department of the Colorado, November 15 (telegram), 20 (telegram and letter), 28, and December 5, 1893, Letters Sent by Fort Bayard.

26. Z. R. Bliss to sheriff of Grant County, Silver City, New Mexico, January 25, 1894; Z. R. Bliss to United States Marshal or sheriff, Deming, New Mexico, January 26, 189[4]; Z. R. Bliss to assistant adjutant general, Department of the Colorado, February 3, 1894, Letters Sent by Fort Bayard; Post Returns, Fort Bayard, January 1894.

27. Twenty-fourth Infantry Returns, August 1892–July 1894; Z. R. Bliss to assistant adjutant general, Department of Arizona, February 13 and March 29, 1892, Z. R. Bliss to acting assistant quartermaster, U.S. Boundary Commission, February 4, 1892; C. J. Crane to J. P. Buker, March 2, 1892, Letters Sent by Fort Bayard; Post Returns, Fort Bayard, January and April 1892; Tenth Cavalry Returns, January 1892.

28. For a contrary view see John M. Gates, "The Alleged Isolation of U.S. Army Officers in the Late 19th Century," *Parameters* 10 (September 1980): 32–45.

29. Barton C. Hacker, "The United States Army as a National Police Force: The Federal Policing of Labor Disputes, 1877–1898," *Military Affairs* 33 (April 1969): 259.

30. See Jerry M. Cooper, *The Army and Civil Disorder: Federal Military Intervention in Labor Disputes, 1877–1900* (Westport, Conn.: 1980).

31. Cooper, *The Army and Civil Disorder*, 115.

32. Twenty-fourth Infantry Returns, July 1894.

33. Z. R. Bliss to assistant adjutant general, Department of the Colorado, September 6, 1894, Letters Sent by Fort Bayard.

34. Samuel P. Huntington, *The Soldier and the State: The Theory and Politics of Civil-Military Relations* (New York: 1957), 261.

35. Z. R. Bliss to assistant adjutant general, October 23, 1888, Letters Sent by Fort Bayard.

36. Z. R. Bliss to acting assistant adjutant general, Department of Arizona, November 5, 1888, Letters Sent by Fort Bayard.

37. J. J. Brereton to P. E. Trippe, July 22, 1890, Letters Sent by Fort Bayard; Post Returns, Fort Bayard, April and November 1894.

38. Z. R. Bliss to assistant adjutant general, Department of Arizona, November 14, 1889, Letters Sent by Fort Bayard.

39. Z. R. Bliss to assistant adjutant general, November 6, 1889; F. Van Vliet to assistant adjutant general, Department of Arizona, December 9, 1889, Letters Sent by Fort Bayard.

40. Post Returns, Fort Bayard, May 1892; Twenty-fourth Infantry Returns, May 1892; Z. R. Bliss, First Endorsement on Rental of Military Telegraph Office at Silver City, New Mexico, December 18, 1894, Letters Sent by Fort Bayard.

41. J. F. Kent, First Endorsement on Telegraph Line Duty, May 16, 1896, Letters Sent by Fort Bayard.

42. Tenth Cavalry Returns, September and October 1889.

43. Post Returns, Fort Bayard, September and October 1892.

44. Z. R. Bliss to assistant adjutant general, Department of the Colorado, August 29, 1893, Letters Sent by Fort Bayard.

45. Twenty-fourth Infantry Returns, October and November 1889.

46. Post Returns, Fort Bayard, September–November 1895, March–September 1896; J. F. Kent to adjutant general, Department of the Colorado, October 5, 1895, Letters Sent by Fort Bayard.

47. Twenty-fourth Infantry Returns, June 1888–July 1893; J. J. Brereton, Second Endorsement on Continuation of L.R. 286, March 17, 1890, Letters Sent by Fort Bayard.

48. C. Dodge, Jr., Endorsement on Charges and Specifications Against Private Elson Lewis, Co. H, 24th Inf., undated; C. J. Crane, First Endorsement on Charges Against Saddler Charles B. Gross and Privates Clay Pointer, John Thornton, Thomas Lane, and Seymour Gardner, Troop D, 10th Cav. and Andre Harris, Co. H, 24th Inf., undated; First Endorsement on Orders No. 121, June 15, 1888; Z. R. Bliss to assistant adjutant general, Department of Arizona, December 23, 1890, Letters Sent by Fort Bayard.

49. Z. R. Bliss to assistant adjutant general, Department of Arizona, February 22, 1893, Letters Sent by Fort Bayard.

50. Z. R. Bliss, First Endorsement on Report on Water Supply, December 31, 1893, Letters Sent by Fort Bayard.

51. Z. R. Bliss to assistant adjutant general, Department of the Colorado, November 2, 1893 (telegram and letter), Letters Sent by Fort Bayard.

52. Post Returns, Fort Bayard, January 1892.

53. Z. R. Bliss to H. G. Brown, January 22, 1892, Letters Sent by Fort Bayard.

54. P. H. Sheridan to R. C. Drum, February [8?], 1881; O. M. Poe to W. T. Sherman, March 17, 1881; J. Pope to R. Williams, January 18, 1882; P. H. Sheridan to adjutant general of the army, Washington, D.C., April 12, 1882; R. T. Lincoln to J. A. Logan, May 11, 1882; W. T. Sherman to R. T. Lincoln, March 30, 1882, Letters Received from Fort Selden, New Mexico, Microcopy No. 689, Records of the Adjutant General (Main Series), 1881–1889, Record Group 94, National Archives, Washington, D.C. (Hereafter cited as Letters Received from Fort Selden.); George Ruhlen, "The Genesis of New Fort Bliss," *Password* 19 (Winter 1974): 188–198; Cohrs, "Fort Selden," 34–37; Hugh H. Milton II, *Ft. Selden, May 1865–June 1891* (N.p.: Privately printed, 1971).

55. Post Returns, Fort Selden, May 1888.

56. Post Returns, Fort Selden, August 1888.

57. J. E. Brett to post adjutant, Fort Bayard, New Mexico, August 30, 1888; H. W. Hovey to assistant adjutant general, Department of Arizona, December 3, 1888, Letters Sent from Fort Selden.

58. These paragraphs on Selden's fire are based upon: commanding officer, Fort Selden, to acting assistant attorney general, District of New Mexico, June 7, 1889 (telegram); J. E. Brett to acting assistant attorney general, District of New Mexico, June 8, 1889, Letters Received by Dist. N.M., 1865–1890; *Las Cruces Daily News*, June 8, 1889. All quotes are from Brett's June 8 letter.

59. *Rio Grande Republican*, June 15, 1889.

60. Post Returns, Fort Selden, June 1889.

61. H. W. Hovey to assistant adjutant general, Department of Arizona, March 2, 1889; J. E. Brett to assistant adjutant general, Department of Arizona, June 20, 1890; J. E. Brett to post adjutant, Fort Bayard, New Mexico, September 2, 1889; J. E. Brett, First Endorsement on L.R. #115, Fort Selden, New Mexico, August 2, 1890, Letters Sent from Fort Selden; Z. R. Bliss to assistant adjutant general, Division of the Pacific, August 11, 1890; Z. R. Bliss to assistant adjutant general, Department of Arizona, November 23 and December 7, 1890; Z. R. Bliss to U.S. quartermaster general of the army, Washington, D.C., October 12, 1890, Letters Sent by Fort Bayard.

62. Post Returns, Fort Selden, October 1890.

63. Post Returns, Fort Selden, January 1891.

64. Robert W. Frazer, *Forts of the West* (Norman, Okla.: 1965), 103. For the story of black soldiers at Selden throughout its history, see Monroe Billington, "Black Soldiers at Fort Selden, New Mexico, 1866–1891," *New Mexico Historical Review* 62 (January 1987): 65–80.

65. Post Returns, Fort Stanton, June–August 1896.

Chapter VIII

1. W. A. Ganoe, *The History of the United States Army* (New York: 1924), 350.

2. Rickey, *Forty Miles a Day*, 104–105.

3. Z. R. Bliss to acting assistant adjutant general, Department of Arizona, June 14, 1888, Letters Sent by Fort Bayard.

4. Z. R. Bliss to assistant adjutant general, Department of Arizona, July 22, 1888, Letters Sent by Fort Bayard.

5. Z. R. Bliss to assistant adjutant general, Department of Arizona, July 19, 1888; J. J. Brereton to commanding officer, Co. D, 24th Inf., July 25, 1888; F. M. Crandal, First Endorsement on L.R. 484–88: Report of Sharpshooters and Marksmen for May and June 1888, undated, Letters Sent by Fort Bayard.

6. First Endorsement on L.R. 619–88: Pistol Practice of Troops D, L, and M, 10th Cav., August 4, 1888, Letters Sent by Fort Bayard.

7. Z. R. Bliss to commanding officer, Fort Wingate, July 20, 1888; First Endorsement on L.R. 608–88: Post Surgeon Calling Attention to Litter Bearers Absent from Drill, July 28, 1888, Letters Sent by Fort Bayard.

8. C. J. Crane to C. Chapman, September 7, 1890, Letters Sent by Fort Bayard.

9. Z. R. Bliss to assistant adjutant general, Division of the Pacific, July 24, 1890; Z. R. Bliss to commanding officer, Fort Wingate, July 26, 1890; Z. R. Bliss to inspector of small arms practice, Department of Arizona, October 2, 1890; H. W. Hovey to G. H. Emus, August 4, 1890, Letters Sent by Fort Bayard.

10. Z. R. Bliss to assistant adjutant general, Department of Arizona, March 8, 1891, Letters Sent by Fort Bayard.

11. Post Returns, Fort Bayard, August 1892; Z. R. Bliss, First Endorsement on Annual Rifle Competition, July 14, 1893; Z. R. Bliss to inspector, small arms practice, Department of the Colorado, May 19, 1894, Letters Sent by Fort Bayard.

12. J. F. Kent, First Endorsement on Practice of Hunting, October 26, 1895, Letters Sent by Fort Bayard.

13. Rickey, *Forty Miles a Day*, 97–98.

14. Z. R. Bliss to commanding officer, Fort Supply, Indian Territory, June 13, 1888; Z. R. Bliss to assistant adjutant general, Department of Arizona, August 13, 1888, Letters Sent by Fort Bayard.

15. Z. R. Bliss to assistant adjutant general, Department of Arizona, January 31, 1891, Letters Sent by Fort Bayard.

16. Z. R. Bliss to assistant adjutant general, Department of Arizona, December 23, 1890, Letters Sent by Fort Bayard.

17. Z. R. Bliss to commanding officer, Company K, 24th Inf., September 30, 1888, Letters Sent by Fort Bayard.

18. J. J. Brereton, First Endorsement on L.R. 630–88: Post Surgeon and the Band, August 5, 1888, Letters Sent by Fort Bayard.

19. Z. R. Bliss to assistant adjutant general, Department of Arizona, January 25, 1890, Letters Sent by Fort Bayard.

20. Z. R. Bliss, First Endorsement on L.R. 1104–90: Requisition for Band Instruments, undated; Z. R. Bliss, First Endorsement on L.R. 1291–90: Band Instruments Repairs, October 11, 1890; J. J. Brereton, First Endorsement on L.R. 1483–89: Band Instruments Supplied from Philadelphia Depot, November 23, 1889; J. J. Brereton to C. L. Collins, March 18, 1890, Letters Sent by Fort Bayard.

21. Post Returns, Fort Bayard, April 1891.

22. Twenty-fourth Infantry Returns, October 1895.

23. *Silver City Enterprise,* June 15, 1888.

24. C. J. Crane to Z. R. Bliss, September 2, 1890, Letters Sent by Fort Bayard.

25. Z. R. Bliss to assistant adjutant general, Department of the Colorado, November 1, 1893, Letters Sent by Fort Bayard.

26. Z. R. Bliss, Fourth Endorsement on L.R. 65–89: Complaint of James A. Smith, January 23, 1889, Letters Sent by Fort Bayard.

27. J. J. Brereton, Second Endorsement on L.R. 441–88: Request of Private Potter, June 22, 1888, Letters Sent by Fort Bayard.

28. Z. R. Bliss to assistant adjutant general, Department of Arizona, April 4, 1892; Z. R. Bliss to J. P. Kelton, March 19, 1895, Letters Sent by Fort Bayard.

29. H. S. Whipple, Endorsement on Charges Against Sergeant Jason J. Jackson, December 25, 1889, Letters Sent by Fort Bayard.

30. C. J. Crane, First Endorsement on L.R. 1129–90: Willis Stanley's Request, September 7, 1890, Letters Sent by Fort Bayard.

31. Second Endorsement on L.R. 611–95: Private James Dickerson's Request, June 5, 1895, Letters Sent by Fort Bayard.

32. Bruce White, "ABC's for the American Enlisted Man: The Army Post School System, 1866–1898," *History of Education Quarterly* 8 (Winter 1968): 488–490.

33. Z. R. Bliss to J. P. Kelton, March 19, 1895, Letters Sent by Fort Bayard.

34. Z. R. Bliss to quartermaster general of the army, June 18, 1888, Letters Sent by Fort Bayard.

35. White, "ABC's for the Enlisted Man," 480.

36. White, "ABC's for the Enlisted Man," 483.

37. J. N. Schultz to adjutant general, January 2, 1869, Selected Letters Received Relating to the Twenty-fourth and Twenty-fifth Infantry Regiments, 1866–1891, Records of the Adjutant General's Office, Record Group 94, National Archives, Washington, D.C. (Hereafter cited as Selected Letters Received by Adjutant General's Office.); Fowler, *Black Infantry*, 93.

38. D. E. Barr to adjutant general, October 1, 1869, Selected Letters Received by Adjutant General's Office.

39. Fowler, *Black Infantry*, 94–97.

40. Fowler, *Black Infantry*, 100–101; *Annual Report of the Secretary of War, 1884–1885* (Washington, D.C.: 1885), vol. 2: 868, 878–879; *Annual Report of the Secretary of War, 1886–1887* (Washington, D.C.: 1887), vol. 2: 11; *Annual Report of the Secretary of War, 1881–1882* (Washington, D. C.: 1883), vol. 2: 579–581; *Annual Report of the Secretary of War, 1882–1883* (Washington, D. C.: 1884), vol. 2: 191–192.

41. Fowler, *Black Infantry*, 103; *Annual Report of the Secretary of War, 1889–1890* (Washington, D.C.: 1890), vol. 2: 62.

42. Quoted in White, "ABC's for the Enlisted Man," 484.

43. Fowler, *Black Infantry*, 104–105.

44. Z. R. Bliss to J. P. Kelton, March 19, 1895; Z. R. Bliss, First Endorsement on L.R. 297–90: School Books, etc., March 19, 1890, Letters Sent by Fort Bayard; *Silver City Enterprise*, June 30, 1888.

45. Z. R. Bliss, First Endorsement on L.R. 204–89: Lieutenant Palmer's Report, February 9, 1889; Z. R. Bliss, First Endorsement on L.R. 297–90: School Books, etc., March 19, 1890; Z. R. Bliss, First Endorsement on L.R. 1381–89: Requisition for Supplies, November 8, 1889, Letters Sent by Fort Bayard.

46. Z. R. Bliss, First Endorsement on Bi-Monthly Report of Schools, September 4, 1888; J. J. Brereton, First Endorsement on L.R. 1457–89: Lists of Men for Instruction, November 18, 1889; C. J. Crane, First Endorsement on Lists of Men Who Require Instruction, October 21, 1890; C. J. Crane, First Endorsement on List of Men Attending School, February 22, 1891, Letters Sent by Fort Bayard.

47. F. M. Crandal to commanding officer, Co. E, 24th Inf., July 1, 1888; Z. R. Bliss to commanding officer, Co. E, 24th Inf., August 31, 1888 and January 31, 1889; Z. R. Bliss to commanding officer, Co. G, 24th Inf., December 31, 1889; Z. R. Bliss to commanding officer, Co. A, 24th Inf., April 30, 1893, Letters Sent by Fort Bayard.

48. Z.R. Bliss to adjutant general of the army, October 19, 1888, Letters Sent by Fort Bayard.

49. Fowler, *Black Infantry*, 106.

50. White, "ABC's for the Enlisted Man," 489.

51. C. G. Ayres, Endorsement on Charges and Specifications Preferred Against Sergeant John D. Sparling, October 28, 1888, Letters Sent by Fort Bayard.

52. D. W. Fulton, Endorsement on Charges and Specifications Preferred Against Private Richard Cox, December 26, 1888, Letters Sent by Fort Bayard.

53. W. Black, Endorsement on Charges Against Private Dick Richardson, December 25, 1889; W. Black, Endorsement on Charges Against Private Lee Chisholm, December 25, 1889, Letters Sent by Fort Bayard.

54. W. Black, Continuation of L.R. 1244–90: Charges Against Private George Tilman, August 3, 1890, Letters Sent by Fort Bayard.

55. Z. R. Bliss to J. A. Lockhart, March 12, 1891, Letters Sent by Fort Bayard.

56. C. L. Collins, First Endorsement on Charges and Specifications Preferred Against Corporal Lawrence J. Julius, October 12, 1888, Letters Sent by Fort Bayard.

57. C. C. Hood, Endorsement on Charges and Specifications Preferred Against Private Edward Williams, November 15, 1888; R. G. Paxton, Additional Charge [Against Private Williams], November 15, 1888; C. G. Ayres, Endorsement on Charges and Specifications Preferred Against Private Charlie Stargall, Troop L, 10th Cav., November 6, 1888; Letters Sent by Fort Bayard.

58. P. E. Trippe, First Endorsement on Charges and Specifications Preferred Against Trumpeter Charles Ridley, March 20, 1890, Letters Sent by Fort Bayard.

59. Endorsement on Charges and Specifications Preferred Against Corporal Ernest Rowland, undated, Letters Sent by Fort Bayard.

60. W. H. Arthur, Endorsement on Charges and Specifications Preferred Against Private Robert Jones, December 31, 1888, Letters Sent by Fort Bayard.

61. F. M. Crandal, Endorsement on Charges and Specifications Preferred Against Corporal Henry James, January 9, 1889, Letters Sent by Fort Bayard.

62. Z. R. Bliss to assistant adjutant general, January 4, 1893, Letters Sent by Fort Bayard.

63. A.S.B. Keyes, Endorsement on Charges Preferred Against Corporal Clay Pointer, August 10, 1888, Letters Sent by Fort Bayard.

64. J. J. Brereton, Endorsement on L.R. 1525–89: Sanitary Report for November 1889, December 20, 1889, Letters Sent by Fort Bayard.

65. Z. R. Bliss to assistant adjutant general, Department of Arizona, January 4, 1893, Letters Sent by Fort Bayard. For a perceptive account of the army's official policies and practical actions concerning the relationship of prostitutes to military personnel on the frontier, see Anne M. Butler, "Military Myopia: Prostitution on the Frontier," *Prologue* 13 (Winter 1981): 233–250.

66. J. J. Brereton, Endorsement on Charge and Specification Preferred Against Sergeant Mailton Ross, December 17, 1888, Letters Sent by Fort Bayard.

67. M. M. Maxon, Endorsement on Charge and Specification Preferred Against Private Peter McCann, undated, Letters Sent by Fort Bayard.

68. C. C. Hood, Endorsement on Charge and Specification Preferred Against Private Henderson Hucksty, August 16, 1890, Letters Sent by Fort Bayard.

69. H. W. Hovey, Endorsement on Charges Preferred Against Private James W. Snyder, September 13, 1890, Letters Sent by Fort Bayard.

70. M. M. Maxon, Endorsement on Charges and Specifications Preferred Against Private William Parker, January 26, 1889, Letters Sent by Fort Bayard.

71. Z. R. Bliss to deputy sheriff, Central City, New Mexico, March 31, 1894, Letters Sent by Fort Bayard.

72. *Rio Grande Republican*, June 26, 1891.

73. J. J. Brereton to post surgeon, Fort Bayard, July 13, August 26, and October 5, 1888; Z. R. Bliss, First Endorsement on Certificate of Disability for Discharge of Private John N. Pyatt, August 16, 1888; C. J. Crane to post surgeon, Fort Bayard, October 9, 1890; First Endorsement on Certificate of Disability for Discharge of Private Reubin E. Douglass, June 19, 1888, Letters Sent by Fort Bayard.

74. C. J. Crane to post surgeon, Fort Bayard, February 9 and April 21, 1891; Z. R. Bliss to assistant adjutant general, Department of Arizona, March 10, 1891, Letters Sent by Fort Bayard.

75. First Endorsement on Certificate of Disability for Discharge of Sergeant John Smith, June 19, 1888; J. J. Brereton to post surgeon, Fort Bayard, July 6, 1888, Letters Sent by Fort Bayard.

76. A.S.B. Keyes, Charges and Specifications Preferred Against Private Charles Waters, November 26, 1889, Letters Sent by Fort Bayard.

77. A.S.B. Keyes, Endorsement on Charges and Specifications Preferred Against Farrier James Livingstone, November 19, 1888, Letters Sent by Fort Bayard.

78. Z. R. Bliss to commanding officer, 10th Cav., October 28, 1890, Letters Sent by Fort Bayard.

79. Z. R. Bliss to sheriff, Grant County, New Mexico, January 29, 1891, Letters Sent by Fort Bayard.

80. Z. R. Bliss, Ninth Endorsement on L.R. 89–89: Complaint of Albert S. Crouch, January 18, 1889; Z. R. Bliss, Second Endorsement on L.R. 1103–88: Letter of Private Peter McCann, December 18, 1888, Letters Sent by Fort Bayard.

81. J. S. Jouett, Endorsement on Charges Preferred Against Private Thomas Pearce, August 5, 1888; Z. R. Bliss to sheriff, Deming, New Mexico, September 10, 1888, Letters Sent by Fort Bayard.

82. J. E. Brett to commanding officer, Co. A, 24th Inf., November 16, 1889, Letters Sent from Fort Selden.

83. Edward M. Coffman, *The Old Army: A Portrait of the American Army in Peacetime, 1784–1898* (New York: 1986), 371.

84. Foner, *United States Soldier,* 223.

85. Coffman, *Old Army,* 371–372.

86. Daniel T. Rodgers, *The Work Ethic in Industrial America, 1850–1920* (Chicago: 1978), 162–165.

87. Coffman, *Old Army,* 373–374.

Chapter IX

1. Post Returns, Forts Bayard and Wingate, October 1898–June 1899.

2. Post Returns, Fort Bayard, June–December 1899; Fort Wingate, January 1899–July 1900.

3. This figure does not include the sixty-two men of Troop M, Ninth Cavalry, who, while passing through Fort Wingate in October 1900 on a practice march, were counted present. See Post Returns, Fort Wingate, October 1900.

4. When Companies E and F, Twenty-fifth Infantry, arrived at Forts Wingate and Bayard in October 1898, they relieved Companies E and G, Fifteenth Infantry, who left a few days later. Two troops of the Seventh Cavalry had ridden out of Bayard in April 1898; they were not replaced until the arrival of the men of the Ninth at Wingate and Bayard in January and June of the following year. Agnew, *Garrisons of New Mexico,* 64–65, 104–105.

5. Post Returns, Fort Wingate, May 1899.

6. Post Returns, Fort Wingate, August 1899.

7. Post Returns, Fort Wingate, September 1899.

8. Rickey, *Forty Miles a Day,* 187.

9. Post Returns, Fort Wingate, July 1899.

10. Post Returns, Fort Wingate, November 1899.

11. Post Returns, Fort Wingate, December 1899.

12. Post Returns, Forts Bayard and Wingate, June 1899; Twenty-fifth Infantry Returns, June 1899.

13. Post Returns, Fort Wingate, July 1900.

14. After New Mexico became a state in 1912, black soldiers returned for a short period. From 1916 to 1922 some troops and companies of the Tenth Cavalry and Twenty-fourth Infantry were stationed at Camp Furlong near Columbus, New Mexico, in response to Pancho Villa's famous raid and generally to provide security for Americans who lived in that region near the Mexican border. For a study of these soldiers and the black community of Columbus that grew up because of their presence, see Horace D. Nash, "Blacks on the Border: Columbus, New Mexico, 1916–1922" (Master's thesis, New Mexico State University, 1988).

Chapter X

1. Michael L. Tate, "The Multi-Purpose Army on the Frontier: A Call for Further Research," in Ronald Lora, ed., *The American West* (Toledo, Ohio: 1980), 198–199.

2. *Thirty-Four*, November 12, 1879.

3. *Thirty-Four*, November 19, 1879.

4. *Thirty-Four*, June 9, 1880. For additional newspaper criticism of not only the black soldiers but also their white officers, see *Thirty-Four*, February 11, May 19, and June 2, 1880, and *Grant County Herald*, quoted in *Thirty-Four*, March 24, 1880.

5. See p. 97–98.

6. Jack D. Foner, *Blacks and the Military in American History: A New Perspective* (New York: 1974), 57.

7. J. A. Corbett to chief, Commissary of Subsistence, District of New Mexico, May 15, 1867; J. A. Corbett to W. E. Sweet, October 22, 1867, Post Records, Fort Cummings.

8. J. A. Corbett to J. Martin, February 16, 1867, Post Records, Fort Cummings.

9. Z. A. Bliss to S. P. Carpenter, July 16, 1893, Letters Sent by Fort Bayard.

10. J. Tempany to adjutant, Ninth Cavalry, September 2, 1879, Letters Received by Dist. N.M., 1865–1890.

11. J. E. Brett to J. H. Nations, May 16 and 17, 1889, Letters Sent from Fort Selden.

12. Quoted in Foner, *United States Soldier*, 144.

13. Quoted in Foner, *United States Soldier*, 145.

14. Quoted in Foner, *United States Soldier*, 146.

15. Allan G. Bogue, Thomas D. Phillips, and James E. Wright, eds., *The West of the American People* (Itasca, Ill.: 1970), 140–141.

16. J. A. Corbett to chief, Commissary of Subsistence, District of New Mexico, February 12, 1867, Post Records, Fort Cummings.

17. E. Pollock to acting assistant adjutant general, District of New Mexico, September 20, 1880, Letters Received by Dist. N.M., 1865–1890.

18. A. Moore to acting assistant adjutant general, District of New Mexico, August 12, 1868, Headquarters Records, Fort Cummings.

19. A. E. Hooker to W. R. Price, January 14, 1876, Letters Received by Dist. N.M., 1865–1890.

20. L. H. Rucker to acting assistant adjutant general, District of New Mexico, January 1, 1877, Letters Received by Dist. N.M., 1865–1890.

21. E. Hatch to assistant adjutant general, Department of the Missouri, September 3, 1879, Letters Received by Dist. N.M., 1865–1890.

22. Thomas D. Phillips, "The Negro Regulars: Negro Soldiers in the United States Army, 1866–1890," unpublished manuscript quoted in Marvin Fletcher, *The Black Soldier and Officer In the United States Army, 1891–1917* (Columbia, Mo.: 1974), 23.

23. Foner, *Blacks and the Military,* 64. Flipper served with the Tenth Cavalry in Arizona and Texas. He passed through but did not serve in New Mexico. For more information on West Point's first black graduate, see Theodore D. Harris, ed., *Negro Frontiersman: The Western Memoirs of Henry O. Flipper* (El Paso, Texas: 1963) and "Henry Ossian Flipper: The First Negro Graduate of West Point" (Ph.D. diss., University of Minnesota, 1971). Other black West Point cadets and graduates have received little scholarly attention, except for Johnson C. Whittaker, whose story of racial tribulations on the banks of the Hudson River is recounted in John Marszalek, *Court-Martial: A Black Man in America* (New York: 1972).

24. Quoted in Foner, *Blacks and the Military,* 61–62.

25. Quoted in Coffman, *Old Army,* 365–366.

26. Fowler, *Black Infantry,* 121–126.

27. Coffman, *Old Army,* 366.

28. J. C. McBride to B. M. Custer, October 7, 1867, Letters Received by Dist. N.M., 1865–1890.

29. J. A. Corbett to assistant adjutant general, Department of the Missouri, September 24, 1867, Post Records, Fort Cummings.

30. W. E. Sweet to post adjutant, Fort Cummings, March 1, 1868, Post Records, Fort Cummings.

31. H. Grovey to L. Day, May 28, 1867, Letters Sent from Fort Selden.

32. C. Steelhammer to acting assistant adjutant general, District of New Mexico, December 11, 1879, Letters Received by Dist. N.M., 1865–1890.

33. Heitman, *Historical Register,* vol. 1: 540.

34. Fowler, *Black Infantry,* 129–130.

35. Heitman, *Historical Register,* vol. 1: 166.

36. Fowler, *Black Infantry,* 129.

37. W. E. Sweet to post adjutant, Fort Cummings, February 19, 1868, Post Records, Fort Cummings.

38. S. C. Plummer to acting assistant adjutant general, District of New Mexico, September 4, 1881, Letters Received by Dist. N.M., 1865–1890.

39. Quoted in Coffman, *Old Army,* 368–369.

40. Quoted in Coffman, *Old Army,* 369.

41. Coffman, *Old Army,* 369.

42. Quoted in Coffman, *Old Army,* 332.

43. Coffman, *Old Army,* 371.

Appendix

1. Frazer, *Forts of the West,* 95–109.

Bibliographical Essay

In introducing this volume on black soldiers in postwar New Mexico Territory, I have spoken briefly about the military service of blacks during and immediately following the Civil War. My comments have been based in part upon the following: Dudley Taylor Cornish, *The Sable Arm: Negro Troops in the Union Army, 1861–1865* (New York: W. W. Norton and Company, 1966); James M. McPherson, *The Negro's Civil War: How American Negroes Felt and Acted During the War for the Union* (New York: Pantheon Books, 1965); Frederick H. Dyer, *A Compendium of the War of the Rebellion* (New York: Thomas Yoseloff, Publisher, 1959), 3 vols.; *The Army Lineage Book. Volume II: Infantry* (Washington, D.C.: Government Printing Office, 1953); and Mary Lee Stubbs and Stanley Russell Connor, *Armor-Cavalry, Part I: Regular Army and Army Reserve* (Washington: Government Printing Office, 1969).

The primary sources for the main subjects of this study are the voluminous military records in the National Archives in Washington, D.C. Information about troop movements and stations and some activities may be found in Returns from U.S. Military Posts, 1800–1916, Microcopy No. 617, Records of the Adjutant General's Office, Record Group 94; and Records of United States Army Continental Commands, 1821–1920, Record Group 393. Available post returns from New Mexico's forts relevant to this study (Bascom, Bayard, Craig, Cummings, McRae, Selden, Stanton, Union, and Wingate) are massive and almost totally complete. Based upon these returns — and generally accurate — is S. C. Agnew, *Garrisons of the Regular U.S. Army: New Mexico, 1846–1899* (Santa Fe: Press of the Territorian, 1971). Agnew has also published *Garrisons of the Regular U.S. Army: Arizona, 1851–1899* (Arlington, Virginia: Council on Abandoned Military Posts, 1974). Supplementing the post returns are Returns from Regular Army Infantry Regiments, June 1821–December 1916, Microcopy No. 665, and Returns from Regular Army Cavalry Regiments, 1833–1916, M744, both in Records of the Adjutant General's Office, Record Group 94; and, finally, Records of United States Regular Army Mobile Units, 1821–1942, Record Group 391.

Considerably more valuable for the activities of the army's enlisted men and its officers are the thousands of extant letters in the military records in the National Archives. Specifically used in this study are: Letters Received by Headquarters, District of New Mexico, September 1865–August 1890, M1088, and Letters Sent by the 9th Military Department, the Department of New Mexico and the District of New Mexico, 1849–1890, M1072, both in

Records of United States Army Continental Commands, 1821–1920, Record Group 393; Letters Received by the District of New Mexico, 1876–81, and Letters Sent by the Post Commander at Fort Bayard, New Mexico, 1888–1897, Microcopy No. T–320, and Special File, Victorio Papers, 1880, all in Records of United States Army Continental Commands, 1821–1920, Record Group 98; Selected Letters Received Relating to the Twenty-fourth and Twenty-fifth Infantry Regiments, 1866–1891, Records of the Adjutant General's Office, Record Group 94; Letters Received from Fort Selden, New Mexico, Microcopy No. 689, Records of the Adjutant General (Main Series), 1881–1889, Record Group 94; Letters Sent from Fort Selden, New Mexico, vol. 7A–7, Records of the Office of the Quartermaster General, Record Group 92.

Also valuable for their correspondence and for other records are: Post Records, Fort Cummings, New Mexico, and Headquarters Records, Fort Cummings, New Mexico, 1863–1873 and 1880–1884, M1081, both in Records of United States Army Continental Commands, 1821–1920, Record Group 393. My account of the 1867 mutiny at Fort Cummings is based on the Records of the Office of the Judge Advocate General, General Courts Martial, 1812–1938, Record Group 153. These records were also used by Lee Myers, "Mutiny at Fort Cummings," *New Mexico Historical Review* 46 (October 1971): 337–350.

A cursory glance at the footnotes of this work will reveal that the vast majority of its sources are these military records in the National Archives. Sources other than the official military records do not exist or are almost impossible to track down. The diaries, memoirs, and personal letters that help fill out the story of the white soldiers are essentially nonexistent for blacks. Few of the remaining entries in this bibliographical essay focus on black soldiers specifically. In reading the following pages, the reader should keep in mind that almost all of the sources mentioned are supplementary to the official records.

Information concerning the army's activities in the West, with occasional references to black troopers, may be found in various *Annual Reports of the Secretary of War*. For this study I have taken specific material from the reports of 1880 (vols. 1 and 2), 1881 (vol. 1), 1881–1882 (vol. 2), 1882–1883 (vol. 2), 1884–1885 (vol. 2), 1886–1887 (vol. 2), and 1889–1890 (vol. 2). These were all published by the Government Printing Office in Washington, D.C., and they were sometimes issued the year following the year covered by the report. Also, the *Annual Report of the Commissioner of Indian Affairs to the Secretary of the Interior for the Year 1877* (Washington, D.C.: Government Printing Office, 1877) yielded pertinent information.

Major parts of the story of black soldiers in New Mexico cannot be understood except in the context of the territory's Indian population. To understand that context, I recommend the following: Rupert Noval Richardson, *The Comanche Barrier to South Plains Settlement* (Glendale, Calif.: The Arthur H. Clark Company, 1933); Dan L. Thrapp, *The Conquest of Apacheria* (Norman: University of Oklahoma Press, 1967) and *Victorio and the Mimbres Apaches* (Norman: University of Oklahoma Press, 1974); Donald E. Worcester, *The Apaches: Eagles of the Southwest* (Norman: University of Oklahoma Press, 1979); and C. L. Sonnichsen, *The Mescalero Apaches*, 2nd ed. (Norman: University of Oklahoma Press, 1972). Dealing with the Victorio era are John P. Clum, "The Apaches," *New Mexico Historical Review* 4 (1929): 107–127; Bruce J. Dinges, "The Victorio Campaign of 1880: Cooperation and Conflict on the United States–Mexico Border," *New Mexico Historical Review* 62 (January 1987): 81–94; Harold Miller, "Nana's Raid of 1881," *Password* 19 (Summer 1974): 51–70; and Stephen H. Lekson, *Nana's Raid: Apache Warfare in Southern New Mexico, 1881* (El Paso: Texas Western Press, University of Texas at El Paso, 1987). Unfortunately none of these books or articles devotes much attention to black soldiers.

Focusing on both the army and the Indians, with passing references to black soldiers, is Robert M. Utley, *Frontier Regulars: The United States Army and the Indian, 1866–1891* (New York: Macmillan Publishing Company, 1973). Utley has written a popular article entitled "The Buffalo Soldiers and Victorio," *New Mexico Magazine* 62: 3 (March 1984): 47–50, 53–54. As Indian scouts and black soldiers often worked closely together, this list would be incomplete if I failed to mention Thomas W. Dunlay, *Wolves for the Blue Soldiers: Indian Scouts and Auxiliaries with the United States Army, 1860–90* (Lincoln: University of Nebraska Press, 1982).

Lenwood G. Davis and George Hill, comps., *Blacks in the American Armed Forces, 1776–1983: A Bibliography* (Westport, Conn.: Greenwood Press, 1985) contains only a few references to black soldiers in New Mexico, revealing the paucity of research and publication on this subject. Arlen L. Fowler, *The Black Infantry in the West, 1869–1891* (Westport, Conn.: Greenwood Publishing Corporation, 1971) is a well-researched study, but unfortunately it has few references to New Mexico, and because it begins with the army's reorganization in 1869 it omits references to the Civil War soldiers stationed in the territory in 1866 and 1867 as well as to the Thirty-eighth Infantry, which was there from 1867 to 1869. William G. Muller, *The Twenty Fourth Infantry Past and Present* (Ft. Collins, Colo.: The Old Army Press, 1972), is much less useful. The most valuable study of black soldiers on the frontier is William H. Leckie, *The Buffalo Soldiers: A Narrative of the Negro Cavalry in the West* (Norman: University of Oklahoma Press, 1967). Leckie devotes attention to the Ninth Cavalry's Indian-fighting activities in New Mexico during the Victorio campaign, although he essentially ignores the garrison life of the everyday soldier there. William H. Leckie and Shirley A.

Leckie, *Unlikely Warriors: General Benjamin H. Grierson and His Family* (Norman: University of Oklahoma Press, 1984) has a paucity of material on New Mexico because the Tenth Cavalry spent little time there while Grierson was its regimental commander. Of almost no value is *Historical and Pictorial Review, 2nd Cavalry Division, U.S. Army* (N.p., 1941).

Older volumes that contain passing references to blacks include: John Gregory Bourke, *On the Border with Crook* (New York: 1891. Reprint. Chicago: The Rio Grande Press, 1962); George A. Forsyth, *The Story of the Soldier* (New York: D. Appleton and Company, 1900); Elizabeth Bacon Custer, *Tenting on the Plains: General Custer in Kansas and Texas* (New York: 1887. Reprint. Norman: University of Oklahoma Press, 1971), 3 vols. An old, general work giving minor attention to black soldiers during the period of the Indian Wars is T[heophilus] G[ould] Steward, *The Colored Regulars in the United States Army* (Philadelphia: A.M.E. Book Concern, 1904. Reprint. New York: Arno Press, 1969). Even though Henry O. Flipper spent little time in New Mexico, he was in both Texas and Arizona, and I would be remiss if I did not mention the memoirs of the first black graduate of West Point: Theodore D. Harris, ed., *Negro Frontiersman: The Western Memoirs of Henry O. Flipper* (El Paso: Texas Western College Press, 1963). An unpublished biography of Flipper is "Henry Ossian Flipper: The First Negro Graduate of West Point" (Ph.D. diss., University of Minnesota, 1971). John Marszalek, *Court-Martial: A Black Man in America* (New York: Charles Scribner's Sons, 1972) tells the sad story of racial discrimination against cadet Johnson C. Whittaker while he was at West Point.

To understand the background of the Colfax County War, the reader should begin with William A. Keleher, *Maxwell Land Grant: A New Mexico Item* (Santa Fe: The Rydal Press, 1942). For the conflict itself, Morris F. Taylor, *O. P. McMains and the Maxwell Land Grant Conflict* (Tucson: University of Arizona Press, 1979) is best. Useful but less trustworthy are Lawrence R. Murphy, *Philmont: A History of New Mexico's Cimarron Country* (Albuquerque: University of New Mexico Press, 1972) and Larry Murphy, *Out In God's Country: A History of Colfax County, New Mexico* (Springer, N.M.: Springer Publishing Company, 1969).

A descendent of some of the participants in the Colfax County War, Norman Cleaveland has written much about that civil conflict. He has compiled and annotated *An Introduction to the Colfax County War, 1875–78* ([Santa Fe: Sunstone Press], 1975), and he has authored *Colfax County's Chronic Murder Mystery* (Santa Fe: The Rydal Press, 1977) and "The Great New Mexico Cover-Up: Frank Warner Angel's Reports," *Rio Grande History* 5 (Summer 1975): 4–9. With George Fitzpatrick as his coauthor, Cleaveland has published *The Morleys — Young Upstarts on the Southwest Frontier* (Albuquerque: Calvin Horn, Publisher, 1971). Cleaveland has added much to our knowledge of Colfax County's problems, even though he assumes conspiracy on limited evidence and assigns only sinister motives to those who opposed his ancestors. Two books by his mother are her recollections as a pioneer woman living in early Colfax County: Agnes Morley Cleaveland, *Satan's Paradise* (Boston: Houghton Mifflin Company, 1948, 1952) and *No Life for a Lady* (Lincoln: University of Nebraska Press, 1969).

Two publications that relate to both the Colfax County War and the Lincoln County War are Lee Scott Theisen, ed., "Frank Warner Angel's Notes on New Mexico Territory, 1878," *Arizona and the West* 18 (Winter 1976): 333–370, and Victor Westphall, *Thomas Benton Catron and His Era* (Tucson: University of Arizona Press, 1973). An article on a specific but crucial event in the history of the disputes is Philip J. Rasch, "Exit Axtell: Enter Wallace," *New Mexico Historical Review* 32 (July 1957): 231–245. For an introduction to the Lincoln County War, see Harwood P. Hinton, "John Simpson Chisum, 1877–1884," *New Mexico Historical Review* 31 (July 1956): 177–205.

Many publications have appeared on the Lincoln County War itself, New Mexico's best known controversy in the history of the American West. Factual data, as well as interpretations of that event, are still in dispute. From the mass of published material, the following books will inform the reader, even though they do not agree in their interpretations of that conflict: Maurice G. Fulton, *History of the Lincoln County War*, edited by Robert N. Mullin (Tucson: University of Arizona Press, 1968); William A. Keleher, *Violence in Lincoln County, 1869–1881: A New Mexico Item* (Albuquerque: University of New Mexico Press, 1957); Frederick W. Nolan, *The Life & Death of John Henry Tunstall* (Albuquerque: University of New Mexico Press, 1965); Donald R. Lavash, *Sheriff William Brady: Tragic Hero of the Lincoln County War* (Santa Fe: Sunstone Press, 1986); John P. Wilson, *Merchants, Guns, and Money: The Story of Lincoln County and Its Wars* (Santa Fe: Museum of New Mexico Press, 1987); and Robert M. Utley, *Four Fighters of Lincoln County* (Albuquerque: University of New Mexico Press, 1986). Except for Utley, who has a chapter on Colonel N.A.M. Dudley, these writers play down the role of the black soldiers in the dispute to the extent that the latter become almost invisible. Dee Dwight Greenly, "The Military Career of Nathan Augustus Monroe Dudley, 1843–1889" (Master's thesis, New Mexico State University, 1986) devotes attention to the major impact of the black soldiers. And to be sure, the role of the black soldiers in the Lincoln disputes is also included in the military records. This section would not be complete if I did not include Lee Scott Theisen, ed., "The Fight in Lincoln, N.M., 1878: The Testimony of Two Negro Participants," *Arizona and the West* 12 (Summer 1970): 173–198.

Black soldiers were used to settle labor disputes, too, and the military records chronicle their participation. For background for their part in the Raton-Trinidad railroad workers' strike in 1894, see Jerry M. Cooper, *The*

Army and Civil Disorder: Federal Military Intervention in Labor Disputes, 1877–1900 (Westport, Conn.: Greenwood Press, 1980) and Barton C. Hacker, "The United States Army as a National Police Force: The Federal Policing of Labor Disputes, 1877–1898," Military Affairs 33 (April 1969): 255–264. Two general works addressing the concept of the army as an extension of the government in regard to civil disputes are Robert W. Coakley, The Role of Federal Military Forces in Domestic Disorders, 1789–1878 (Washington, D.C.: Government Printing Office, 1988) and Samuel P. Huntington, The Soldier and the State: The Theory and Politics of Civil-Military Relations (New York: Alfred E. Knopf, 1957).

Robert W. Frazer, Forts of the West (Norman: University of Oklahoma Press, 1965) includes brief histories of New Mexico's forts, vital background for any military study of the territory. More interpretive is Lee Myers, "Military Establishments in Southwestern New Mexico: Stepping Stones to Settlement," New Mexico Historical Review 43 (January 1968): 5–48. Studies of the histories of individual New Mexico forts give further details of the environment in which black soldiers served, and some of these studies contain occasional references to them: Chris Emmett, Fort Union and the Winning of the Southwest (Norman: University of Oklahoma Press, 1965); Dale Frederick Giese, "Soldiers at Play: A History of Social Life at Fort Union, New Mexico, 1851–1891" (Ph.D. diss., University of New Mexico, 1969); Thomas J. McLaughlin, "History of Fort Union, New Mexico" (Master's thesis, University of New Mexico, 1952); James Monroe Foster, Jr., "History of Fort Bascom, New Mexico, 1863–1870" (Master's thesis, Eastern New Mexico University, 1955) and "Fort Bascom, New Mexico," New Mexico Historical Review 35 (January 1960): 30–62; William Thornton Parker, Annals of Old Fort Cummings, New Mexico, 1867–8 (Northampton, Mass.: Privately printed, 1916); Hugh H. Milton II, Ft. Selden, May 1865–June 1891 (N.p.: Privately printed, 1971); Timothy Cohrs, "Fort Selden, New Mexico," El Palacio 79: 4 (March 1974): 13–39.

Relevant to the demise of Fort Selden is George Ruhlen, "The Genesis of New Fort Bliss," Password 19 (Winter 1974): 188–217. For the story of black soldiers at a single fort, see Monroe Billington, "Black Soldiers at Fort Selden, New Mexico, 1868–1891," New Mexico Historical Review 62 (January 1987): 65–80.

New Mexico Territory had a number of newspapers; the fairly complete files of many of these are available. Unfortunately, specific references to black soldiers are few. This book's footnotes make occasional references to the following New Mexico newspapers: Santa Fe Weekly New Mexican, Santa Fe Daily New Mexican, Santa Fe New Mexican, Rio Grande Republican (Las Cruces), Las Cruces Daily News, Thirty-Four (Las Cruces), Mesilla News, Mesilla Independent, Grant County Herald (Silver City), New Southwest and

Grant County Herald (Silver City), *Silver City Enterprise,* and *Las Vegas Gazette.* The *Rocky Mountain News* (Denver, Colorado), June 17, 1877, also has an article relevant to the Ninth Cavalry.

The presence of the army and its soldiers in the West related to more than Indian subjugation; the army was a significant factor in the western economy. Two books dealing with this influence before the Civil War are Francis Paul Prucha, *Broadax and Bayonet: The Role of the United States Army in the Development of the Northwest, 1815–1860* (Lincoln: University of Nebraska Press, 1953) and Robert W. Frazer, *Forts and Śupplies: The Role of the Army in the Economy of the Southwest, 1846–1861* (Albuquerque: University of New Mexico Press, 1983). Carrying Frazer's narrative further — and more relevant to the story of New Mexico's post–Civil War black soldiers — is Darlis A. Miller, *Soldiers and Settlers: Military Supply in the Southwest, 1861–1885* (Albuquerque: University of New Mexico Press, 1989).

A number of books, chapters in books, and articles have been written about various aspects of the non-Indian-fighting life of the American soldier on the frontier after the Civil War. Don Rickey, Jr., *Forty Miles a Day on Beans and Hay: The Enlisted Soldier Fighting the Indian Wars* (Norman: University of Oklahoma Press, 1963) is an excellent study dealing with almost every aspect of this life, including routine duty, food, clothing, pay, health care, discipline, crime, vice, punishment, recreation, relaxation, and outside interests. Unfortunately its paucity of references to black soldiers leaves the impression that the frontier army was all white. It would seem, from the numerous references to white units and white men, that for Rickey the Ninth and Tenth Cavalry regiments and the Twenty-fourth and Twenty-fifth Infantry regiments did not exist. Although it is true that white and black men had essentially the same experiences — except in regard to racial prejudice and discrimination both on and off the posts — this does not justify treating the black men as if they were invisible. Furthermore, Rickey virtually ignores New Mexico in addition to treating only white troopers. The chapter entitled "Army life on the Border" in Utley's previously mentioned work suffers from the same shortcoming, as does Edward M. Coffman, "Army Life on the Frontier, 1865–1898," *Military Affairs* 20 (Fall 1956): 193–201. Coffman's essay may be considered as an early overview of the long chapter on enlisted men in the army between the Civil War and the Spanish-American War that appeared in his later work, *The Old Army: A Portrait of the American Army in Peacetime, 1784–1898* (New York: Oxford University Press, 1986). In that exhaustively researched magnum opus published thirty years later, however, Coffman rectifies the earlier omission with numerous perceptive statements about black soldiers during the era of the Indian Wars.

Jack D. Foner, *The United States Soldier Between Two Wars: Army Life and Reforms, 1865–1898* (New York: Humanities Press, 1970) and *Blacks and the*

Military in American History: A New Perspective (New York: Praeger Publishers, 1974) overlap somewhat, but they acknowledge the presence of the black soldier in the military as well as address the problems of prejudice and discrimination. Because the army's schools involved black troopers quite extensively, Bruce White, "ABC's for the American Enlisted Man: The Army Post School System, 1866–1898," *History of Education Quarterly* 8 (Winter 1968): 479–496, is pertinent to this study. The lives of the soldiers off the posts, both white and black, involved many activities, one of which is dealt with in Anne M. Butler, "Military Myopia: Prostitution on the Frontier," *Prologue* 13 (Winter 1981): 233–250.

To insure correct spellings of names and to find biographical information of army officers, I used Francis B. Heitman, *Historical Register and Dictionary of the United States Army, From Its Organization, September 29, 1789, to March 2, 1903* (Washington, D.C.: Government Printing Office, 1903. Reprint. Urbana: University of Illinois Press, 1965), 2 vols. Unfortunately no such work exists for enlisted men. Based upon a long, well-documented but un-available, unpublished manuscript is Thomas D. Phillips, "The Black Regulars," in Allan G. Bogue, Thomas D. Phillips, and James E. Wright, eds., *The West of the American People* (Itasca, Ill.: F. E. Peacock Publishers, 1970), a brief but informative overview of the life of the black soldiers from 1865 to 1898.

Ten references which contributed in a minor way to specific sections of this work are: Monroe Billington, "Black History and New Mexico's Place Names," *Password* 24 (Fall 1984): 107–113, 156; Horace D. Nash, "Blacks on the Border: Columbus, New Mexico, 1916–1922" (Master's thesis, New Mexico State University, 1988); John M. Gates, "The Alleged Isolation of U.S. Army Officers in the Late 19th Century," *Parameters* 10 (September 1980): 43–45; Thomas C. Railsback and John P. Langellier, *The Drums Would Roll: A Pictorial History of U.S. Army Bands on the American Frontier, 1866–1900* (London: Arms and Armour Press, 1987); Marvin Fletcher, *The Black Soldier and Officer In the United States Army, 1891–1917* (Columbia: University of Missouri Press, 1974); Daniel T. Rodgers, *The Work Ethic in Industrial America, 1850–1920* (Chicago: University of Chicago Press, 1978); Michael L. Tate, "The Multi-Purpose Army on the Frontier: A Call for Further Research," in Ronald Lora, ed., *The American West* (Toledo, Ohio: University of Toledo, 1980); Russell F. Weigley, *History of the United States Army* (New York: Macmillan Company, 1967); W. A. Ganoe, *The History of the United States Army* (New York: D. Appleton and Company, 1924); *Statistics of the Population of the United States at the Tenth Census: 1880* (Washington, D.C.: Government Printing Office, 1883), 2 vols.

Finally, I used the following combined references to determine those black soldiers who won Medals of Honor while serving in New Mexico during the Indian Wars: Preston E. Amos, *Above and Beyond in the West: Black Medal of Honor Winners, 1870–1890* (Washington, D.C.: Potomac Corral, The Westerners, 1974); W[alter] F. Beyer and O[scar] F. Keydel, *Deeds of Valor: How America's Heroes Won the Medal of Honor* (Detroit: The Perrien-Keydel Company, 1900–1901), 2 vols.; *Army and Navy Journal* 14 (May 12, 1877): 18; Ralph Emerson Twitchell, *The Leading Facts of New Mexican History*, vol. 2 (Cedar Rapids, Iowa: The Torch Press, 1911–1917), 5 vols.

Index